THE ENGLISH HOUSE

THE ENGLISH HOUSE

CLIVE ASLET

BLOOMSBURY

First published in 2008

Text copyright © 2008 by Clive Aslet

Illustrations copyright © 2008 by Mai Osawa

The moral right of the author has been asserted

Bloomsbury Publishing Plc
36 Soho Square,
London W1D 3QY

Bloomsbury Publishing, London, New York and Berlin

A CIP catalogue record for this book is available from the British Library

ISBN 978 0 7475 7797 3
10 9 8 7 6 5 4 3 2 1

Illustrator: mai-osawa-art.com

Typeset by Hewer Text UK Ltd, Edinburgh
Printed by Clays Ltd, St Ives plc

The paper this book is printed on is certified by the © 1996 Forest Stewardship
Council A.C. (FSC). It is ancient-forest friendly. The printer holds
FSC chain of custody SGS-COC-2061

For Constance

'Every Mans proper Mansion House and *Home*, being the Theater of his *Hospitality*, the *Seate* of *Self-fruition*, the *Comfortablest part* of his owne *Life*, the *Noblest* of his *Sonnes Inheritance*, a kind of private *Princedome*; Nay, to the *Possessors* thereof, an *Epitomie* of the whole *World*, may well deserve by the *Attributes*, according to the degree of the *Master*, to be *decently* and *delightfully* adorned.'

Sir Henry Wotton, *The Elements of Architecture*

'It was a sweet view – sweet to the eye and the mind. English verdure, English culture, English comfort, seen under a sun bright, without being oppressive.'

Jane Austen, *Emma*

'To my farther great benefit, as I grew older, I thus saw nearly all the noblemen's houses in England; in reverent and healthy delight of uncovetous admiration, – perceiving, as soon as I could perceive any political truth at all, that it was probably much happier to live in a small house, and have Warwick Castle to be astonished at, than to live in Warwick Castle and have nothing to be astonished at; but that, at all events, it would not make Brunswick Square in the least more pleasantly habitable, to pull Warwick Castle down.'

John Ruskin, *Praeterita*

CONTENTS

Foreword

This is a story told through houses I have known. Some of them I encountered when writing articles for *Country Life*, where I became an architectural writer in 1977, occupying the editor's chair for thirteen years. (I am now editor at large.) A number of the houses I wrote about for *Country Life* reappeared in *The Last Country Houses* (1982), about the period from 1890 to 1939, and in *The American Country House* (1992); I have not drawn on those here. Rather, I have tried to span the range of houses in which the English still find it comfortable to live today: some small, some not so small, none – with one exception – monstrously big. That exception is Elveden, an example of the country house at the zenith of its domestic elaboration, and to that extent an essential addition to the story. If it seems too much of a cuckoo in the nest, I hope that readers will be prepared to indulge my partiality for it, acquired, wearing a heavy overcoat and in close proximity to an electric heater, during a cheerful if bitterly cold January week while the contents of the house were catalogued around me.

An Ordinary London Terraced House

The year is 1851, the place is London. In Albertopolis, the exhibition zone around Hyde Park, a marvelling public wanders through the vast conservatory of the Crystal Palace, eyes aching from the prodigality of ornament that industry has brought forth to be celebrated in the Great Exhibition. In Parliament, Lord John Russell's administration falls, only to be reinstated when no other can be formed. At the Kennington Oval, Richard Manks performs the feat of walking a thousand miles in a thousand consecutive half-hours. In an area beside the Thames, until recently market gardens but now the scene of the largest single development ever achieved by one man in London – that man being Thomas Cubitt – two families settle into a newly finished house at the end of one of the many terraces that have just sprung into existence.

The head of one of these families, Mr Filmore, describes himself as the Dispenser – of medicines rather than punishment – to the Millbank Penitentiary, occupying the site of what is now Tate Britain, a neighbourhood described in *David Copperfield* (1850) as 'oppressive, sad, and solitary by night'. With his wife and two daughters, he shares the house with a builder, Job Matthews, his wife and their seven children; thus the house, of three floors above a basement, is pretty crowded. (English houses, the German Prince Pückler-Muskau had observed twenty years earlier, were all the same, the inhabitants being stacked one above the other like cheeses in a warehouse.) But Mr Matthews will move on. It is common practice at this time for new houses to be first occupied by the tradesmen who build them. The Filmores will probably move on, too – everyone does. Tenants do not regard newness as a virtue; they fear the damp of drying plaster.

In the 1870s, a fulsome newspaper article will call Pimlico 'a paradise of peace'. In 1851 it is no such thing. There are wooden scaffolding poles everywhere, as well as painters, plumbers, black-smiths and hundreds of bricklayers. Heavy horses – as many as eighty of them – haul cartloads of timber, railings and stone from Cubitt's great yard on Thames Bank, land that will soon be transformed by the Victoria Embankment. The main thorough-fares have no houses on them, only hoardings. The new streets do not sit on the ground. They are raised up, to run along the tops of the vaults into which, in due course, grimy coalmen will upend the contents of their black, oily, acrid-smelling sacks. Next to Mr Matthews's house, another eleven shells are waiting to be finished. A century and a half later, the one adjoining Mr Matthews's house – then 119, now 154 Tachbrook Street – will become home to the Aslet family.

Our house belongs to a standard London type. The front door opens onto a narrow hallway, from the side of the hallway rises the staircase; there are two rooms to each floor, a precipitous area at the front and an umbrageous yard at the back. Each house front along Tachbrook Street is about the same as the next. But not quite. A few houses have a window each side of the front door (they are double-fronted). The interiors are broadly similar but not identical; quirky details make each house slightly different from its neighbour. This is how the English like their houses: individuality keeps bubbling to the surface.

I always thought that Tachbrook Street took its line, as well as its name, from a stream which, until the area was developed, had gossiped its way to the Thames. But I was wrong. The name comes from Tachbrook, in Warwickshire, the birthplace of Henry Wise, Queen Anne and George I's gardener. Wise owned land around Pimlico and used it as his nursery. His occupation was until recently commemorated in the local pub The Royal Gardener (though the head on the sign was that of 'Capability' Brown).

But the curve of Tachbrook Street does follow that of a water-course: the central channel of what might be thought of as the Tyburn delta. The Ty Burn had lent its name to the notorious gallows that stood at the junction of London's principal east/west road – the present Oxford Street – and the main route leading north – once Watling Street, now Edgware Road. But the name of Tyburn had been replaced by one that was more noxious still: King's Scholars' Pond Sewer. This began, innocently enough, in the pond on Tothill Fields where the King's scholars of Westminster School disported themselves. En route to the Thames it acquired a noisome cargo, the ordure issuing from the drains of Buckingham Palace and the grand houses of the West End. By the time this stream reached the site of what would become Tachbrook Street, it was a sea of water-borne excrement twenty feet wide. Not a terrific advertise-ment for the locality.

Until the 1820s, fish still swam in the Thames. That is because of the sound environmental principles on which Georgian London – however seemingly fetid – was run. Most householders relieved themselves in an earth closet, the contents of which would be removed, while the family slept, by night-soil men, who then sold them to farmers to spread on the land. It was not a perfect system – the tramp from privy or cess pit to street door inevitably took the night-soil men through the house – but it was green. As London expanded, the farms came to be further away; increasingly household waste was discharged into streams. Little was done to control this practice until legislative minds were concentrated by the Great Stink of 1858, which caused the corridors of the Palace of Westminster to be hung with sheets soaked in chloride of lime. The result was the smooth-walled, egg-sectioned glory of the civil engineer Joseph Bazalgette's sewers, which, as anyone who has walked (slitheringly) through them will confirm, were Victorian England's equivalent of the Pyramids. Bazalgette not having yet begun his mighty work, Thomas Cubitt covered over the King's Scholars' Pond Sewer, building houses to either side of it, its memory surviving in the line of our street.

Pimlico came to be known, by some, as Stuccoville, after the Roman cement that covers the fronts of buildings, in our case to the top of the first floor. Stucco had come into vogue at the beginning of the eighteenth century, when John Nash had built the fashionable terraces around Regent's Park. Nash's object was to make each terrace, comprising a string of individual houses, look like a palace. Painted sand colour and scored in imitation of jointing, the stucco resembled stone. Photographs suggest that in the Victorian period stucco was painted in the rich, dark colours that were then in mode. Painting may have been a nuisance, but it was also a virtue: while expensive, it ensured that the front of the house was regularly refreshed. The air of London was so freighted with soot and smuts, a residue of which would be unloaded onto its houses each time it rained, that most buildings were black.

By any standards, stucco is a poor material, with the dubious virtue of concealing, in cheaply built houses, the poor materials and workmanship that would otherwise be on view. This fertile ground for moralists was tilled with vigour by the young Gothic Revivalist A. W. N. Pugin, a fierce, religiously zealous propagandist who inveighed against shams. And the practical Robert Bakewell, writing a builder's manual in 1834, knew what was what: '. . . even when most perfect, we know [stucco] to be a deception, and intended to hide deformity and worthlessness.' Still, there is a limit to what stucco can cover up, and no amount of it can obscure the fundamental truth that London is a brick city.

Brick-making was regarded as a singularly wretched industry even by the tough-minded Victorians. London has no good building stone, but the Thames basin abounds in clay, used to produce bricks of various grades and with fantastic names – paviours, pickings, rough paviours, washed stocks, grey stocks, rough stocks, grizzles, place bricks, shuffs. The best – malms – contained a proportion of chalk; inferior bricks were made from loam, to which chalk was added in the form of a paste. When fired, the chalk gave them a buff or brownish cast, which the trade described as yellow. Yellow London stocks were the atoms from which the metropolitan universe was constructed. To produce them, small brickyards set themselves up just ahead of the developers.

Just as our house was being envisaged, in 1850, the brick-maker Edward Dobson wrote a treatise on the manufacture of bricks and tiles, detailing the processes involved. The season began in April, when the brick earth was turned over by men with shovels. The clay was then wheeled to the pug mill to be mixed and ground. Next, it was moulded by hand on a rough table; the moulding was skilled work, often performed by women, while men brought the raw material and took away the shaped bricks on barrows. From the barrows, wet bricks were carefully stacked, eight high, until they hardened. In London, the dried bricks were fired in clamps rather than permanent kilns, fuelled largely by the ash left over from domestic hearths, sifted to ensure that it was fine enough; this was then left to smoulder for six weeks.

It has been calculated that at the time our house was being built, five hundred million bricks a year were being made within a five-mile radius of London Bridge. Or, put another way, five hundred million bricks every other six months. For that was the brick-makers' problem. Production was seasonal; it could not proceed in months that were subject to frost. As a result, the labourers, who were paid per thousand bricks, worked every hour that they could during the period that was available to them. For the rest of the year, they were idle. Hard, dismal, damp, heavy work it was, too, when they were at it, beginning at 4.30 in the morning and working through, with half an hour for lunch, until 8 o'clock at night. Wives and children were not spared. A report in *The Graphic* found a child of four helping to carry clay for her seven-year-old sister. Families needed the money from child labour. The job was such that many of the men spent their wages on drink. (The brick-maker whom the religious busybody Mrs Pardiggle visits in Charles Dickens's *Bleak House* has been drunk for three of the four days since she last visited.) Sometimes even the children were drunk. Clergymen were sent on missions to reform the brick-makers, as though they were considered some foreign, uncivilized tribe.

But who gave a thought to the brick-makers when viewing the houses in Tachbrook Street? The area was intended to be eminently genteel. By the time it was begun, Belgravia, a little to the north, had been successfully developed for the aristocracy; the intention was that Pimlico should be a Belgravia for the middle classes. As a result, there were none of the town palaces that subsequently became embassies, and no house had a private garden, with the exception of the one that Thomas Cubitt built for his daughter on the corner of Warwick Square. The status of our house, in the Victorian hierarchy, was defined by what it did not have. There were no separate back stairs for servants: they would have had to share the same staircase as the family. There was no servants' hall; no mews at the end of the non-existent garden for horses (horses were kept in commercially operated mews and hired when necessary; Tachbrook Streeters would have walked, used the omnibus or taken a cab); no billiard room, no ballroom. For all that, Pimlico, as a newspaper article of 1877 simpered, was intended to be respectable,

> . . . the abode of gentility – a servant or two in the kitchen, birds in the windows, with flowers in boxes, pianos, and the latest fashions, of course. People are here always dressed in their best, and though not the cream of the cream, can show on occasion broughams and pairs, opera cloaks of surpassing gorgeousness and dress suits that would satisfy Poole or Worth. Where people do not live on their property they are artists – they teach the piano, singing, dancing, drawing, languages, or are in the City . . .

It was all a bit of a fraud, in fact. A more worldly, and truer, note was sounded by Trollope: 'For heaven's sake, my dear,' a well-wisher advises Lady Alexandrina de Courcy, considering the houses that her future husband, a civil servant, is prepared to offer her, 'don't let him take you anywhere beyond Eccleston Square!'

According to the 1871 census, our house was occupied by five women: a widow of seventy-two; her daughter, also a widow (her husband had been a piano maker); Mary Priest, who was the wife of a house steward, presumably employed in Belgravia; her three-week-old daughter; and a lodger, Elizabeth Wyatt, described, with shades of *Bleak House*, as 'occupied in Court of Chancery'. Next door lived Amos Waller, a draper's clerk, with his wife, daughter, three sons and two nieces. There was a ladies' school down the street, and a professor of music. At No. 74, we find Henry Stevens, 'linguist and tutor'. But some of the other auguries are not good. William Jacques, in No. 101, was a pawnbroker. There were a number of ornamental carvers, ironmongers, dressmakers and oil-men, but the words that fall most often on the eye are 'lodging house'. This was to be Pimlico's fate. Unable to attract residents who could afford their own houses, it descended to letting out rooms – eventually to be known as bedsits. Some of the lodging houses were respectable, but others were not, becoming a byword for prostitutes. This reputation survived into the 1960s, when the estate agent Roy Brooks placed a newspaper advertisement for a 'Brothel in Pimlico' (this would become the title of a collection of such advertisements published after his death).

By 1949, when the Ealing Studios released a film called *Passport to Pimlico*, the area had become something of a joke. The polite pretensions of 1877 had been singularly unfilled, and the memory of them, preserved in the architecture, seemed merely risible. Pimlico had, for somewhere so central, always seemed cut off from the rest of the capital, first by the Grosvenor Canal, then by the railway. It was on the way to nowhere, without being a destination in itself. In the film, it declares independence from the rest of the country and mentally floats away altogether: its cockney inhabitants, fed up with making do in the austerity of post-war Britain, abandon their ration coupons and decide to open Continental-style pavement cafés.

Since then, swathes of the old Pimlico have disappeared, along with half of Tachbrook Street, replaced around 1970 by a vast Council estate by the architects Darbourne and Darke. The estate was regarded as a model for the future, with balconies cascading with creeper. Architectural students made pilgrimages to see it. But it turned its back on Cubitt. Darbourne and Darke took their inspiration from the Victorian architect G. E. Street's church of St James the Less, on Vauxhall Bridge Road, built of red brick. So from our front windows, we look out onto a red-brick terrace of shops that include a small supermarket, a chemist, a dry cleaner, a bakery and a pub.

In the *Passport to Pimlico* days, our house would have been divided up into bedsits. We know that from the telltale panel in the surround to the front door; it marks the place where a row of buttons would have been, each meant to ring in a different flat. At some point, like almost all the houses in Pimlico, the place received a mansard roof, hiding behind the Cubitt parapet, to provide another floor. Our immediate predecessors converted the property back into a single dwelling, as it was in 1851 and as it remains today.

What does this tale signify? Our house is as unremarkable as the almost identical ones that were built under Cubitt's eye by the thousand. On your way to Pimlico tube station, you would hardly notice it. Yet stop for a moment before this house – or any house – and it tells you more than you might expect. The curve of the street has a history to it. The perfectly ordinary bricks of which the house is built hold their mystery. The house does not look just as it did in 1851, or 1877, or even 1949; yet it is the same building. By studying the friend of sixty we can imagine the boy that he was at eighteen. It's the same with houses.

1. A Stone-Built Norman Home
Boothby Pagnell Manor House

Noise. That is what is absent from medieval houses today. They are so wretchedly mellow and serene. Imagine what the manor house at Boothby Pagnell, five miles south of Grantham, would have been like under construction. Somewhere, perhaps on the site itself, certainly nearby, stone was being split from the living rock. A man was pushing a wedge into a hole that he had chipped out and clouting it with a sledgehammer. Hard work, but more than that, clanging and monotonous. The stone does not split at first, so he makes another hole, pushes in his wedge. This time it is the wedge that breaks, not the stone, so he trudges off to the blacksmith. The blacksmith, in the leaky workshop that has been thrown together on the building site, hammers out another wedge on his anvil, thumping and tinging; half his time is spent replacing tools. The masons who shape the stones – tap tap *tap*, tap tap *tap* – spoil an average of three chisels a day each.

There is a little village of workshops on the building site. The carpenter made them, rough wooden structures with walls of woven sticks covered in a daub of clay mixed with straw. The thatch that has been shoved onto the roofs is already mossy and rotten, but it keeps off most of the rain. There is a tree trunk outside the carpenter's shop. The carpenter chose it himself, when it was still growing in the wood. Two men sawed through the trunk before knocking in wedges; once it fell, it had its branches trimmed off. Then a squat, powerful horse dragged the trunk to where it was needed. The carpenter has squared the trunk off, using an adze. It could be made into planks for the scaffolding, or into a beam to tie the new house together, or into floorboards for the first floor. In fact it will be none of these things. The carpenter wants it to provide timbers for an open-work domed structure he is assembling: the frame on which the masons will construct a vault.

Vaults are wondrous things, understood only by carpenters and masons. The masons cut the stones to exactly the right shape; they must dovetail neatly. The template that the masons use to check their work is a wooden jig made by the carpenter. Lime, poisonous stuff, seals the joints between the stones; it comes from rocks burned down to a powder. The people who do the burning cannot help breathing the gas that comes off; they never live very long. The lime is mixed with sand and water to form a paste. When the vault is made, the scaffolding has to be taken away before the paste becomes hard; it is the pressure of the stones pushing down on each other that makes the vault stand.

Wood smoke drifts from another part of the site. It is the kiln, firing tiles for the chamber floors. They have been baking for nearly a week. The basket maker shouts to the tile maker. His craft will leave no evidence behind it in the structure of the building, but it is essential all the same. There are baskets for tools, baskets that you put on your back when you go up a ladder, baskets for carrying mortar – these are quickly rotted by the lime. The craftsmen at Boothby – Bodebi, as the parish is called in the Domesday Book – form a community. They have been there, working in their sheds during all but the coldest months of winter, for a year or two; they will be there for a year or two more. So far the house has risen only to the first floor. The lord who will live in it is not all that rich, and nothing is done very quickly when it depends on handwork.

The villages east of the A1, the old Great North Road, lie in serious farming country, a land of big, open fields, sheep and billowing trees. These are not self-consciously picturesque places, as in the Cotswolds, but workaday communities. Boothby Pagnell shelters between two woods, Boothby Great Wood to the east and Boothby Little Wood to the west. There are freshly built houses in developments like Bluebell Close. Driving through, you might stop and look at the church – clearly Norman in origin, to judge by the round-headed arch and two-light window in the tower, though remodelled by the Victorians – although you would probably not be detained by very much else.

But stand by the church and you will notice a gap in the dense belt of trees that lines the other side of the road. This is the beginning of a gravel drive that soon sweeps past some tall Wellingtonias (there was a craze for them in the nineteenth century, when they were introduced from America) to reveal Boothby Pagnell Hall. Cream-coloured, all Tudor-ish gables and dormer windows, it was built in 1825, replacing a seventeenth-century building. Beyond it is another structure: a compact little building, no more than 55 feet in width and 23 in depth, sitting modestly in the centre of a lawn, its demure silvery stone occasionally breaking out into a becoming blush of pink, rust and pale yellow. This is one of the earliest English houses to survive; it dates from around 1170.

There are of course many that didn't survive. Five thousand years ago, a community of farmers and fishermen built a settlement on the western shore of Orkney, off the north coast of Scotland. They made the straightish walls of their dwellings nestle into a shoulder of rubbish – or midden – piled up to protect them from the wind.

(Wise move. The wind blows hard on Orkney.) They slept on stone beds, sat on stone benches, stored their utensils in stone cupboards and kept the bait they used for fishing in boxes made of stone. Older than the Pyramids or Stonehenge, Skara Brae was abandoned around 2500 BC and forgotten.

There is nothing like Skara Brae in England. It has survived because of a peculiarity about Orkney: on this windswept island, trees grow with difficulty. Therefore the people who built it used stone. The earliest houses in England were built of more manageable but less permanent materials.

In 1982, a mechanical digger unearthed some unusual timbers from Flag Fen outside Peterborough. These turned out to come from a Bronze Age settlement, carbon-dated to about 1000 BC. Archaeologists have now reconstructed one of the Round Houses: a large, dark dwelling, its walls daubed with mud to keep out the wind, and a heavy conical roof, covered in turf. As turf became very heavy when wet, the roof had to be supported by internal posts.

When the Romans conquered southern Britain in the first century AD, they found a population still living in such round huts (though by now the roofs were no longer supported internally, being of thatch and therefore lighter in weight). By far the most impressive structures that confronted the invaders were hilltop forts, whose banks, ditches and gateways can only have been built by whole communities working together. There were eight hundred of these forts in England, some of the biggest occupied permanently. Maiden Castle in Dorset was so crowded with huts that it had to be cleared and reorganized, the huts being rebuilt in straight rows to allow better movement between them. The Romans dignified some Iron Age settlements with the term *oppidum* ('town'), but they were not much more than clusters of huts. A Celtic village built after the Roman invasion survives at Chysauster in Cornwall. There are eight dwellings arranged along a street – perhaps the first village street in England. Each of the structures has a central courtyard surrounded by enormously thick stone walls (fourteen feet in places). Within these walls are small chambers of different shapes. Although the inhabitants of Chysauster may have supplemented their farming with money made from selling nuggets of tin, life there cannot have been much more comfortable than it had been several millennia before.

The Romans began a programme of urbanization, building fifty towns, most of which were to become the nuclei of towns that still flourish today. Laid out on a grid pattern, these settlements, often associated with forts, included all the comforts that could be found elsewhere in the Empire. Wealthy Britons were encouraged and financially helped to build houses. Towns and armies required food, and to provide the necessary surplus, farming became more efficient. Big farms were run from villas that sometimes evolved into sumptuous country houses with mosaic pavements, bath complexes and underfloor heating. The villa at Fishbourne, probably built for a pro-Roman chief, is of such swaggering opulence as to be called a palace. Most such houses were distributed around southern and central England, below a line from the Severn to the Wash. The sites of some of them are still inhabited, though nothing of these villas remains above ground, except for archaeological finds.

After the legions left Britain in AD 410, the great organizational machine ran down. Weeds grew up through the stones of the roads. Inhabitants drifted away from cities such as London and Exeter. Peasant farmers probably made their homes in parts of some opulent villas before finally abandoning them. But in the centuries that followed, England could not support the population it had known under the Romans: the number of people living there when Boothby Pagnell was being built more than seven hundred years later was two-thirds that of the Roman period. The Saxons pillaged Roman monuments for their building materials. As Roman skills were forgotten, the structures they left behind came to inspire awe; the author of a poem called 'The Ruin', written in the eighth or ninth century, called them 'the work of giants'. The technique of brick-making was lost. When William the Conqueror began Colchester Castle above the foundations of a great Roman temple, his team quarried whatever Roman buildings they could find for hundreds of thousands of bricks: they could not have made a single one of them for themselves.

In the early twelfth century, the Norman monk William of Malmesbury settled himself in the scriptorium of Glastonbury Abbey and began to write, or dictate, his *Gesta Regum Anglorum* (Deeds of the English Kings), primly comparing Saxon domestic priorities – their love of riotous drinking parties, their mean and despicable houses – with the austerity of the Normans under William I, who lived moderately but built well. William had begun building as soon as he had landed in Sussex, erecting a castle at Hastings that would be the pattern for many others. The Bayeux Tapestry shows his men at work heaping up a mound, or motte, with curving sides like a pudding. On the flattened top is a stronghold: the donjon, as it would have been known throughout the Norman period and Middle Ages, later known as the keep. Around the motte, using the trench which had supplied the earth, would have been a moat. The Normans generally constructed a palisade, called the bailey, outside the motte. To begin with – for reasons of speed, if not expense – both palisade and keep were made of wood. After the Battle of Hastings, William rushed up castles of this type all around his new territory – in the crook of the old Roman wall at London, commanding the English Channel from an old Roman site at Dover (it took just eight days to build the motte), dominating the river Avon at Warwick. These castles, intended to secure England, were the forerunners of hundreds of lesser ones built throughout the land by the new caste of Norman feudal lords, who held their lands from the King in return for military service.

Building with wood was quick, but second-best. The Normans loved stone. They were more skilled in working stone than the

Saxons had been, and they liked to build big. The first stone-built castle was Chepstow, on a superb but rocky site above the river Severn, begun in 1067. In London, William I's keep – the White Tower, so-called because of the taste for whitewashing even stone buildings – would eventually become one element in an immense defensive complex.

Emphasizing its role as a palace as well as a fortification, the White Tower contains the first fireplace in England. (It was, however, a crude affair, with no chimney stack to create an updraught to draw out the smoke.) Lesser castles functioned as defensible family homes. They might have *garde-robes* (lavatories) positioned above the moat, chapels with traceried windows, and gardens where the ladies grew herbs. There was a degree of one-upmanship about castle-building; great lords wanted to impress visitors by stage-managing the route by which their properties were approached, as for example via a long flight of steps and a waiting room at Castle Rising in Norfolk.

Even before 1066, Edward the Confessor, who had been brought up in Normandy, had begun to grant land to Norman religious foundations. Around 1050, a Norman by the name of Osbern Pentecost built a motte in Herefordshire. It can still be seen outside the village of Ewyas Harold, a mound of more than thirty feet in height which probably had a stone keep on top of it. Such an advanced fortification – one of four Norman-style castles in England to survive from before the Conquest – represents an early attempt to keep the bandits of the Welsh borders in check. The idea of a private castle from which to dominate the surrounding population would have been distinctly alien to contemporary Saxons and admirably demonstrated one side of the Norman character: brutal, arrogant, warlike and domineering.

But the Normans, including William I himself, were also pious. Soon after the Conquest, William began a campaign to rebuild all the existing cathedrals and abbeys in England, stamping Norman identity on the country. The Normans also gave money to religious foundations. In Lincolnshire, the de Bothebys followed in this tradition; in 1114 Theodoric and Lezelina de Botheby are recorded as donors to Crowland Abbey, where they watched a foundation stone being laid. Abbeys such as Crowland owned large tracts of sparsely populated countryside.

After a century or so, the Normans settled down. It was then that they founded towns (sixty of them by 1130) and built houses like Boothby Pagnell. Boothby Pagnell had a moat, possibly dating from Saxon times. John Leland, the Tudor antiquary who travelled throughout England as Henry VIII's Keeper of Libraries, mentions it in his *Itinerary* (c. 1540), and parts are still visible in a sunken track. Other defensive features included a flight of steps you had to climb before entering the manor house on the first floor. But these measures were intended to deter gangs of robbers, or belligerent neighbours, rather than full-scale military assault. Henry II's sons, Richard and John, were fighting a civil war around the time Boothby Pagnell was being built; but although the de Botheby lord may, as a knight, have been required to turn out in favour of one side or the other, such disturbances did not normally trouble the routine of the countryside. The de Bothebys felt sufficiently secure to make themselves comfortable. Not a castle, Boothby Pagnell was the centre of an estate, a seat of justice – and a home.

The clutch of early English houses of which Boothby Pagnell is one are a disparate lot. Fyfield Hall in Essex stands out because it was constructed out of timber. To the historian, this is a great boon: wood can be carbon-dated, sometimes even ring-dated, so we know that the trees which went into Fyfield were cut down between 1167 and 1185. There is a scattering of other timber manor houses of this date, but most early houses which have survived were built of stone. They include a number of town houses in Lincoln and Bury St Edmunds associated with Jewish financiers of the early Middle Ages. Since there were no banks, these businessmen needed strong houses to protect themselves from attack by debtors as well as envious neighbours. The need for credit itself reflected an increase in economic activity which was making people in the countryside rich as well. Although altered, Saltford Manor in Somerset and Hemingford Grey in Huntingdonshire may be even earlier than 1170. These were manor houses, each the centre of an agricultural estate ruled by its lord. Again their builders used stone, which cannot be dated as scientifically as wood.

This was not a choice to be made lightly. 'It was a hand-made world throughout, a slow world, a world without power, a world in which all things were made one by one,' wrote the twentieth-century sculptor Eric Gill, who knew all about stone – '. . . a world dependent upon human muscular power and the muscular power of draught animals'. Human muscle power was in limited supply. It has been calculated that Lincoln, one of the biggest cities in England, did not contain more than four or five thousand inhabitants at the time of the Domesday Book. Near Boothby Pagnell, Grantham, with its 1,200 inhabitants, was no bigger than a modern village. At the end of the twelfth century there were still fewer people in England than there had been during the Roman period. For any family to build a stone house was a major undertaking.

But stone endures. It is due to this that the Jew's House in Lincoln, Moyses Hall in Bury St Edmunds, the Music House in Norwich, fragments in Bristol and Southampton, Saltford Manor and Boothby Pagnell Manor House still exist, unlike so many of their contemporaries, which have perished.

The particular stone used at Boothby Pagnell was a type of limestone. Look at a geological atlas of England, and you will see where limestones occur. Britain has a most intricate geology. Drive from the north coast of Scotland to the south coast of England, and your tyres pass above half a billion years of the world's history – all the geological periods that have existed. This has affected the landscape, which seems to change character every few miles.

Traditional buildings were generally built of materials that came to hand easily, so their variety is also witness to the local rocks and soils. For building, the best stones were seemingly those that were the least spectacular: the fine-grained limestones from which many of England's most beautiful buildings were made, including the Palace of Westminster in London. (Although the Anson stone used there was so low grade that it decayed quickly in London's soot-laden atmosphere.)

England seems to wear a band of these limestones like a sash. Slung over her shoulder at Yorkshire, it slants diagonally across Lincolnshire, Gloucestershire and Dorset before trailing into the English Channel around Lyme Regis. Around 250 million years ago, England was submerged beneath a shallow tropical sea. Punctuated with islands and coral reefs, the scene would have looked something like the Caribbean today – not surprising given that the landmass was located at a much more southerly place on the globe. As the tiny creatures swimming in the sea died, their shells drifted down to the ocean floor. Over hundreds of thousands of years this layer of shells built up to a depth of many feet.

Under the magnifying glass, sometimes with the naked eye, you may still be able to see fragments of shell in limestone today. This is the stone known as lias. In time, the land was pushed up above sea level, leaving a landscape of river deltas. Much of southern England was covered by a vast, calm lagoon, supersaturated with the mineral calcium carbonate. Tiny circular deposits of it accumulated around grains of sand to form what geologists call ooliths. After millions of years, these dots began to fuse together into butter-smooth oolitic limestone.

Before the coming of the railways in the nineteenth century, hauling heavy materials around the country cost too much for ordinary people, so anyone living far from the limestone belt had to make do with what they could find. Flints might be picked up from the open fields, but their rounded, knobbly shapes are not good to build with: the gaps had to be filled with strong mortar. In the thirteenth century builders developed the technique of splitting flints to reveal their hearts of glassy blackness. Flint knapping shaped the split flints into squares – a perilous job when undertaken on a large scale because of the silica dust which flew up and damaged the lungs of the workers. The corners of flint buildings had to be made out of stone.

Flints were at least stone of a kind. In Cumbria, Buckinghamshire and the New Forest, country people made their houses of mud; mixed with straw and gravel, pummelled down between the sides of a wooden form, walls of *cob*, *dabbing* or *wychert* – dialect names for this rammed earth, more fancifully called *pisé de terre* – could last for centuries, as long as the water was kept off them. But if the plaster covering was allowed to decay, they would simply dissolve back to mud. A similar material, used in East Anglia, was clay lump, made out of clay incorporated with straw (by means of a horse being led round and round over ground that had had the top soil stripped off it) which was then put into wooden moulds to dry. The blocks were built into walls, smeared with clay, coated with coal tar and colour-washed. Roofs were made of thatch.

People who lived near the limestone outcrops along the greeny-yellow sash in the geological atlas had an advantage in life: their houses could have strong walls. Where the stone could be easily split (having been left out in the frost), they might also have sound, if tremendously heavy, roofs. That said, stone was expensive. Until 1500 most English houses were built of wood.

Types of limestone range from so-called Purbeck 'marble' – it made the tall polished shafts clustering around the pillars of thirteenth-century cathedrals – to Portland stone, washed ghostly white by the rain; because it can be quarried in large blocks, Portland has been used to dress many London buildings. Such different stones, and yet the Isle of Purbeck, near Poole, and the Isle of Portland, near Weymouth, lie quite close together. The quarries around Bath provide the luminous stone which makes one feel that town is always smiling. Bath stone can be easily carved into capitals, urns, garlands – any fetching detail you can think of – but, being porous, it is apt to decay. The broad-shouldered Cotswolds are made of limestone, and so are the pretty villages and manor houses that snuggle up to them. Around the beautiful town of Stamford in Lincolnshire are many quarries, producing what is generically called Lincolnshire limestone – although confusingly most of them are in Northamptonshire, hence its exceptional number of fine churches. Sir Christopher Wren favoured Ketton stone. Earlier, the best-known quarries were Barnack, Weldon and – ten miles from Boothby Pagnell – Ancaster.

I like the word 'freestone': it has a proud, independent ring. It means stone that can be shaped into a flat surface in any plane. It would have been worth the effort of carting freestone some distance. Even so, ten miles was a long way on twelfth-century roads, as creaking cartwheels bumped over ruts and got sucked down into mud. Fortunately Ancaster stone is not only found at Ancaster, but in outcrops across the surrounding area; probably the de Bothebys' freestone came from one of them. Only the outer surfaces of the walls were built of it, laboriously chipped smooth; the parts that the eye would not see were filled with irregular boulders, inferior stone that was the wrong size or wrong quality to be shaped. The rubble stone would have come from the site itself, perhaps having been dug out of the moat.

Not that the freestone blocks in the walls at Boothby Pagnell are perfectly shaped. They came out of the quarry in different sizes, and that is how they have been laid, in jumbled courses. The stone is now draped in a filigree of grey lichen, liver-spotted with tan blotches. Under a magnifying glass, the stones themselves change character, often becoming a beach of shattered shell fragments – the lias – or revealing the smooth texture of oolite. Here and there can be seen an orange-coloured stone, high in iron content – there had been iron-masters at work in nearby Rockingham Forest since Roman times.

If there was a house at Boothby Pagnell (in earlier times known as Bodebi) before the Conquest, perhaps controlling the same area of land, in the decades after 1066 the old Saxon establishment was pushed aside. The de Bothebys were a Norman family, occupying a place within the feudal system imported from France. Boothby Pagnell is, even now, in the Hundred of Boothby, a Hundred being a unit capable of supplying a hundred soldiers. No doubt the de Botheby men were often called away to fight on one side or the other, but they must have been good businessmen as well as knights. They owned a single manor. Even with the standard perks – fines extracted from peasants for poaching or infringing other feudal laws, charges levied for milling corn at the lord's mill (local people could go nowhere else) – this would not have been sufficient to finance an ambitious building project. But Lincoln was now at its zenith of prosperity as a wool town. Everyone needed clothes made out of wool, yet not everywhere could support sheep. In an otherwise subsistence economy, wool could be traded, even exported. The de Bothebys' new house could well have been built on profits from the wool trade.

But man cannot live by wool alone. A church existed at Boothby Pagnell when William I commissioned the Domesday Book, and it was probably the de Bothebys who rebuilt it. Often a stone church would be built before the stone house that stood near it. The presence of God or his opposite, the Evil One, was felt everywhere. The church was a vital structure, the largest space that most villagers entered on a regular basis, and like the manor house, an unimaginable contrast with their own flimsy dwellings. (In Yorkshire, an entire village is said to have blown away in a gale.) The lord's hall was the secular equivalent of the church: a microcosm of England as the de Bothebys saw it, on the same scale as the church, if not bigger.

In Roman life, public activity had been kept separate from the private realm, and family life had taken place in buildings that were different from those provided for law, theatre, religion and politics.

But feasting was not a private matter in the Saxon and Norman traditions. As a matter of course, all members of the lord's family and his senior dependants would take part. Oft-repeated usages helped bind them together as a unit, imbued with a strong sense of shared values. This esprit de corps inspired Saxon households as they stood together on the battlefield. The thought of being exiled from the hall and its community – the fate of the Wanderer in the famous Old English poem of the same name – was unbearably dismal. In this respect Norman habits were little different from Saxon ones.

Dozens of people – stewards, bailiffs, reeves, clerks and other manorial officers, house servants, gardeners, grooms – were directly dependent on the de Bothebys. Life for the family would hardly have been possible without them. These servants, extended family members and hangers-on made up the household. Twice a day, they ate together in the hall. Households experienced an inflation of numbers as the centuries wore on, reaching a zenith in the late Middle Ages and only declining in the sixteenth century. So halls could be crowded. Order was imposed through carefully graded seating arrangements which expressed the hierarchy by which the entire country was structured.

When in the thirteenth century Bishop Grosseteste of Lincoln drew up some guidance for a lady in governing her household, he urged that eating outside the hall should be strictly forbidden. Only the sick or the truly exhausted could be excused attendance. The lady herself was to preside – as no doubt the de Bothebys did – from the centre of the high table, which would have been placed across the top of the room. The elevated status of the high table was symbolized by its being raised a foot or so above the floor on a dais. At right angles to the dais, other tables stretched down the length of the hall. Benches rather than chairs were drawn up to them. (The system survives in Oxford and Cambridge colleges and the Inns of Court in London.) Order was ensured by the presence of a marshal, who supervised the service at the high table, kept the lower ranks from quarrelling or making excessive noise, and – in large households – stopped freeloaders (known as lechers) from seizing food from the dishes before they had been put on the table. Interestingly, Bishop Grosseteste attached much more significance to the ceremony with which the meal was conducted than to the food itself.

In the Bayeux Tapestry, diners appear to be taking whole birds and pieces of meat off the spits on which they have been roasted with their hands. There were as yet only knives, spoons and hands to eat with – no forks. When fowl or meat was being carved, it was held steady using the fingers; this was still good form when Wynkyn de Worde's *The Boke of Keruynge* (The Book of Carving) was published in 1508 (however, according to Wynkyn, no more than 'two fyngers and a thombe' should be allowed to touch the meat). The etiquette books of the later Middle Ages place an understandable emphasis on the washing of hands before and after eating; in monastic houses there is always a *lavatorium*, for washing, next to the refectory. The tables were made up of boards placed on trestles. When the eating was finished, they would be dismantled, leaving an uncluttered space where justice could be dispensed (fines were a useful source of income to the manorial lord), dances held, conversation pursued, guests received, games played and announcements made. At night, the hall underwent another transformation, this time into a dormitory, for it was there that most of the household slept.

A great hall that was built about the same time as the one at Boothby Pagnell can be seen not far away, at Oakham. It looks not unlike a church, with arches to either side forming aisles. The internal divisions are clearly expressed in the roof, which rises at a steeper pitch in the centre than at the sides. There would have been plenty of ventilation, whether desired or not, from the draughts that whistled through the wooden shutters (there would have been cloth rather than glass in the windows). The draughts helped kindle the logs on the big central hearth, which provided the only source of heat. One can imagine people sitting around it, with their shoes off, warming their feet: this is a practice shown in numerous medieval carvings and illuminations. Smoke gusted upwards into the tall roof and eventually out through louvres in it. But it would have got into people's eyes on the way, and the smell would have permeated everything. Not that wood smoke was the worst of the smells in the hall. Personal hygiene was scant. As late as the sixteenth century, Erasmus was outraged by the state of English floors, almost all of which he found to be bare clay covered in 'rushes from the marshes, so carelessly renewed that the foundation sometimes remains for twenty years, harbouring there below spittle and vomit and urine of dogs and men, beer that hath been cast forth and remnants of fishes and other filth unnameable'. This would probably stand as a fair description of the floor at Boothby Pagnell, only in the twelfth century it was nothing remarkable.

Man's short life is like a sparrow flying through a hall on a winter's night. This simile, though contrived by the Venerable Bede several centuries before Boothby Pagnell was built, would have been easily understood by its owners. Dogs and cats wandered into the hall in search of scraps. It was not unknown for horses to be ridden into halls, at least in romances. Rats and mice would hardly have been worth comment. The de Bothebys may have wrinkled their noses at this hugger-mugger existence, sometimes, one would imagine, longing for the moment when they could withdraw to more comfortable space where they could speak French in private and play chess. For with its dais and collapsible furniture, the hall was less like a home than a theatre where the family was always on stage. Even very great people found the experience uncomfortable. Neither King Richard nor King John much cared for the sharp-tongued wit that even they had to suffer in hall on occasion.

So the de Bothebys constructed a more intimate building for their own use, which in fact would have been one of many structures on the site. Norman manors were built rather like tribal encampments, contained within a ditch or bank; different functions occupied different buildings, which only later came to be grouped in a coherent relationship to one another. But whereas the existence of the great hall has only recently been deduced by archaeologists, and the other buildings on the site have disappeared without trace, at least so far, this private structure survives. This is as it should be, in the story of the English house. For the hall and its values, though lingering in very large houses into the seventeenth century, ultimately disappeared, despite attempts by paternalistic Victorians and romantic socialists to revive them. Instead, comfort and privacy – expressed in the de Bothebys' chamber block – became, in modern times, the essential qualities of a home.

Seen just as the place to which the de Bothebys withdrew into their own world of quiet and warmth, Boothby Pagnell Manor House no longer looks so very small. It is unquestionably solid. The walls, built mostly of randomly shaped stones but with squared stones, or ashlar, at the corners and openings, are more than three feet thick. Originally the roof would have been thatch; the staircase to the first floor is a modern replacement, and a larger window was inserted about 1500. Otherwise the east front is much as the de Bothebys would have known it. A narrow window, divided into two by a stone mullion, lights one of the first-floor rooms; above it is a round-headed arch. A buttress adds its support to walls built on shallow foundations. In its completeness, Boothby Pagnell Manor House is an exceptional survival.

This was a serious piece of architecture. The two ground-floor rooms are both vaulted, one with the barrel vault that you would expect in a Norman building, the other with a vault supported on stone ribs – a harbinger of the Gothic style – the spaces between the ribs being filled with stone tiles set on their edges. This technique implies a refined knowledge of construction. The ribs would have been laid out first on a wooden framework, that framework being quickly removed once the stones had been set in place and the mortar laid, so that the mortar would strengthen under compression. A triumph of construction, and yet the space that it covered was probably used mainly to store the large quantities of grain and wine that were needed to see a medieval household through the winter.

The two family rooms lay upstairs, and here one begins to understand the level of comfort that this chamber block represented. For what do we see in the west wall of the larger of the two chambers, but a fireplace? We have seen that there was a fireplace in the White Tower in London, built a century before, and wall fireplaces had been used in Normandy itself since the 1020s. But the White Tower functioned as a royal palace; Boothby Pagnell was on no such scale. It is easy to imagine what a pleasure it must have been for the de Bothebys, on a blustery winter's day, to leave the hall, its central fire giving a very uneven distribution of heat, and hurry the few paces, probably under a covered way, to the chamber block, its walls hung with tapestries or painted cloths, perhaps with a favourite falcon sitting on a perch or rail, and draw a stool up close to a fireplace that was more than six feet wide. The hood alone looks welcoming; it is a massive work of masonry, supported on corbels and with sides that slope up to the ceiling. It does not project very far: the flue snakes back into the thick wall, and then up and up – as children like to discover when they stand inside it – to a neat circle of sky far above, which is the mouth of the chimney. Externally, the presence of the fireplace is marked by an architectural flourish appropriate to its importance: the chimney stack at the back of the building steps up to a gabled base, supporting a tall cylindrical stack. In the matter of chimneys, Boothby Pagnell was one up on William I's Tower of London. In the wall is a recess, quite small but faced with carefully shaped stones; at the top, two stones meet each other to form a triangle. It looks like a recess in the chancel of a church. Perhaps the de Bothebys kept a jug of wine here.

The next-door room has no great and luxurious fireplace but probably contained a bed heaped with coverings (it had to be well covered: people slept naked in the Middle Ages). A window seat hints at the charm the room must have held for its first occupants (though it may not have been so pleasant in rough weather: water came in, and there are runnels at the foot of the windows to channel it and little drains to let it escape). The technical term for such an upper chamber is *solar*, sometimes said to derive from the Latin *solarium*, a room designed for the enjoyment of sunshine, on the grounds that such spaces were more amply lit than penumbrous halls. This is probably fanciful, but suggests the allure of a room filled with light at a time when candles were very expensive. Bedrooms did not need to be kept dark when most people rose at dawn. On the other hand, these rooms, with their narrow windows, were never flooded with light. Windows had to be small: glass was rare and quite possibly not used in a building like this, the de Bothebys, as we have seen, having always had defence at the back of their minds. Peasant houses were certainly far darker, and smokier.

Houses like Boothby Pagnell, made up of several detached structures, existed in England before the Conquest. In the eighth century, King Alfred, summarizing St Augustine's soliloquies, evoked the disposition of a royal palace with the words '. . . some men are in the chamber, some are in the hall, some on the threshing-floor, some in prison.' Alfred's 'royal halls and chambers marvellously constructed of stone and wood' were the subject of praise from his biographer. Archaeology has revealed that late Saxon manors were composed of separate hall and chamber blocks, on the same principle as Boothby Pagnell: interestingly, there was one in Lincolnshire, at Goltho. Archaeological excavations suggest that they had their chambers on the ground floor, but clearly more elaborate complexes existed where the chamber was raised. The King's house at Calne must have been one of them: the *Anglo-Saxon Chronicle* describes how the chamber floor collapsed under the weight of the royal council. The Bayeux Tapestry shows King Harold feasting at Bosham in a room over a round-headed arcade, while a companion on the steps urgently points to the sea; similarly, Edward the Confessor is shown dying in an upper chamber. So it would seem that the Norman de Bothebys were following a Saxon precedent, though it probably did not strike them as such, as by then there were very similar manors under construction in Normandy. The Normans, having invaded England, liked this native building type and took it back with them to France.

Once work on the manor house had been finished, the de Bothebys must have surveyed their new home with satisfaction. Grooms tended their horses. Cooks were busy at their endless task of preparing food, perhaps setting fires in the open air. Feeding the quantities of people who ate in the hall was a major undertaking. Everything consumed at the manor, bar a few spices, would have been grown at home. But then the manor was itself a kind of giant larder, organized to supply a constant flow of food. Doves fluttered from the dovecot – they would be served up in due course, a welcome addition to the monotonous winter table. Perch and bream glided through the moat and the fish ponds. Fruit swelled on the trees in the garden. The woods teemed with game. Rabbits bobbed in the warren. Shepherds herded sheep from pasture to pasture. In the great open fields, peasants tilled their strips for part of the week, providing a few eggs or a hen by way of rent. On other, carefully specified days, they worked on the de Bothebys' land. Their round would have been much the same as that depicted in a book of psalms commissioned by another Lincolnshire lord, Sir Geoffrey Luttrell, more than a century later. This psalter is not only decorated with religious scenes and grotesque beasts, but with vignettes of rural life: peasants getting drunk, millers grinding corn, snails, oxen, a woman scattering crumbs for farmyard birds, ploughing, aiming slingshots at crows, getting in the harvest, serving a feast in a hall.

The Luttrell Psalter was made about 1320, by which time the male line of the de Bothebys had died out, though their name was perpetuated in that of the village. In 1309, the heiress Agnes de Botheby married Sir John Pagnell, who came from a prominent family descended from one of the Conqueror's favourites, Ralph Paganel, who held forty-five lordships, among them Newport Pagnell. It says much for the charms of Bodebi and its manor house that the Pagnells transferred their allegiance to it. Later members of the family went to the bad. John Leland tells of two John Pagnells, father and son, both knights and 'great lechers', the younger of whom fathered an incestuous child with his daughter. In 1565 another Pagnell took the altarstone from the church to use as a hearth.

Of course the de Bothebys who built the manor house had no reason to foresee scandal or disaster. The system of which they were part seemed immutable, and the next century would see England's population grow as its wealth increased. Aspects of the de Bothebys' way of life would filter down the social hierarchy, until they reached the level of the prosperous families who farmed southern England. They too needed halls and private chambers, though on a different scale from those of a Norman lord, and probably not ones built of Ancaster stone.

2. A Yeoman's House of Wood
The Clergy House, Alfriston

In the mid-fourteenth century, travelling from Boothby Pagnell to Sussex would have been a luxury, albeit a strange one, being hardly comfortable or even safe. Few people except clergy, who belonged to the multinational institution that was the medieval Church, armies and territorial magnates shuttling between their possessions, made long journeys. To the tillers of the land, travel was generally an unimaginable concept, daunting and bizarre; they had little reason, and may not even have been allowed, to go beyond their immediate neighbourhood. More prosperous individuals could afford a broader view. In the *Canterbury Tales*, Chaucer's pilgrims not only go to pay homage to St Thomas à Becket at Canterbury: the Wife of Bath had made other pilgrimages, to Santiago de Compostela and Jerusalem (three times), and the Knight had fought in Spain and North Africa as a Crusader. Travellers of this kind brought back new tastes in food and luxuries. But there were not many of them.

An emissary from Lincolnshire to Sussex would not have travelled alone. No man left home at that time without a sharp-bladed weapon hanging from his belt, and prudent travellers took provisions to sustain them on the journey, perhaps even a makeshift shelter, in case they could not reach an alehouse or inn, or find a welcoming private hall (Bishop Grosseteste of Lincoln put particular store on hospitality, insisting that strangers had to be embraced into a household). As he trotted his pony over dry, sandy tracks and splashed his way through the clinging puddles of clay ones, our Lincolnshire friend would have had plenty of time for his own thoughts, and fears, the journey would have taken a week or two. When Edward I's Queen Eleanor had died in 1290, it had taken a fortnight for the funeral cortege to make its way to Westminister; the speed of travel had not increased since then.

We can understand what the journey to Sussex would have been like from an extraordinary map that survives from 1360. Preserved in the Bodleian Library in Oxford, it is a unique document, centuries ahead of its time in attempting to show the correct geographical relationships between the different parts of Great Britain. Although nobody in the fourteenth century would have carried a map on their travels, only an itinerary of villages to count off like a rosary, the Gough Map shows how medieval people envisaged moving around England. Rivers curl into the land mass like fat eels. Roads, by contrast, are red veins no more than a pen stroke thick. There are not many of them, and they generally follow the course of the ruts gouged out of the paving stones by Roman carts and chariots. Indeed they would have been wide enough for two carts to pass each other, but no more.

Ancaster is marked on the map; so is Grantham, shown with an enormous church. But this is a rural landscape, with few centres of population, and some of those – from the modern standpoint – eccentrically chosen. We make our way towards Stamford, and thence south along Ermine Street to Caxton (once a town, now a village), Royston, Ware, Waltham Abbey – and London. Roads stride on over streams and rivers: nearly as many bridges existed by the end of the Middle Ages as were found in the eighteenth century. There are few towns, but we see many people, moving slowly across fields with backs bent – not as many, however, as there were before the Black Death visited in 1348.

Our traveller is out by first light, while noctural badgers are still nosing through the nettles of the waysides. Everyone is up early, and outside. Fourteenth-century England was a land of villages, not big towns and cities – a mere eighty thousand people lived in London at the time. As much land was farmed then as now, perhaps more, but the countryside would have been far busier with people. Men would have been sowing, children scaring away birds (greedy doves from the lord's dovecots among them), shepherds driving sheep across fallow land, foresters making their way to the woods, warreners tending rabbits (introduced to England by the Normans), ploughmen carting dung, gardeners pruning orchards and women carrying the sticks to their homes; on the road itself there may well have been friars, pardoners, itinerant beggars, sometimes the great train that proclaimed the presence of a travelling lady, and others from among the crowd imagined by Piers Plowman in his vision of 'feir feld full of folk'.

Twenty miles south of London, the road passed among great oak trees, centuries old, growing on what had been farmland to the Romans but which had reverted to scrub once the ancient social structure had broken down. The scrub grew, over the years, into forest. Parts of the forest would have been cleared; there was iron ore in the rocks, and the miners needed the trees to make charcoal in order to melt it. This was the Weald. The word is the same as Wold, meaning 'wooded place' (it survives in 'Cotswolds' and the York-shire and Lincolnshire Wolds). Our traveller would have had good reason to sing loudly and spur on his pony while darting anxious glances at the shadows that lay behind the trees; isolated farmsteads had become established around Saxon *dens* or *deans* (meaning clearings made for pigs), and hursts (wooded eminences) but there were few hamlets; outlaws to which the Weald gave shelter were not at all likely to behave with the chivalry of Robin Hood. What a relief it would have been to emerge onto the waves of chalk downland that roll towards the coast! Sheep grazed contentedly among the cowslips and violets of the pasture, then scrubby though later nibbled almost bald. Eventually the road approached the marshy plain where the river Cuckmere loops its lazy meanders towards the English Channel. Beside this river lies the village of Alfriston, the end of the journey.

The Clergy House lies next to the river, a watery location to build on, you might think, despite the bank of earth to protect it from flooding. Water, though, was the medium of medieval life. The rivers were essential to getting around fourteenth-century England. Flooding watermeadows would bring on an early bite of grass for sheep, giving a farmer an advantage over his neighbours on higher ground. Water, like most resources in the countryside, was too precious not to manage carefully.

There is a church a few yards away from the Clergy House, a remarkable building which stands on a Saxon mound, perhaps once a prehistoric burial site, some way from the village High Street. Begun around 1360 and dedicated to St Andrew the Apostle, it is constructed to an almost centralized Greek-cross plan (with the tower over the crossing) that erases all memory of the more modest structure which preceded it. Mysteriously, the stones that had been brought to build it on a different site kept being moved – how else but by the will of God? – to the present one. And four oxen were found with their rumps touching and their bodies placed at right angles to each other. This is what dictated the plan, or so we are told. The church was so big that it would eventually be known as the Cathedral of the South Downs.

Was it a thanks offering? Whoever built it would have lived through the terrible decade that followed the Battle of Crécy in 1346. After Edward III's victory, the English had retaken the French port of Calais. This would have been welcome news to the people of Sussex, geographically so close to the Continent – the county's well-being had been bound up with events across the Channel since William had landed at Pevensey in 1066. Life was constantly being disrupted by the need to produce soldiers for the King's armies, and the county often played reluctant host to troops en route to the coast. But an unwelcome byproduct of the newly invigorated trade with France was rats, which slipped from the French quayside into the holds of ships, then out again into English ports. The rats carried fleas, and the fleas spread plague. The summer of 1348 was one of the wettest in memory. It rained on the dresses of great ladies, plundered from French towns, at the tournaments organized to celebrate Edward's victory. It rained on the corn in Sussex fields, ruining the harvest. The poor were short of food, and this weakened their resistance to disease. The Black Death broke out in Dorset and was thence carried around the coast by ship; once it reached London, it was sent out all over the country. Sussex caught it early. In sumptuous Battle Abbey, erected by William the Conqueror himself, the abbot and over half the monks died. Near Alfriston, eight of the thirteen canons of Michelham Priory perished. Within a few months, the population of Sussex had been reduced by as much as a half. Villages were deserted. The Black Death was followed by chaos, as civil order collapsed; in 1351 the bailiff of Pevensey seems to have extorted protection money from the Prior of Michelham, to the tune of 30s a year.

In the Church of St Andrew, the painting of the Doom, or Last Judgement, which accompanied the Consecration of the Cross and various images of saints and bishops, would have had a particular resonance in these difficult times, when life, even by contemporary standards, must have seemed unusually precarious. Those who survived the Black Death emerged from the trauma into a new economic reality. As in any period of change, people with the quickness of mind to understand what it meant could profit from the wreckage. Anyone with labour to sell suddenly found that he could gain up to 75 per cent more for his efforts. The feudal system, with its complex web of obligations, could not be sustained; there were not enough people left to provide the services or to police the system. Some villages disappeared altogether. Alfriston, by contrast, came out on top.

The Clergy House (a name it acquired in later centuries) is built on a glebe, land owned by the Church and farmed by the Church's administrator, or rector; Michelham Priory acquired it in the fifteenth century. It was constructed at the end of the fourteenth century. We do not know the identity of the original builder: it could have been the Church, wanting to improve the income from its glebe or even to house clergy (it has been suggested that the original arrangement of doors separated the living quarters, perhaps occupied by priests, from the service end of the house, where women might have worked). An alternative theory, which I shall accept for convenience, is that it was built for a yeoman, one of the rising class of farmers who rented their land, in this case from the Church. His position in society lay somewhere between the lesser nobility and the peasants; presumably he and his forebears were among those clever enough to do well out of the economic turmoil that characterized the second half of the fourteenth century. Yeomen hardly figured before 1348; by the end of the century they featured in the *Canterbury Tales* (the Devil wears a green yeoman's jacket in the Friar's Tale). Hundreds of houses like the Clergy House would be built across Hampshire, Sussex and Kent over the next hundred years.

The life of a yeoman and that of a priest were not worlds apart. Priests were in the habit of keeping pigs, sheep, cows and, for visiting the parish, a pony; '. . . the Vicar of Chieveley in 1314 had as many as twelve cows, a hundred sheep and twelve pigs, while a flock of fifty or sixty sheep with half a dozen milking cows was quite common. Pigs were also very popular with the clergy,' commented Dr J. R. H. Moorman in *Church Life in England in the Thirteenth Century* (1945). Tithes had to be stored in barns, sometimes of great size, making a parsonage resemble a farmyard. Most people in Alfriston would have farmed in some manner. But the village was also bustling its way towards becoming a town, its prosperity supported by foul-smelling leather-tanning. On the other side of the village green, known as the Tye, from the Clergy House, two inns were built in the High Street during the late fourteenth century, and Alfriston would soon be granted the right to hold a market and fair.

The whole of the Yeoman's home is about the size of the chamber block at Boothby Pagnell, its hall, solar and service rooms companionably crowded together under a single tea cosy of a thatched roof (although the original covering could have been Horsham stone). But size is not the only difference. The Clergy House is built of wood.

Originally the whole of Britain was a forest. It used to be thought that much of it remained in this condition until the Norman period. Now it seems that most of the immense primordial trees were cut down long before 1066, before even the Romans had come, during centuries when woodsmen only had stone axes and fire to do the job. Only about fifteen per cent of England was wooded at the time of the Domesday Book. But wood, like water, was essential to medieval life. So trees were treated like other crops and husbanded to produce a harvest year after year.

Every manor had its woods. Like so much of the economy, they were controlled by manorial laws. Lordly halls and abbots' parlours, castle guard rooms and royal palaces, shared the same heat source as the peasant's hovel. Even fallen branches and spindly trees had their value, if not to smoulder into the charcoal made by itinerant charcoal burners in turf-covered shelters in the forest, then to be carved into tables, chairs, plates, spoons, clogs – nearly everything that could be found in poor homes, even in well-to-do ones, was made of wood. Whippy young shoots were gathered to make fences, poles and basketwork; they came from coppiced trees, often hazel, which had been cut down to the stump, or from oak pollards, truncated about six feet from the ground, above the height of grazing animals: both techniques cause supple new growth to sprout in crowns. Pollarding helps trees to survive to immense ages; some of the ancient, hollow trees in Windsor Great Park and Sherwood Forest today would have been alive back in the fourteenth century.

Firebote gave peasants the right to collect firewood. *Pannage* allowed them to fatten their pigs on fallen acorns in wood pasture. *Fencebote* conferred the right to gather wood for fencing, *plough-bote* to make agricultural tools. These and other rights were policed by the wood ward, an official whom the lord employed to look after his precious woods. *Housebote* was the right to fell timber to build or repair a house.

Different species of tree have different qualities. Elm is tough; its wood makes the best floorboards and coffins (it takes the longest to rot in water). Yew, being flexible, is particularly suited to longbows. So is ash; but ash can also take knocks, making it the wood for cart shafts and wheels. Fine-grained box is extremely hard: ideal for pestles and mortars, and the making of mathematical instruments. Sycamore was chosen for milk pails because it imparted no taste. Oak was medieval England's commonest tree, and it yielded the best building timber: easy to work when green and then almost impenetrably hard once the sap had gone from it, while the frame of a house locked together as the wood dried and shrank. This gave strength, and after a while the house would cease to move. But it should be remembered that structures built of green wood in this way are akin to living organisms. As the timbers change shape, walls can twist and bow, bulging like saddlebags or leaning jauntily. Few of the angles in the Clergy House are precisely true. Wooden houses, like their occupants, evolve with the years, and this one might have expired altogether in the 1890s if it had not been rescued by the National Trust. Having sunk into use as two poverty-stricken cottages, it was on the point of being demolished.

As we have seen, nearly all the houses built in England before the Tudor period, even in areas with good building stone, were made of wood. Many more survive than meet the eye, hiding behind fronts of brick or mathematical tiles that were added to give an air of fashion and prosperity to the street in the seventeenth or eighteenth century, while the interiors went unchanged.

Wood, even oak, has its disadvantages. If exposed to damp it eventually rots. As a result, the posts supporting the earliest wooden houses, which were inserted directly into the soil, did not survive for long. Every few decades, the houses had to be rebuilt. One can imagine that this would have been an opportunity to clear out the animal life with which they would have become thoroughly infested. Saxon houses were always of this 'earth foot' construction, so none have come down to us. Only around 1200 did householders start to raise their vulnerable timbers off the ground, standing them on a wooden beam, or sill, supported by a low wall of stones. From the second half of the thirteenth century, the number of timber-framed houses that would survive into the twenty-first century began to increase. The Clergy House rests on a sill of flint.

Far away from Sussex, in the north and west of the country, the frame of a house might be built out of crucks. Crucks are massive timbers that stand like pairs of straddling legs – the word has the same derivation as crutch and crotch, meaning fork. They could be made from trees that in craggy areas had grown up with a bend in them, or carpenters might select a naturally curving lower branch. There is some thought that branches were pegged to the ground to encourage bends. Pairs of timbers were then matched up, or an exceptionally thick trunk or branch would be split into two, each half forming a mirror image of the other when raised. Carted to the site of a new house, the crucks were laid on the ground and joined with a crosspiece to form an A. Neighbours helped the householder to haul – or perhaps walk – the A into an upright position. Another pair of crucks would be raised, making one bay of the house – then more crucks for as many bays as the house would be long. The A's were held together by horizontal beams. The size of a cruck-built house was limited by the height of the original trees.

Crucks were not used in the south and east of England, regions that were richer than the rest of the country and closer to the Continent – factors which could have influenced the preference for box-frame construction. Another explanation could be that fewer great oaks grew in these areas; therefore builders were forced to rely on younger trees, grown in plantations, whose trunks would have been both thinner and straighter. As its name implies, the box frame was made of timbers which were assembled together like a box – the principle upon which the Clergy House was constructed.

The frame was shaped away from the place where it was finally erected, in the carpenter's woodyard. Standing astride the rough trunks, the carpenter and his apprentices would have chipped away at them with a sharp-bladed tool like a hoe. As they walked backwards, they would have left a more or less smooth surface in front of them. The timbers would then have been cut to length; joints would have been formed; the structure would have been put together to try it out. The joints are variations on the mortice and tenon, the mortice being a notch cut into the wood and the tenon being a tongue that projects into it, secured into position with a wooden pin. There are many refinements on this principle, designed to lock the parts of a building together, some looking like elaborate geometrical puzzles. Often these intricacies would be hidden from view once a building had been constructed. Nails were not used at all.

The timbers available for such houses were not perfect in every respect. Those that were to be visible on the outside of the building, or that faced into principal rooms, looked as regular as possible, but blemishes such as knots might crop up in passages. Timbers would therefore be laid on the ground with their better faces downwards, while the carpenter took his 'pryking' knife and notched Roman numerals, or a version of them, into their backs, to serve as a code for when the whole structure was re-erected. Eventually, the timbers were loaded onto carts and taken to the building site. So such houses were effectively built as kits. Trees for a box-frame house did not have to be very large – no longer than fourteen feet in the case of one Weald of Sussex house. But a lot were required. It has been estimated that as many as 360 trees could go into a medieval house; a substantial farmhouse outside East Bergholt in Suffolk, owned by the National Trust, was built of fifty acres' worth of three-year-old trees, along with some reused timbers and offcuts.

Not just the frame of the Clergy House is made of wood, but also the floorboards and the panelling. Good timber did not come cheap. Some might have been obtained by *housebote*, or grown on the Yeoman's own land, but most of it probably had to be purchased. The cost of buying and felling the trees was not the end of it. They would then have been hauled off to the wood yard – a time-consuming and therefore expensive operation in itself. But none of this expense would have equalled the cost of shaping the timbers. Carpenters were said to practise a 'mystery' – suggesting that they had arcane knowledge. To an extent they did; whether individual craftsmen consciously understood mathematics or not, they ultimately benefited from the translation of Euclid from

Arabic into Latin which was done around 1120. Geometry enabled carpenters – and also masons – to work with precision, and they could charge good money for their services. (Although, like builders of other ages, they did not always turn up on time. Having been contracted to build a house at Temple Balsall in Warwickshire in 1415, John Bonde would begin work variously at prime – early morning – or midday, according to documents in the subsequent lawsuit. *Plus ça change*.)

Carpenters naturally wanted to encourage an aura of rarefied knowledge to heighten their standing in the community. And timber architecture in England did develop an element of mystery, as its dizzyingly projecting upper floors were built ever outward, seemingly in defiance of gravity. Something of this can be seen in the Clergy House. The centre is occupied by the hall, open to the rafters. To either side of the hall are two-storeyed cross-wings, the upper floors of which projected forward from the main line of the building. They seem to hover by themselves. These projections are called jetties. Jetties were being used by at least 1286, the date of a house called The Old Canonry in Wingham in Kent. Generally, the projecting timbers were hidden by a fascia board in early houses. One no longer exists, if it ever did, at the Clergy House, leaving the beam ends clearly visible. Later, the beam ends of jettied houses would attract the attention of carvers, who would adorn them with geometrical patterns or turn them into dragons.

What were jetties for? In a crowded city, householders might have valued the extra space that they would provide by encroaching over the street. That cannot have been necessary on an open site. Even today, historians are hard put to find a practical explanation. Jetties may have had a benefit in throwing water away from the lower floor of a house; medieval houses were built without gutters, though their eaves projected to compensate. There is another possible explanation. Jetties may simply have been an exuberance.

Wood – a light form of construction, unlike ponderous masonry – can be used to play structural tricks, and one can imagine that people like the Yeoman, living in places where wood was easily available, would have delighted in such things.

The Clergy House uses jetties in a particular way. The type to which it belongs is known as the Wealden House, although its presence was not confined to the Weald proper, but became common throughout Kent, Sussex and Hampshire. While the upper floors of the cross-wings jump forward with projecting jetties, the centre block containing the hall stays put. A continuous roof sails over the whole thing, supported by a massive beam, or eavesplate; the eavesplate is in turn supported by a pair of arched timber braces. In the case of the Clergy House, one of the jetties disappeared when that part of the house was rebuilt in the sixteenth century (at which point it gained a massive brick fireplace, which must have seemed a fair exchange to the occupants). The Wealden House type seems to have emerged in the years after the Black Death. Trees Cottage at Froxfield in Hampshire, which has a two-bay hall comparable to that of the Clergy House, has been ring-dated to 1360.

Gaps between the timbers of the Clergy House were filled with a weave made of oak strips or laths and thin withies onto which was sloshed a daub of mud mixed with straw, dung and cow hair – fairly stiff, to avoid excess shrinkage. This was protected by a coating of lime. Walls made by this method were cold, if not draughty, and liable to disintegrate if they got wet. In later centuries, a variety of coverings was introduced to keep out the weather. The most common was plaster (lime, obtained by burning limestone, mixed with chalk) or 'Roman' cement (lime mixed with clay). Elsewhere, walls were faced with overlapping boards (weatherboarding), or hung with tiles or slates. Here was another opportunity to decorate: both slates and tiles could be arranged like fish scales or in other fancy patterns. As coverings improved, the quality of the timbers beneath them declined. Which was the cause and which the effect? We can only say that fewer and less robust timbers were used in seventeenth- and eighteenth-century timber-framed houses than had been the case in earlier times.

By the sixteenth century, carpenters were contriving the fantastic tiers of jetties seen in The Feathers at Ludlow in Shropshire, the Rows at Chester in Cheshire, and houses like Little Moreton Hall in the same county. Panels were adorned with geometrical arrangements of struts and braces, making herringbone or lozenge patterns, particularly in Cheshire, Lancashire and the West Midlands: they might be criticized by an austere age for being unstructural, but they suited the Elizabethan taste for fantasy and artistic elaboration. It is as though their creators were painting with wood.

Let us return to our Lincolnshire visitor. We find him needing to make his presence known in the hall of the Clergy House. The front door is placed about a third of the way along the entrance front, its top shaped with a Gothic arch. In a grand country house, this would have led into a screens passage with three openings: to the pantry (*panetrie*, or bread room, where food was kept), the kitchen (detached from the main building) and the buttery (the *bouteillerie*, or bottle store, which would now be called the cellar for wine and beer). An echo of this arrangement survives in the Clergy House, but on a far more modest scale. There was no screen, unless a movable one, and only two door openings (with shaped tops) giving onto what would have been the servants' wing.

The hall was a supremely adaptable room type, forming a domestic common currency; from the age of the Saxons until that of the Tudors, noblemen, clergy, innkeepers and yeomen all had their halls, varying only in size. The hall at the Clergy House is modest in comparison to Boothby Pagnell, not so much as 25 feet long. It is cold underfoot. Beneath a scattering of rushes, the floor, in the Sussex way, is made of chalk lumps, rammed down to make a smooth, hard surface and then coated with sour milk to seal it. Logs smouldered on a central hearth. Hazily, lazily, the smoke found its way up to the roof beams 25 feet overhead, where there was a louvre for it to escape through. In time the smoke would blacken the timbers at the apex of the roof, as can still be seen at the Clergy House; the Yeoman may have lived in greater state than the poor widow in Chaucer's Nun's Priest's Tale but might have sympathized with the condition of her 'full sooty' hall. In *Piers Plowman* (*c.*1360–99), William Langland gives a vivid description of smoke smiting the eye of the householder, making him hoarse so that he 'cougheth and curseth'. Not until the Elizabethan period could people of middling rank aspire to a fireplace in a chamber. Writing his *Description of England* in 1577, William Harrison recorded the changes that had come over Radwinter in Essex during the lifetime of older men, the most conspicuous of which was the 'multitude of chimneys lately erected'. Even aristocratic halls continued in possession of their central hearths until the sixteenth century, and their disappearance was still being lamented by traditionalists in the reign of Charles I.

The cock Chantecleer and his three 'wives' wandered in and out of Chaucer's poor widow's house. Most country people lived close by their animals; in the West Country cow byres were built under the same roof as the farmer's living accommodation, the result being the long house – a form that made maximum use of available heat. The Yeoman at the Clergy House lived at a further remove from the farmyard. Nevertheless, we can imagine birds fluttering up to the rafters and perching on a fine piece of structural carpentry called the king post. This was a stout post rising from an even stouter transverse beam tying the walls of the hall together. The king post supported a pair of rafters in one direction, while, at an angle of ninety degrees, two arched braces supported the roof ridge.

The king post was one of many carpentry structures that evolved for the purpose of strengthening roofs – queen posts, crown posts, arched braced collar beams and the like – which must also have been enjoyed for their sculptural qualities. By the end of the fourteenth century, carpenters had so developed their 'mystery' that the roofs of very grand buildings could be graced by virtuosic hammerbeam roofs, providing a means by which widths greater than the height of a tree trunk could be spanned.

The Yeoman's hall is not a long structure like the de Bothebys', but more of a cube; there were, of course, fewer people to accommodate. Nevertheless, as at Boothby Pagnell, the household still sat at tables to either side of the central hearth. In this comparatively small space, there is no sign that the high table stood on a dais, but its dignity was marked by the mouldings on the beam behind the Yeoman's chair, one corner having been carved with an oak leaf in tribute, perhaps, to the trees from which the Clergy House had been built. It might be that the table was not in this case a trestle, for the Yeoman, like the Franklin in the *Canterbury Tales*, may have preferred a 'table dormant' – an ordinary solid table which could not be taken apart for storage. This was a sign of generosity: the table stood always ready, under starter's orders so to speak, and eating could begin at a moment's notice. The Yeoman's hall was on its way to becoming a dining room. With his modest establishment and position, he does not need it to fulfil as many different roles as did the de Bothebys'.

Our visitor from Lincolnshire tucks his knees under the expansive tablecloth, well washed though still marked by the evidence of past meals which it has been impossible to scrub out (the skirts being used instead of napkins). Placed before him are slabs of very coarse bread – trenchers, from the French *tranchoirs*, 'things for carving upon' – which serve instead of plates. A pitcher of water is brought for him to wash his hands, he says a prayer (as in the Norman period, little happens in the fourteenth century without reference to God), and he can begin heaping food from the dishes standing in the centre of the table. 'It snowed in his house of meat and drink,' wrote Chaucer of the Franklin's hall; let us hope that the Yeoman is another such gourmand, although luxuries such as partridge are almost certainly beyond him. Instead visitors probably find robust fare: soup, bacon, tripe, mutton, fried eggs, roast ox tongue, fish caught in the Cuckmere or in the sea. There are loaves of bread, though you need strong teeth for it. When this course is finished, the dishes are removed and replaced with cheese, fruit and tarts. Diners put down their spoons and knives, and rinse their hands again. It is tempting to eat the trencher, now soaked with the sauces and gravy that accompanied the meat; this used to be the habit, but now it is polite to put these in the bin of leftovers that will be distributed to the poor.

If the visitor is on good terms with the Yeoman, he will be taken to his chamber at the end of the meal. At Boothby Pagnell, the de Botheby lord would have led his guests outside to the detached chamber block. Now, though, the solar has been joined to the end of the hall. The practicalities of this arrangement are obvious. Life takes place under one roof; the integrated chamber is less costly to build. As at Boothby Pagnell, the solar is still on the first floor, and more comfortably furnished than the hall. The walls are hung with curtains or tapestries; there is a chest or coffer for clothes and precious objects; a small table, or the trestle and board that make one, at which the Yeoman and his wife can dine alone; and perhaps a cabinet.

As we have seen, the Clergy House came in time to be owned by Michelham Priory, that is until the next great upheaval in English life: the Dissolution of the Monasteries ordered by Henry VIII. As one of the lesser monastic houses, Michelham, whose buildings were already dilapidated, was among the first to go; the Prior left with his pension of £20 in 1536. The site and property of the priory were thereupon granted to the Dissolution's chief architect, Thomas Cromwell. As we shall see, a revolution in land ownership had begun. This would have a profound effect on the land market and therefore on the number, the distribution and the look of the English house.

Meanwhile, another quieter revolution was under way that would suffuse much of the face of England with a rosy blush: the rediscovery of brick.

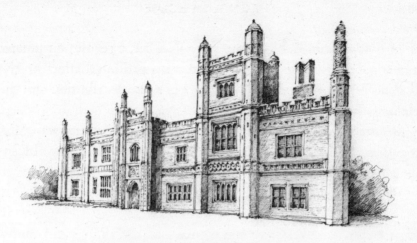

3. Showing Off in Brick
East Barsham Manor

Boothby Pagnell in Lincolnshire is made of stone; the Clergy House at Alfriston is made of wood. East Barsham in Norfolk is made of brick. England today can fairly be called a brick country; there are more English houses built from brick than from anything else. The Tudor builders of East Barsham Manor must have loved the material, for they rejoiced in its exuberant possibilities. Like many other brick buildings of this date, it has had a difficult history; but the decorative ingenuity displays such joie de vivre that you cannot stand in front of it and feel sad.

Brick is an enormously old material. The ancient Egyptians made bricks from moulds and left them out to be baked by the sun; there is a wall painting showing this process in a tomb in Thebes of about 1450 BC. Brick-making is part of the 'hard bondage' suffered by the children of Israel in the first chapter of Exodus. There is some evidence to suggest that the technique of baking clay to make it hard was known in Britain before the Romans arrived. But the Celtic tribes seem not to have built much from it. By contrast, the Romans fired millions of bricks during their four centuries of occupation, and some can still be seen in ruined walls and foundations today. Roman bricks generally took the form of large, flat tiles – some eighteen by twelve inches in surface area, and an inch or so deep. They were most commonly used as engineering courses to bind together flint-and-rubble walls, as at Richborough Castle in Kent or Burgh Castle in Suffolk (two courses were laid at an interval of four feet). The lighthouse in Dover Castle also incorporates bricks in this way. Some small Roman buildings were constructed entirely of bricks, which were also laid to make arches, domes and vaults. After the legions left in the early fifth century, Roman sites served as giant reclamation yards, supplying building materials into the Norman period. William I's Colchester Castle, an enormous building for its day, is largely built of bricks from the Roman town. The skill of brick-making was lost in England in the Dark Ages, however, perhaps because life was too unsettled for this time-consuming activity.

Once brick-making was revived in the late Middle Ages, bricks came to serve as a substitute for stone in areas that did not have it, particularly in East Anglia, where East Barsham lies. The new material had some advantages over stone. Each brick was made so that it fitted easily into the hand, and while an early brick wall might be massively thick, individual bricks were not enormously heavy. As a result, they could be handled more easily than stone. Laying bricks was generally quicker than hauling masonry. On the other hand, bricks are relatively soft and easily broken; they were not, therefore, the material of choice for castle walls. (Herstmonceux in Sussex is an unusual brick castle built in the 1440s; it survived both the Wars of the Roses and the Civil War without harm, the interior only being demolished in the eighteenth century.) In the early years following its reintroduction, brick was pre-eminently a material for manor houses like East Barsham and churches. It helped satisfy the aspiration of the rising middle class, which had made money from sheep farming and weaving, for houses to match their new status. Brick, being a novelty that was then not widely available, delighted Henry VIII, several of whose sixty-three palaces were built of it, including Greenwich, Nonsuch, St James's and Hampton Court. Ingenious bricklayers knew how to make the most expensive examples look showy and deluxe.

The very first examples of English brick-making after the Roman period seem to have dated from the twelfth century. There was a brick yard in Hull in 1303, its workers bearing English names. By the end of the fourteenth century they were able to produce enough bricks to rebuild the town's walls. Often it is difficult to be sure whether early bricks were made in England or imported from Flanders. (Bricks are popularly said to have come over as ballast in ships, although this seems unlikely; they were too costly to have been carried without an end use.) Brick-making skills were also brought over by Flemish craftsmen. Little Wenham Hall on the Orwell estuary in Suffolk, built in the 1270s, is the first wholly brick-built house in England: the small size of the bricks suggests that Flemish craftsmen had some hand in making them. Flemings were at work in 1416–17 on Stonor in Oxfordshire, the records of which include the first known use of the word *brick*. 'Baldwin Dutchman' ran the kiln that supplied the 322,000 bricks for Lord Cromwell's Tattershall Castle in the 1430s, and Peter Lyndon, who laid them, was a 'Docheman', too. But Henry VI turned to an Englishman, William Vesey, when he established a brick yard at Slough in 1437, supplying bricks for his grandiose new Eton College as well as Windsor Castle.

Naturally, production for these works was on a bigger scale than most private builders could achieve. Until the coming of the railways in the nineteenth century, most bricks were made from clay dug out near building sites, the resulting pits being left to form ponds once construction was finished. 'Brick earths are found almost everywhere,' notes Nathaniel Lloyd in *A History of English*

Brickwork (1925). But the quality of the clay varied, and that is one factor that determines colour in bricks: muddy yellow in the case of Little Wenham (there they were made from the chalky clay known as gault); silvery 'Woolpit Whites' at Hengrave Hall in Suffolk, where they combine harmoniously with the stonework; elsewhere pink, vermillion, plum and mauve. Firing bricks for longer turned them deeper colours, from purple to slate, which could then be used to create diamond, or 'diaper', patterns on façades.

The colours of East Barsham are mostly dull crimson and orangey red. From a distance, it gets its sparkle from the thick lime-mortar joints, characteristic of Tudor brickwork and necessary because of the irregularity of the bricks. A coat of arms on the gatehouse shows that the principal builder was almost certainly Sir Henry Fermor, who acquired the manor by marrying the widow of the previous owner, John Wode; there was a Speaker of the House of Commons of that name in 1482, probably the same man. It may be that Wode began the house on a more modest scale about 1500; there seems to have been a change of mind at some point, to judge from the slight asymmetry of the entrance front. Fermor, one can imagine, was a more pushy individual. When his stepson Roger Wode died on a pilgrimage to Jerusalem, he bought out his step-daughter's interest and plastered East Barsham with his heraldry. By 1523, he was the richest man in Norfolk, according to the subsidy roll, and Norfolk, which developed a home textile industry in response to export difficulties caused by the Hundred Years War, was one of the richest counties in England. In 1533, Fermor was High Sheriff of the county. East Barsham bubbles with self-confidence and pride, its red bursting out of a landscape whose palette is otherwise confined to green and (at harvest time) gold.

The Tudor age valued fantasy. Balance and symmetry had their place in a world already being influenced by Renaissance ideas, themselves ultimately derived – though at several removes – from the classicism of ancient Rome. But not austerity or restraint. East Barsham's silhouette is all tower and turrets, crenellations and chimney stacks. The house is approached through a gatehouse. Gatehouses once formed part of the defensive apparatus of fortified houses, or *castes*; this one is merely for show. The surface ripples with decorative bands, ornamental panels and heraldic ostentation. The façade of the main house revels in its large number of chimney stacks. As well it might: at the time most people still had to blink their way through halls with smoky central hearths. At East Barsham, every chimney stack shimmers to a different design: fluted, criss-cross, wavy, covered in fleurs-de-lis. Some are clustered together in double banks of five. Of necessity the grouping of chimney stacks was a relatively recent development, having emerged in the fourteenth century – before that there had not been enough chimney stacks to group. Now the chimney stack was a status symbol, to the extent that some houses vaunted them purely for show.

Most Tudor bricks have a pleasingly rough texture, the result of the mould having been coated with coarse sand before the clay was put inside. The decorative fireworks at East Barsham, however, required bricks of a finer kind; they were produced from different-shaped moulds to make panels and latticework. Once baked, bricks could be carved using a chisel, either before laying or in situ. The surface might be rubbed down to achieve a precise result. (Some shapes were impossible to make in moulds. Besides, carving and rubbing baked bricks avoided the distortions that came during firing.) More elaborate decorations, such as portrait heads and heraldic beasts, were protected with a surface glaze; they would then generally be termed 'terracotta', although it takes an expert to tell the difference between true terracotta and glazed brick. Terracotta supplied the splendid supporters to the Fermor arms on the East Barsham gatehouse, now sadly eroded. The house runs the entire gamut; it is even possible to identify some bricks that were given an extra layer of surface colour by means of a technique known as rougeing. It would seem that the same craftsmen also worked at Great Snoring, two miles away, although only fragments remain of the original manor house. Who they were and where they came from remains a mystery. The use of terracotta panels suggests a Continental origin; the terracotta portrait medallions at Hampton Court are the work of the Italian sculptor Pietro Torrigiani. But as a whole, East Barsham represents the flowering of a peculiarly English tradition.

Inside the house, brick is used in yet another way: to make vaults, two of which survive. Barrel vaults made out of brick had been one of the features of Roman bath houses; East Barsham, however, has Gothic groin vaults with ribs – and since they can hardly have been a structural necessity, one can only think of them as a *jeu d'esprit*. Contemporaries might well have been impressed by another, more practical innovation, found between the window mullions. Glass could hardly be called new, having already been made, in some form or other, for four and a half millennia. The Romans had discovered the trick of making clear glass (adding manganese oxide to remove its otherwise greenish cast), but the collapse of their empire had seen all but the end of glass-making in Europe. While techniques were revived in the Norman period, stimulated by the need to make stained glass for cathedrals, in England glass was not used in any but the grandest of houses before 1300. The Clergy House had no glass in its windows; it is unlikely that Boothby Pagnell did. At the time when East Barsham was built, glass was becoming increasingly commonplace in prosperous homes, but it remained expensive.

Tudor and Georgian glass was made by heating the raw ingredients in a furnace, extracting a blob, blowing it – by means of a long iron pipe – into a globe, continuing to blow while waving the globe until it became a cylinder, or 'muff', splitting the muff from end to end with shears, and then flattening it on an iron plate. It was thick, full of imperfections and could not be produced in anything but small panes. But what joy it gave to householders who could afford to buy it! Glass developed into an obsession in the later sixteenth century; Elizabethan aristocrats built country houses with enormous banks of windows through which light flooded into rooms that were bright with gaudily coloured tapestries. 'Hardwick Hall, more glass than wall' ran one couplet, in tribute to Bess of Hardwick's Derbyshire seat; 'Bright as Holdenby' was another saying, inspired by the extravagant glazing at Holdenby Hall in Northamptonshire. The result was not flawless as regards comfort. Small panes of glass, not more than six inches square, were held together by lead 'cames', which got loose in time; windows which opened did so on frames and with hinges made by blacksmiths – after a time they let in draughts. But how pretty the effect of light, strained through the irregular glass, was during the summer, how the windows sparkled when the sun caught them – and what an impetus the flood of light must have been to decoration! For the first time the inhabitants of English houses had a reason for staying inside, other than shelter and warmth.

Rules for planning a Tudor manor house were set out by a doctor called Andrew Boorde in his *Dyetary of Health*, written in the 1540s: 'Make the hall under such a fashion that the parlour be annexed to the head of the hall, and the buttery and pantry be at the lower end of the hall; the cellar under the pantry, set somewhat above from the pantry, coming with an entry by the wall of the buttery; the pastry house annexed to the kitchen.' Stables, slaughterhouse and dairy were to be located a quarter of a mile from the house, and the moat 'should be divers times scoured and kept clean from weeds'. It is difficult to imagine from the placid condition of Tudor and Elizabethan manor houses today the bustle that must have surrounded them when they were first built. With their dependent buildings the scene must have resembled a small village.

The manor houses of England have come, for many people, to represent a domestic ideal: mellow, full of architectural interest, their mature gardens punctuated with topiary, they are big, but not too big for modern life. But they were often regarded quite differently in the eighteenth and nineteenth centuries. Large numbers of them – Great Chalfield in Wiltshire, Owlpen in Gloucestershire, Athelhampton in Dorset, Brockhampton in Worcestershire, Markenfield Hall in Yorkshire – fell into decay. They were tenanted, divided into cottages, gently allowed to rot. They had come to seem old-fashioned, with their draughty halls and dark rooms, and the sixteenth-century preference for sheltered, often low-lying sites was condemned as damp. Some disappeared altogether; many were only rescued in the late nineteenth and early twentieth centuries, when William Morris and the Arts and Crafts movement taught a new respect for such buildings, and the Settled Land Acts made it possible for estate owners to sell them (often they had previously been entailed). East Barsham's decline was parlous. By the time John Adey Repton visited in 1808, his drawings subsequently being engraved by the Society of Antiquaries, half the house behind the façade had disappeared, while the rest was in use as a farmhouse. In the course of the next century it decayed further, such rooms as there still were being left open to the elements, their ceilings and back walls having gone. Fortunately it was caught just in time. What is in large part a new house was built behind the surviving façade. As a result, we can see little of the original fabric, although a plan drawn by Repton shows that it broadly conformed to Dr Boorde's prescription. Beyond that, we can only glimpse what life was like from a few scant documents, such as Sir Henry Fermor's will, made in 1533. While his son William inherited most of his property, his widow, Dame Winifred, was to be provided with 'a lodging in the east end of the house during her widowhood, with £20 towards hanging the same and trimming the chamber, a basin and ewer of silver, a nest of gilt goblets, a dozen of silver spoons, two goblets, two salts and a plain piece, with meat and drink for herself, two maids and a man'. This gives us a picture of rooms hung with tapestries, tables handsomely furnished with silver and silver gilt, and life made easy by the presence of servants – three to look after one woman.

Although manor houses were treated badly, even at their lowest ebb they had the power to inspire imaginations sensitive to their charms. In the early nineteenth century, East Barsham Manor was a wreck; yet William Wilkins, a product of the Picturesque movement who is best known for his Greek Revival National Gallery in London's Trafalgar Square, borrowed its silhouette for two houses in the Tudor taste that were built in the 1810s: Dalmeny in West Lothian, for the 4th Earl of Rosebery, and Tregothnan in Cornwall, for the 4th Viscount Falmouth. The social climber Henry Fermor might have been pleased.

4. A House Made from a Church
Buckland Abbey

Legend has it that the likeness of Amicia, the dowager Countess of Devon who founded Buckland Abbey in 1278, can still be seen over a door on the south side of the building. 'The countenance would not be ugly,' wrote Lady Elliott-Drake in *The Family and Heirs of Sir Francis Drake* (1911), were it 'not for the ears, which are astonishingly large'. The monks at Buckland came from Quarr on the Isle of Wight, then part of the family estates. If, as the Cistercian Rule demanded, they valued remoteness and seclusion, Buckland must have seemed particularly satisfactory. It was the Cistercians' most westerly foundation, and although on a fine day it is possible to recognize the great Cornish historian A. L. Rowse's description of 'a green sheltered nook fed by the streams running down to the Tavy', with gardens and closes hiding behind walls, while 'the silver streak of the Tamar' flashes in the distance, fine days can by no means be guaranteed on Dartmoor. When the rain drives relentlessly, it can seem wild and tempestuous even now. There is no park, so fields come down to the house and its garden on all sides.

Even for Devon, Buckland was not a particularly rich abbey, but the monks must have managed their agriculture efficiently, to judge from the evidence of their stupendous barn. Built about 1300, this was retained after the abbey was repurposed, and it is on a majestic scale: some 180 feet long, with a roof, built in the fifteenth century, that the carpenters who erected the Clergy House in Alfriston would have admired. Light filters in through lancet-like windows. The barn has something of the solemnity and spatial scope that must once have belonged to the church before the latter was divided up internally to form the house. Though the barn was substantially bigger; wealth was stored up on earth as well as in heaven.

It is easy enough to make out the bulk of the abbey church since the nave and chancel walls survive. It was not enormously ambitious by Cistercian standards. In Cistercian foundations, the nave was used by lay brothers, uneducated helpers responsible for working the land, while the 'choir monks' occupied the chancel and crossing. At Buckland the nave had only four bays. Above the crossing the square tower remains a prominent feature, more prominent, indeed, than it would have been when the abbey was built. This is because Buckland ceased to be a religious foundation in 1539 and, over the ensuing decades, was turned into a solid, if somewhat peculiar, country house, convenient for Plymouth. Wearing the undyed habits that gave them the name of 'white monks', the Cistercians were one of a series of reforming orders which sought to bring new rigour to monastic life, and they frowned on towers as vainglorious. Buckland's tower would originally have risen only a small way above the ridge of the roof, the line of which is still visible in the masonry.

Until 1536, the Church owned a vast swathe of England. Nobody has been able to calculate how much exactly: some say as much as a third, though a more cautious estimate would be between a twentieth and a sixth. By 1540, all this land was in secular hands and could be bought and sold freely. Whatever the other religious and social consequences of the Dissolution of the Monasteries, it was a stimulus to the land market and a help to the new men of the age, who wanted to build country houses. The number of good sites available for building had greatly increased. So had the revenue to fund works.

There had been some two hundred monasteries in the country, and the materials of which they were built and with which they were furnished were systematically pillaged for reuse. Lead, which was difficult to mine, was stripped from the roofs and melted down; bells were hauled away to be recast as cannon; stone was carted off for use in local towns; precious vestments were turned into bed hangings; the parchment of old books was used, it was said, to mend holes in shoes; there was not so much as a hook from the holy kitchens that did not go for something, and at a price. (By the end of it, once Henry VIII's costly wars had been paid for, the royal finances were not in a much better state than they had been at the beginning, but that is another story.) Often monastic buildings, or parts of them, were converted into new dwellings: Newstead Abbey in Nottinghamshire and Lacock Abbey in Wiltshire were fashioned out of old cloisters; the monks' *dorter* (sleeping quarters) and *frater* (refectory), the abbot's lodging and part of the cloister were to form part of the great house that would arise at Forde Abbey in Dorset; at Hilton in Somerset, the gatehouse was kept as a residence. Abbey churches often survived as cathedrals or parish churches. At Buckland Abbey, on the other hand, the new owner had no scruples in turning the church itself into a house: hardly the most elegant in the county, but, as an expression of Protestant bloody-mindedness, one of the most radical. True to the order's reforming spirit, the architecture of the church was sober. The grey stone that the monks used for their buildings, including the church, is a kind of slate, quarried locally and known as shillet; the walls came to be covered, still more soberly, in roughcast as an added protection against the vigorous weather.

Some of Buckland's other conventual buildings survived into the eighteenth century, being shown in the topographical artist Samuel Buck's print of 1734; these include what are now two private houses. Their original functions are unclear, but Tower Cottage is thought to have been part of a detached abbot's lodging or of the infirmary. The Cider House seems to have been part of the refectory. In 1988, an archaeological dig revealed what may be a fragment of cloister, unusually placed on the north side of the church – as at Quarr. A little to the east of the abbey lie what appear to have been the foundations of the gatehouse. We can only be tentative, for at Buckland, as at other former abbeys, buildings for which the new owner had no special use were comprehensively pulled down for the Tudor equivalent of architectural salvage.

Who was Buckland Abbey's new owner? After the departure of the monks, it was leased to George Pollard, who may have been brother to the commissioner taking surrender of the religious houses in the west, Hugh Pollard; another brother, Richard Pollard, bought Forde Abbey. However, within a couple of years, the abbey was sold by the King to Sir Richard Grenville, from a West Country family whose origins lay in the Norman Conquest. A. L. Rowse described the dominant characteristic of the Grenvilles as 'a harsh, domineering note, proud in the extreme, unyielding, betraying signs of overstrain and unbalance, forceful, highly strung, bent on action, capable of the highest devotion; above all, exciting'. In 1539 Grenville was in the middle of a six-year stint as High Marshal of Calais. This, he felt, entitled him to some of the pickings of the Dissolution. But despite writing to Henry VIII's Chancellor Thomas Cromwell, he was not considered sufficiently important for a gift, and when it came to making a purchase, he would have preferred a property in his native Cornwall, rather than Devon. But like many other buyers, he had to accept the nearest thing to his ideal that he could get (a phenomenon that will be familiar to many people who have searched for a dream home since then).

It may have been that Grenville was more interested in what surrounded the abbey than in the buildings themselves. Until the agricultural depressions of the nineteenth century, land was regarded as the soundest investment and the most substantial embodiment of wealth. Originally, the monks had themselves farmed with the help of lay brothers, but as fewer young men came forward to serve in the latter capacity, most of their estates were let out to tenants. The new owners simply took over as landlords, leaving the tenants unchanged. In addition to Buckland, Grenville acquired the rectory of Morwenstow in Cornwall, previously owned by the Priory of Bridgewater in Somerset.

Before Grenville made his first payment for Buckland, an official auditor, Mathew Colthurst, drew up an inventory of the property that he would be allowed to buy, listing the 'apple orchards, gardens, lands, meadows, feedings, and pastures'. This amounted to about a third of the estate that had been owned by the monks. Presumably there was, or had been, a windmill in 'Wyndemyll parke', while the presence of sheep can be deduced from the meadow called Shepewaishe. Altogether the farms on offer were calculated to yield an income of £23 3s 5d per year, and Grenville's purchase price was set at ten times that figure. (This was the multiple generally used at the beginning of the Dissolution; later on, the price of monastic lands went up steeply.) Usually, a certificate of woods was attached to valuations of this kind; at Buckland this seems to have been overlooked, and the woods were thrown in as a bonus.

What is perhaps surprising, from the point of view of the future house, is that the monastic buildings are not described. Presumably this is because they were tenanted. But it also reflects the low value that the Tudors seem generally to have placed on such structures: there was little immediate profit to be had from them, and converting them to houses was a source of expense. Indeed, Sir Richard, who died in 1550, never lived at Buckland; it was left to his son, Sir Roger, to make it his home. However, Sir Roger's tenure was brief. He had the unfortunate distinction of captaining the pride of the King's navy, the *Mary Rose* – second only to the *Great Harry* – when, top-heavy from the fitting of too many cannons, the lowest rank of its gunports was rushed by water and the ship sank off Portsmouth in 1545. Sir Roger was among the six or seven hundred men who drowned.

His heir, another Richard, was no more than a toddler at the time. Richard's mother remarried, but their new home, encircled by the Tamar, could be reached easily by boat, the Tavy, on which Buckland lies, being one of the Tamar's tributaries. Buckland had been settled on Richard by his grandfather. Given the undying fame that he would achieve as captain of the *Revenge*, it is permissible, perhaps, to imagine him as a lad, sailing to Lopwell Quay, bird-nesting, hawking and exploring the abbey buildings at Buckland, with its great empty, forbidding church. Work on the conversion may already have begun, to judge from an entry in old Richard's will, directing his wife to use timber from the woods for the purpose. It is unlikely to have got very far, though, because she died soon after her husband. The future now lay in young Richard's hands. Before his thoughts turned to building, however, he had first to make his mark on the world, and to that end he went to London, with the object, like any ambitious young man of the age, of studying law.

By temperament, though, young Richard was a Grenville, not a lawyer. In 1562, he killed a man in a street brawl; we do not know the precise circumstances of the affair, and in any case, since life was held cheaper in the Elizabethan age, he was pardoned. A companion on that occasion, Nicholas Specott, bought some land at Buckland which Richard sold to finance his London lifestyle. Soon enough, Richard had found a more appropriate outlet for his aggression in soldiering. About the age of twenty-one, he married a girl called Mary St Leger. Following one of his new in-laws, Sir Warham St Leger, he attempted to settle some land in Munster, again selling a parcel of his Buckland inheritance to fund it; but the investment disappeared into the political soup of Ireland. Richard's next move was to enter Parliament as a Member for Cornwall; but one does not have to look long at the portrait that he had painted at the age of twenty-nine (now in the National Portrait Gallery in London) to know that a Parliamentary career was unlikely to occupy him for long. Menacing black armour, a thin frill of ruff, a head of neatly clipped gingery hair, a tightly set mouth in the midst of a finely combed beard and moustache, one hand resting on his sword, the other clasping a baton – these details might pass as conventional were it not for the eyes, looking not at the spectator but over his shoulder, as though on the qui vive for some enemy to fight, or slight to be overturned. Rarely in the stiff corpus of Elizabethan portraiture does a painting convey such an impression of barely controlled agression.

With his fellow West-countryman William Hawkins, Grenville shared a privateer with the deliciously inappropriate name, were you to be one of its victims, of *Castle of Comfort*. Not himself a sailor, he thirsted after the profit that could be made from the sea. To that end, in 1574, he put himself at the head of a consortium of West Country friends and gentry, proposing a voyage of exploration to the Queen. The idea was to seek out new trade routes and lands for England; not only would these be claimed for Her Majesty, but – and this was the first time anyone had suggested it – they would be settled by her subjects. Buckland now came into its own; being so handy for Plymouth, it must have seemed an excellent base of operations. But the Queen never gave her consent; there had been a temporary rapprochement with Spain. His plans baulked, there followed years in which Grenville, in his early thirties, was at home more than he would have liked. This was when he transformed Buckland.

In Tavistock, the churchwardens' accounts for 1574 contain a payment to one Walter Luggar 'for bringinge home the bell from

Buckelonde': they were rehanging the bells, and the Buckland bell augmented their number. This suggests that the work of converting the abbey was under way. The date 1576 appears over the hall chimneypiece, presumably indicating that the conversion had been finished. Sadly, we have no letters to indicate what Grenville or his lady may have hoped for from their home; nor do we know the name of their architect, if they had one. One can imagine, though, that their priorities were not so different from those of Thomas Wriothesley at another abbey where the church became part of the house, Titchfield in Hampshire. There the conversion, which took place as soon as the abbey had been dissolved in 1538, can be followed in a series of letters from Roland Latham, the King's commissioner, and his clerk John Crayford to the new owner. Uppermost in Wriothesley's mind was the cost, estimated to be at least three hundred marks. For this price he could punch a hole through the centre of the nave and build a gatehouse over it; turn the abbey *frater* into the great hall; and use the cloister as a courtyard. One of the conveniences of the abbey was that it provided a suitable kitchen and other service rooms near the great hall; by now, kitchens were accommodated within the main house, a promising arrangement for anyone who cared more about eating his food whilst it was hot than the old practice of building kitchens in a separate block.

Latham and Crayford did not hesitate to recommend the 'plucking down' of those parts of the Titchfield church that were not otherwise being used; '. . . it is,' they wrote, 'but a small matter, minding (as we doubt not but you will) to build a chapel.' Plucking down was perhaps the easy bit; churches were not very adaptable to houses. In Grenville's case, his determination to make his home in this way seems almost perverse. The gusto with which he set about it may have reflected his bullish Protestantism; later in his career he was to be a zealous persecutor of Catholics. In eyes such as his, the church may not have seemed holy at all; indeed, the reverse may have been true, since it represented a way of worship that led its followers into error.

Typically, the means by which Grenville achieved his transformation were bold and unusual. Two floors were inserted into the church, along with the necessary partitions to make rooms. By lopping off the south transept, he obtained light for the great hall under the crossing tower. A wing was formed between the south transept and the choir to make a kitchen: the arcades to the old chapels can still be made out in the wall. Building work was kept to a minimum.

Economical though this scheme was, it made no use of the great spaces of the abbey. Even Grenville's great hall is only one storey in height, and rather low-ceilinged at that. The great hall was no longer the communal heart of the house as it had been at Boothby Pagnell; it was now little more than another room. On the other hand, the unexpected appearance of some of the carved architectural details in the upper rooms – the winged ox of St Luke in a corner of what later became known as the Georgian Dining Room, for example – is an appealing, if unintended, feature. Outside the dining room the ribs of a Gothic arch – part of the structure of the old church – loom unexpectedly out of the walls.

The result was not a sumptuous house, though it included one great decorative flourish in the form of the plasterwork of the great hall. A series of weird male caryatid-cum-satyrs conceal the brackets above the cornice; they seem to have no parallel. Less perplexing is the engaging frieze of two knights who have given up the worldly life; they are shown contemplating skulls while their warhorses rest in the meadow. It is an appropriate image for a soldier and adventurer at home, confronting his own mortality, though there was no hint in Grenville's own life that he had any thoughts of retiring. Paint analysis suggests that at least the many shields in the room were originally coloured, no doubt because they bore Grenville's own coat of arms. Over the fireplace are the figures of Justice, Temperance, Prudence and Fortitude. The first three seem as inappropriate to Grenville's own life as the scenes of the knights in the meadow.

In 1577 Sir Richard – he had been knighted, like most of his forebears, by then – served as High Sheriff of Cornwall. The role of Buckland as his home can be gauged from the christenings that took place in the parish church: first that of his daughter Bridget in 1578, then of a cousin in 1579. We occasionally glimpse the man himself in contemporary records. Of his wife we hear nothing, though we can imagine her assuming the responsibilities that fell to any Elizabethan wife of her station. She would have supervised the scouring of knives and the polishing of armour with sharp river sand and the plant known as horsetails. Fine clothes would have had to be stored, shaken out regularly to prevent moth and, when necessary, cleaned. Or rather, an attempt would have been made to remove stains, with varying degrees of effectiveness; the only fabric that could be kept truly clean and fresh was linen, which is why rich people wore linen shifts – looking like nightdresses – next to their skin. The washing of these was not work for delicate fingers. Fine lace would have been starched (the starch came from a plant called cuckoopint) in boiling water, and the material generally used to bleach whites was human urine.

In 1580, Sir Francis Drake returned triumphant from his round-the-world voyage. Now fabulously enriched and indisputably the man of the hour, he had fulfilled the ambition of exploring the seas and plundering the Spanish that had been frustrated in Grenville. And yet Drake was an upstart, the son of a mere parson, which is why, indeed, he had become a sailor. Only weeks after Drake's reappearance, Grenville decided to leave the orbit of Plymouth, withdrawing westwards to the family's ancestral seat of Stowe in Cornivall. Once Drake was ready to establish himself in the country, his eye lit upon the mansion that Grenville had recently carved out of old Buckland Abbey. Perhaps the rivalry that had grown up between the two men made the idea of acquiring it particularly sweet. Drake had sixteen years to live at Buckland; his time there can be tracked from the string of messengers sent from Plymouth on official business, their visits recorded in the Widey Court Book there. It is likely that Drake's principal interest in the property was the building up of the estate, which he did by the acquisition of several manors in the 1580s. Of the house, he changed practically nothing, beyond adding a fireplace with his coat of arms. He was not a land animal. Besides, Sir Richard had built well.

What did subsequent generations make of the house that Grenville had formed out of a church? After Drake's death, Buckland passed to his brother Thomas, a litigious character, and remained in his family until the twentieth century, with a brief interregnum during the Civil War. To celebrate the Drakes' return, the Sir Francis of the day put his coat of arms, dated 1655, over a fireplace on the top floor. Following his death in 1661, however, the house was let, and by the next time we have a description of it, in 1754, it was in a sorry condition. 'To see this place makes me, if possible, lower than before,' wrote a family friend, Nicholas Rowe. 'It rains into all the rooms of the house. Part of the ceiling of the room where you dine has fallen down. The gardens look wild . . . the hall ceiling, I fear, will come down too.'

In the later part of the eighteenth century, however, the fortunes of Buckland revived. Restoration in the twentieth century revealed the date 1772 on the back of the panelling in the dining room, and the Georgian staircase is probably also of this time. The agriculturalist William Marshall stayed at Buckland in the early 1790s to gather material for his *Rural Economy of the West of England* (1796). In the Advertisement of the first volume he pays tribute to 'my valuable and lamented friend, the late Sir Francis Drake', while in the second he describes in detail the model farm buildings erected at Buckland. The 'DUNG YARD of a semi-octagon form, inclosed, on one side, with cattle sheds' was found to be 'in every point of view . . . very eligible'. It can still be seen.

After Sir Francis's death in 1794, the estate passed to his nephew Lord Heathfield, who decided to put Buckland back into more habitable condition. His 'Particular of Works' in the Devon Record Office at Exeter is unusually specific:

It is intended to fit up this House merely for an occasional residence for a Month or two at a time to have spacious and cheerful access to the Master apartments & convenient communications to the Servants Offices. If there is a good dining Parlour or common Room a Pleasant Drawing Room with a Master Bed Room & two dressing Rooms that will be sufficient, on the first floor, especially if a Cabinet Master Apartment can be got near it – at all Events no alteration must be attempted to the character of the Building.

Heathfield's architect was Samuel Pepys Cockerell, best known for the Indian-style Sezincote in Gloucestershire which he built for his nabob brother Sir Charles. A long letter in the Devon Record Office dated 27 April 1801 describes the work that he executed, which included covering Buckland in roughcast, which within a year, he noted approvingly, had 'already the Character of Age & Rust upon it'. It had been Cockerell's intention to hasten this effect by staining the roughcast in different tints, but apparently his orders were countermanded by Marshall, who naturally considered himself to be an expert on practical building. As a result Cockerell was forced to lament that some of the roughcast 'is at present of the Tone of a newly Repaired Village Cott, instead of the Venerable Rust of an Abbey, whose character & features denote the possession of many generations, & the Idea of which it appears to have been Your intention to maintain'. After a detailed account of the interior decoration, he ends his letter by proposing that the tower of what is now Tower Cottage – then the stable – be given the present termination, which takes the form of a castellated dovecot, for 'fancy Pigeons'. Cockerell believed that this 'would have a good Effect from the two North Rooms'. The projecting staircase tower on the south front of the abbey was also added at this time.

Buckland was too tough for the character that the monks and Grenville had given it to be erased, however. It remains their house: an aesthetically unstable mixture of monastic austerity and pushing, fiery, uncomfortable ego, for which the safest place to let off steam is the countryside.

5. A Classical Sporting Pavilion
Lodge Park

'Sherborne is up!' On hearing this cry, a faithful butler bodily lifted his master, owner of Sherborne Park in Gloucestershire, and carried him from the gaming table. Such was the family legend, recorded in a great history of the Duttons published in 1901. If it actually happened – it would be nice to think that it did – it would not have been such a difficult feat. For John Dutton, generally known as Crump, was a puny, hunchbacked man, with what looks like a saintly disposition to judge from his monument in Sherborne church (it shows him pre-packaged, so to speak, in his winding sheet, tied up at the top like a haggis). His portrait by Franz Cleyn at Lodge Park shows a pair of anxious eyes staring out above a worried mouth, framed by a Puritan collar, long grey locks and a sober, broad-brimmed hat. But monuments and portraits do not tell the whole truth. Crump was a cavalier who is supposed to have died after falling from his horse during a night ride. His favourite sport was deer coursing, which combined his love of dogs and gambling. Lodge Park – compact, formal, rich in architecture, standing stiffly to attention in the open countryside – is the result. It looks so improbable in its setting among the cornfields that you might almost think that some wizard transported it from another, more elaborate location.

That may have been precisely the effect that Crump and his architect intended. The Elizabethan age had put a high value on ingenuity; wit, wordplay, costly apparel, extravagant building and elaborate genealogies were proof that the Elizabethans had never been afraid of showing off. By the troubled reign of Charles I, however, prodigality had been replaced by a more reserved taste. Caprice was still highly regarded; the court delighted in vastly expensive masques, one of the principal features of which were ingenious transformation scenes. But it was only the King, his family and courtiers who saw them. In architecture, the Queen's House at Greenwich, begun for James I's Queen Anne of Denmark and finished for Charles I's Henrietta Maria, spanned a public road. It was a private joke. Lodge Park is in this tradition: an exquisite building, whimsically constructed for the purposes of sport.

The road to Lodge Park runs straight. It is narrow, the over-grown thorn and elder trees to either side unrecognizable as the hedge they must once have been – they are garlanded with briar rose in summer. We have climbed out of the Windrush Valley, on the other side of the A40, and are crossing a broad, high plain of cornfields and blocks of trees. And here, in the middle of the great flat expanse of eminently unremarkable landscape (except that it is not quite so unremarkable, as we shall see) comes the astonishing spectacle of Lodge Park.

Lodge Park only just scrapes into this story as an English house because no one lived in it permanently until the twentieth century. But to judge from the huge fireplaces (exposed though the lodge was, it must have been a warm little place: look at the bank of a dozen chimneys on the roof), the basement kitchen (two bread ovens and a pastry oven) and the wine cellar, Crump and his friends must have had a jolly time even if they did not spend the night. At the end of the day, they would have rolled back to the place they had come from that same morning: Sherborne Park, a couple of miles away. Sherborne had been the largest of the estates belonging to the Abbey of Winchcombe. In 1551, it had been acquired, along with the site of Lodge Park, in one of the long legal wrangles that were such a feature of Tudor landownership, by Thomas Dutton. As the younger son of a Cheshire squire, Dutton had presumably done well out of the Dissolution of the Monasteries and knew all about the value of property, being Crown Surveyor of Gloucestershire.

The new men of Elizabeth I's England were desperate to show off, frantic to build houses. It was a competitive age. Courtiers, lawyers and merchants wanted to flaunt the fortunes that they had made. Their love of profusion led them towards elaborate ornament and fantastic skylines. They were so obsessed by their lineage that James I was moved to remark, after a genealogical lecture from Lord Lumley, that Lumley must have been Adam's 'ither name'. But they were equally anxious to parade their erudition and cleverness. At Blickling in Norfolk, the plasterwork allegories in the ceiling seem to have been made almost deliberately obscure, with layers of meaning that, presumably, would have kept guests talking for hours. Tiers of allegorical sculpture at Burton Agnes in Yorkshire make the hall a three-dimensional sermon; one glimpses the society that relished the verbal richness of Shakespeare's plays. On the whole, these builders of houses were a harsh lot, violent, vindictive and obsessed by status, hubristic in their ambition. One can imagine that Thomas Dutton was a man of this stamp.

But the mansion which Dutton built, in a heavenly valley overlooking a tributary of the Windrush, was interesting. It had close affinities to calmly grand, well-ordered Longleat in Wiltshire. Not enough is known of its history to say whether it was Longleat that influenced Sherborne or vice versa. Although Thomas had a good library, later owners were more careless about historical records. (While the house was being rebuilt by the 2nd Baron Sherborne in the 1820s, many of its muniments were entrusted to the vicar of Windrush for safekeeping; alas – as the 4th Baron Sherborne told the Bristol and Gloucestershire Archaeological Society in a presidential address in 1887 – he burned those of an ecclesiastical nature in case they were put to base uses. A servant seems to have disposed of the others to whomsoever would buy them. The village shoemaker was seen cutting up ancient parchments and black-letter folios as patterns for shoes.)

By the nineteenth century, the passion for field sports had become so remote from high culture that Matthew Arnold pictured the aristocracy as 'Barbarians'. There was no such idea current when Lodge Park was being built. Educated gentlemen read Latin easily and saw country pursuits through the idealizing medium of Virgil. Crump's Lodge Park may seem self-indulgent in view of the purpose, but it was also pioneering. Whereas Elizabethan grandees set their hunting lodges in high and remote places and designed them in fantastic styles, the nature of the sport at Lodge Park required a level stretch of ground – and the building is not so much fantastic as intensely architectural. It represents one of the first instances of pure Italianate classicism in England, from which the Roman style had been absent for more than a thousand years.

This reflected the great development that had overtaken English architecture since Buckland. When the Romans had left Britain, they had taken the classical tradition with them. Over the next millennium and more, nothing that was built in England could have been called classical. For Northern Europe, the reawakening began around 1500. France copied Italy, and England, under the ambitious, young, Europe-focused Henry VIII, copied France. While, as we have seen, the Dissolution of the Monasteries brought architectural dividends, as private individuals like Grenville and Dutton acquired building sites – sometimes with monastic buildings out of which they could carve houses – it also had the effect of putting Italy, crucible of the Renaissance, out of bounds. An excessive interest in Italian classicism would have caused suspicion in the not unreasonably paranoid world of the Tudor court. So to begin with, except for a few houses like Longleat and, it would seem, Sherborne, English classicism was a hand-me-down affair. Early use of the Doric, Ionic and other architectural orders was mixed with a good deal of whimsy, unsettling the effect of calm, harmonious grandeur which was the chief object of classical taste. By 1600, some smaller houses, such as Chastleton in Oxfordshire, were being compactly planned on strictly symmetrical – i.e. classical – lines. But you would hardly know it to look at them: the pointed gables and battlements of the Northern tradition died hard. The building that came to be called Kew Palace was built for a rich merchant in 1631; although the mason was able to construct pilasters and cornices out of brick, the shaped and curved gables – three to each front – make it very different from any building known to the classical world.

Lodge Park is one of a group of buildings which diverted English architecture into a new channel. Once it was thought to have been designed by Inigo Jones; it was not, but it almost certainly emerged from within his circle. The 1634 account of a visitor, Lieutenant Hammond, dates it to the early 1630s – about the time that the very different Kew Palace was being built. Jones was then streaking like a meteor across the architectural sky; the architect of Lodge Park had not had much time to absorb his radical example.

By the seventeenth century, a new class of professional architect had begun to emerge. John Shute was the first, although little is known of his activities; Robert Smythson had a large practice (Longleat, Wollaton, Hardwick, Burghley, Burton Agnes) and passed it on to his son. Jones hovered on the edge of another tradition. The Renaissance made design an intellectual activity,

separate from its practical aspects. It was therefore open to gentlemen and others who had no claim to hands-on experience.
Although Jones was not a gentleman-amateur, he arrived at architecture by an indirect route, being forty before becoming Surveyor
of the King's Works. As yet he did not have a single building to his
name, though he had established himself as a painter, masque
designer, antiquarian, connoisseur and all-round man of taste.

Jones found his style in Italy. While there he was by no means
exclusively interested in architecture: a sketchbook suggests that he
was perhaps more concerned to study the Mannerist painters whose
work he admired. Nevertheless, he bought architectural textbooks,
notably the *Quattro libri* of Palladio, and set out to visit the buildings
illustrated in them; he also met Palladio's disciple Scamozzi. These
masters seemed to understand classicism as a structural grammar, as
opposed to a vocabulary of ornament; by comparison, the English
interpretations seemed provincial. Jones preferred the severity
of ancient ruins and Palladio's 'sollid, proporsionable . . . and
unaffected' style to the 'aboundance . . . brought in by Michill
Angell [Michelangelo]'. It was a highly individual taste, as out of
step with prevailing fashion on the Continent as it was in England.

In the summer of 1617, a courtier reported that James I's Queen
was building 'some curious devise of Inigo Jones' at Greenwich.
This was the Queen's House. Anne did not live to see it finished,
and James, never flush with money, lost heart in the project; it had
to wait until Charles I was on the throne to be completed. By then
the design seems to have changed. A painting of Greenwich Park by
Driaen van Stalbemt and Jan van Belcamp that is in the Royal
Collection hints at a red-brick building with arched windows; this
scheme was abandoned in favour of the crisp white box that we see
now, the inspiration for hundreds of crisp white boxes across
Britain during the eighteenth century. Work on this second phase
began in 1630 and went on until 1635, just when Lodge Park was
being built.

As a court architect, Jones's opportunities were limited by the King's lack of money. The Stuarts had hoped to rebuild the Palace of Whitehall; the first step towards doing so – and all that they achieved – was Jones's Banqueting House. This is a richer building than the Queen's House, and the debt to Palladio is more pronounced. England had not seen anything like it before. To the few eyes that, at this date, had been educated in the meaning of classical architecture, it was a literate building. With its orders and entablatures, the classical language symbolizes load-bearing construction. Before Jones, English architects had borrowed individual decorative elements from the classical repertoire without applying this logic. Rigorously rectilinear, the Banqueting House made sense.

Contemporaries saw the aura of Jones at Lodge Park from an early date. Lieutenant Hammond found it to be 'one stately, rich, compacted Building all of Freestone, flat, and cover'd with Lead, with strong Battlements about not much unlike to that goodly and magnificent Building the Banquetting House at Whitehall'. From a distance, the rectangular profile and tight discipline of the façade substantiate the comparison. Inside, the proportions of the Great Room are even more Jonesian: it is a double cube, the form that Jones used at Wilton House in Wiltshire.

But even at first glance Lodge Park seems a little too frantic with architecture to be comfortable. Pediments jostle shoulder to shoulder along the cornice line. On closer inspection, the detail shows that Jones's ideas have only been partially understood; quirks keep breaking out in an unseemly manner. Fussy niches pop up to either side of the central first-floor window. The pediments on this floor are broken with decidedly Jacobean-looking busts. The balusters of the parapet taper towards their feet. What we seem to be looking at is Jones's Italian classicism being overlaid by details of an earlier, or at least a different style, one with its roots in the French Renaissance. There is a flavour of

the mid-sixteenth-century patternbooks of J. A. du Cerceau and
Philibert de l'Orme in the crowded character of the façade. The
heavily banded columns of the loggia suggest the work of Salomon
de Brosse.

Lodge Park thus belongs to what might be called a series of
credible first attempts at Jonesian classicism. Another is Godolphin
House on the western extremity of Cornwall. The owner, Sir
Francis Godolphin, who moved in a sophisticated, architecturally
minded circle, procured – or drew – a plan for a radically classical
house, entered by a double loggia (the entrance front is supported
on a row of sturdy Tuscan columns, repeated on the courtyard side
– the only time this was done in England). The Cornish masons
who executed the work in local granite added their own, distinctly
un-classical touches, such as battlemented parapets. We know that
the house was roofed by 1634 because someone scratched that date
into the already-dry plaster of a window embrasure. (Although the
scheme was never completed: Sir Francis lost every last penny
supporting the royalist cause in the Civil War.)

The master mason Valentine Strong was a more workaday figure
than Jones. His family owned a stone quarry near Sherborne, and it
is known that he worked for Crump Dutton at Sherborne in 1651–3.
Could he have been the architect of Lodge Park? It seems unlikely.
His few securely attributed works, such as the manor houses at
Fairford and Lower Slaughter, both in Gloucestershire, are far
more tight-lipped than Lodge Park and do not share any stylistic
traits with it. Maybe Lodge Park was the work of the equally
elusive and no less picturesquely named Sir Balthazar Gerbier, a
diplomatist and painter as well as an architect. Very little of
Gerbier's oeuvre survives beyond the swaggeringly Baroque York
Watergate, now in Embankment Gardens in London. Did Gerbier
see the Banqueting House and filter its ideas through his own florid
temperament? It is as good a guess as any other, though at present
no theory about the architect of Lodge Park carries conviction.

The interior originally comprised only two grand rooms, each taking up the whole of one floor. The ground floor was occupied by a hall, with an immense fireplace, an archway through to the staircase and, to one side, panelling that contained two doors (a memory of the screens passage). The first floor comprised a Great Room, dominated by an even bigger fireplace, for feasts. From here, you would step out onto a broad balcony above a loggia, or you would go up another staircase and emerge onto the leads. Lodge Park was essentially a viewing platform for following sport.

The custom of using the roof of a building for walking and taking the view was long established; once they had got up there, visitors might mark their ascent by carving their footprint into the lead. Some forms of hunting – closely associated with gambling – gave the roof as observation post a special point. For gentlemen of Crump's era not only chased game on horseback, making their way across largely undrained country on heavy horses, following sturdy, slow-running hounds; they also watched it as a spectator sport, particularly when pairs of greyhounds were coursing stags and hares – 'a very noble and worthy pastime', according to Gervase Markham, writing in 1631. Since the owners would bet on the outcome, it is easy to see how this practice would have appealed to Crump Dutton. Lieutenant Hammond concisely (and admiringly) stated the raison d'être of Lodge Park as having been 'built at the great Cost and Charges of a noble true hearted Gentleman, more for the pleasure of his worthy Friends, than his owne profit; Itt is richly furnish'd to entertaine them to see that Kingly sport [of deer coursing]'.

It may be that the Queen's House at Greenwich was also intended as a grandstand, from which to watch hunting in Greenwich Park. What otherwise appear to be the whimsically tall proportions of Ashdown House in Berkshire – even more of a doll's house when it was built about 1663, because the wings did not appear until twenty years later – may be explained in the same way:

it stands at the centre of what were four great avenues through the woods, planned for Lord Craven's hunting as well as for scenic effect. Though Lodge Park is not as tall as Ashdown, it rises high enough to command fine views of open countryside. On the balcony, niches serve conveniently as seats.

A bird's-eye view from the 1740s shows that, by that date, the back of the house was sheltered by a plantation – as well it might have been, given the wind that can sometimes whistle over the plain there. The important view was to the east. The course – a mile-long straight of turf between two walls – can be seen in the old paintings. It was about two hundred yards wide at the start, funnelling to half that width at the finish at the Lodge Park end, which was marked by a ditch. The first hound to jump the ditch was the winner. There was a second, wider ditch that the deer could jump, but the hounds could not – though if £20 was put up, a 'fleshing course', ending in a kill, was expected.

There had been a park at Sherborne in the sixteenth century, but Crump began enclosing a new one as soon as he inherited in 1618. Deer from the park were caught and kept in what Hammond describes as 'handsome contriv'd Pens and Places' before being 'turn'd out for the Course'. With money at risk, there had to be rules, and these are found in a document entitled 'The Articles and Orders of the Paddock Course at Shirborne in Gloucestershire', probably compiled in the eighteenth century. The course was shaped like a long funnel, wider at the start than the finish. At some point down its length was a marker known as a pinching post; judges stood there and at the end of the course, in front of the grandstand. If a hound reached the deer before the post, the match was declared invalid. There were rules for every eventuality – the escape of a deer, its running the wrong way, the non-appearance of a competing hound. The sport began with a 'Slipper' hound breathing the deer; the Keeper was expected to 'put up his Deer at a day's warning for any Gentleman to run his Dogs paying his Fees'.

Lodge Park was just the sort of bubble that might have been blown away by the Civil War. But Crump, for all his gambling, was too wily for that. In his early years he had shown Parliamentary leanings; as MP he was jailed before the Civil War for refusing to collect the King's hated Ship Money tax. But once hostilities broke out in 1642, he offered to lend Charles I the enormous sum of £50,000, and joined him at Oxford. There he is described by the Oxford historian Anthony Wood, in his *Athenae Oxonienses* (1721), as 'active in making the defence and drawing up the articles of Oxon when the garrison was to be surrendered to the Parliament; for which, and his steady loyalty, he was afterwards forced to pay a round sum in Goldsmith's Hall, London'.

After the Civil War, Crump must have exercised the 'sharp understanding and cleer judgement' attributed to him on his memorial. Though fined heavily for supporting the King, he managed to re-establish friendly relations with Oliver Cromwell. Whatever else Cromwell may have banned, he did not ban hunting. In 1655 a warrant signed by him allowed Crump to take bucks and roes from Wynchwood Forest to stock his deer park. Crump continued to course from Lodge Park; he also arranged for his nephew and heir, William, to marry Frances Cromwell, the Protector's daughter. In his will he appointed Cromwell his nephew's guardian, referring to the proposed marriage, 'which I much desire and if it take effect shall account it a blessing from God'. The marriage did not take place in the end, but on Crump's death in 1656 Cromwell wrote his condolences to the widow, lamenting the 'great loss of your noble husband, my very good friend'. No doubt Crump's cavalier friends concurred with his memorialist in remembering his 'great hospitallity farr and neer', personified by Lodge Park.

Whatever the authorship of Lodge Park, it deserves to be called one of the first Palladian buildings in England. As such it attracted the interest of the connoisseur and architect Lord Burlington, who set himself a mission to reform the nation's architectural taste in the early eighteenth century. Around 1730 William Kent updated the Great Room, and since Burlington was his patron, it may well have been he who told Kent about it. Burlington accepted the attribution to his hero, Inigo Jones. He commissioned the architect Henry Flitcroft to draw Lodge Park for him; Flitcroft did so, omitting some of the exuberance. At least by 1740 a portrait of Jones was hanging in Sherborne House, for the accounts mention brass plates having been bought for it that year. Lodge Park became assimilated into the canon of approved models for Burlington's neo-Palladian movement, with its emphasis on purity of style and proportion.

As the redecoration shows, Lodge Park was still being used in the 1730s. The landscape was being reshaped by Charles Bridgeman, in a foretaste of the naturalistic style of Lancelot 'Capability' Brown: what now seem to be awkwardly placed blocks of trees in the 'unremarkable' landscape are in fact a rare survival of Bridgeman's work. By this date deer coursing was beginning to look old hat. But the Duttons kept at the forefront of sporting, as well as architectural, developments, being one of the first families to pioneer a brisker form of hunting. In December 1748 the *London Evening Post* carried a report of a 'most remarkable' day out with the combined Chedworth and Sherborne hounds: 'They ran a Fox five hours without a Check over the finest Country in England; no Chace could afford more Entertainment, no Hounds could pursue their game with more Steadiness and Resolution, no Fox could more boldly run over a fine County, and no Sportsman could pursue with more Spirit and Judgment in Riding.' Until the 1670s, foxes had been considered vermin that should be exterminated by any means possible, and beneath the dignity of gentlemen to hunt. However, it had become sufficiently fashionable by 1730 for Burlington himself to design Fox Hall – a starkly upright, if perfectly proportioned, brick box with a pediment – as a banqueting hall for the Charlton Hunt in Sussex.

By the 1890s Lodge Park had become two gamekeeper's cottages. At the end of the century, however, Lady Sherborne converted it to a house. Two not unworthy pieces of architecture survive from this time in the neo-Baroque gate lodges. It was as a house that I first saw it in the early 1980s; the National Trust has since then bravely but sensitively returned Lodge Park to the form it took in Crump Dutton's day.

What is the importance of Lodge Park, as built in the 1630s? Little in terms of direct influence on other buildings perhaps. But it shines like a star whose light reaches us from the dawn of a universe – that of Italianate classicism. For a century and a half after Lodge Park was built, nearly every house in Britain was constructed in a classical style. The pediments over the first-floor windows of a London terraced house descend, however distantly, from those designed by architects like Jones, Gerbier and Strong.

6. The Town House of a Puritan
The Merchant's House, Marlborough

One April morning in 1653, some workers in a tannery in Marlborough High Street were drying bark. Tanners used the bark of trees to extract the preservative tannin, from which the name of their trade derives. Tanning was an unpleasant trade; one of the agents used to cure leather was urine, and dead flesh was always among the refuse. Another disadvantage was the use of fire, an omnipresent danger to medieval and later towns.

On this occasion the bark caught fire, and the conflagration soon spread to the tanner's house. The tanner himself, Francis Freeman, was away from home; neighbours were prevented from entering the house to extinguish the flames by servants who barred the way, presumably fearing theft. The fire exploded from the roof, showering sparks and carrying up burning wads of thatch which the wind blew along the High Street. Piles of wood, neatly stacked behind houses, were an invitation to the flames, as were neighbours' thatched roofs. By the end of three hours nearly the whole of Marlborough was destroyed.

The Great Fire of Marlborough has its compensations for the historian; such was the devastation, and the consequent need to seek the help of others in rebuilding the town, that the town is unusually well documented as a result. Amazingly, one of the houses on the High Street survives in something very much like its original condition. Unlike many town houses, it can be dated exactly, and we know who lived there. Given the popular image of England under Oliver Cromwell as a land of grim, black-suited Puritans averse to sensory indulgence, it is remarkable to find that the owner, Thomas Bayly, was a seller of luxurious silks, and, as we shall see, he and the son who succeeded him loved colour.

Some of England's Roman towns grew up on the sites of Iron Age hill forts; some evolved out of Roman *castra*, or camps; others, like London, developed in response to the needs of commerce and trade. There are III boroughs recorded in the Domesday Book; by the early fourteenth century that number had more than doubled. The urban weave was loose in comparison to modern towns and cities: townsmen often had enough land to grow vegetables and keep a couple of pigs and a cow; they did not want to rely on food of sufficient quality arriving from the countryside. Nevertheless, to prevent one person's space and activity impinging on another's, building had to be regulated. This was recognized, for example, in the foundation of Salisbury in 1219; future citizens developed their plots according to a rule book. They would hardly have expected to do otherwise in a world that was still based, like that of Boothby Pagnell, on hierarchy and control.

One pressing reason for building controls was the presence of trades in towns, pursued either in houses or near them. We have seen that tanning was an unsavoury business; in London it was banished beyond the City walls. Marlborough, a country town of only some three hundred houses in the mid-seventeenth century, was a different proposition. There was no congestion, and consequently less sensitivity towards noxious trades. Not only was Freeman's tannery firmly embedded in the wide High Street, broad enough to hold a market on Wednesdays and Saturdays, but the centre of the street was occupied by a shambles, or abattoir. Presumably meat was butchered and sold there, too, but in an age before refrigeration the place would not have made an attractive centrepiece. Towns earned their livings in different ways. Leicester, for example, was famous as a 'vast magazine of wool', as Daniel Defoe put it, the sheep being 'without comparison, the largest,' finest and greatest bearers of fleeces 'in the whole island'. Marlborough was also a wool town; weaving had taken place there since the thirteenth century. By the time of the fire, the town possessed only three weavers, but had developed quite a business making clothes: Johanna Green has identified at least seventeen tailors, seven shoemakers, five linen drapers, four mercers, three woollen drapers, three weavers, three felt makers, two silk merchants, two hatters, one hosier and a button maker. The High Street displayed a sumptuous range of 'Silks and Tafety, Cloath and Lace, Linnen and Woolen, Gold and Silver', according to an account of 1653. In addition, like other country towns, Marlborough had a special line in food, in the shape of cheese, for which it remained famous until the eighteenth century, when for some reason cheesemaking declined.

Marlborough was also a coaching town. When Samuel Pepys visited in June 1668, five coaches from Bath passed through in the early morning: his entertainment the night before had been so enjoyable that he missed seeing them all. This gave shopkeepers a more than local market for their goods; it was said that 'no braver Wares can be had or bought in London, than was to be had in the famous Towne of Marlborough.' Presumably some of the coaching traffic perused Thomas Bayly's silks, invitingly set out in a ground-floor room of his house, open to the street during the day and locked up at night behind a stout shutter. Textiles would have been displayed on a counter that formed a barrier to the street; this was the standard practice, also followed by Shakespeare's father, John, a glover in Stratford-upon-Avon.

But Marlborough, despite its luxuries, was a Puritan town. A 'town most notoriously disaffected', full of 'obstinacy and malice', according to Clarendon, it sided with Parliament during the Civil War – much to the annoyance of the royalist Lord Seymour of Trowbridge, who held the castle. At one point, the town was seized by a royalist force under Lord Digby, whose soldiers ran riot, looting cheese and destroying the stock of the town's bookseller. They did not hold it for long, although towards the end of the war raiding resumed, largely by troops hungry to plunder the Saturday market (they would camp out on the Downs on Friday nights for the purpose). Marlborough had not long picked itself up after these frights when another day of 'sad miseries and afflictions' dawned, and the town burned.

Thomas Bayly stood in the ashes of his shop and lamented Marlborough's ruin to an absent townsman, John Lawrence, two days later: 'All the heart and principal parts of it laid in the dust, to the utter undoing of a multitude of families, that now want bread. And I have a great share in this sad affliction, my houses [in fact two joined together to make one larger one] being burned down to the ground, a good part of my wares plundered, and lost, and burnt.' The author of *Take Heed in Time, or a Briefe Relation of Many Harmes which Have of Late been Done by Fire in Marlborough* ... laid it on thick. 'It was not the houses that were burned alone,' he wailed, 'but also the Goods that were in them, there was Brasse and Pewter, Gold, and Silver melted, the value whereof cannot be made knowne, there was Silkes and Taffety Woollen and Linnen cloth and many other rich commodities consumed to ashes.' He went on to paint a picture of almost biblical woe:

It would make a heart drop tears of blood that had but heard the dolefull
cryes and heavy moanes that past between men and their Wives, Parents
and Children. The Wife crying out to the Husband, O dear Husband
what will become of us and our Children; The Husband answering the
Wife, we are all undone, I know not what to doe.

It was only later that he remembered that four Dutch prisoners,
taken during the naval wars with Holland, lost their lives in an
attempt to rescue some of the town's cheese (no doubt they
required considerable encouragement, of a forcible nature, to make
the attempt). The other dead were a postboy and a tailor's wife. Not
an enormous toll, given the fire's ferocity.

Without insurance, and with most of their possessions destroyed,
the townspeople petitioned Oliver Cromwell to allow them to issue
a brief, a petition read in parish churches throughout the land
asking for charity. Cromwell seems not to have favoured the
system: fewer briefs were issued during the Commonwealth than
under either King Charles I or his successor, Charles II, and as yet
none at all had been issued since the Civil War. Marlborough's
stoutness in support of Parliament softened Cromwell and a brief
was authorized. (The brief – *Take Heed in Time* – was written with
an eye on churchgoers' pockets.) Superficially, Marlborough returned to normal remarkably quickly for a town that had been all
but wiped out. When John Evelyn passed through in June 1654, he
found it 'now new built'. It may have been that he was looking only
at façades which had been rushed up quickly, leaving the buildings
behind them unfinished. But careful study shows that rather more
of the old fabric of the High Street has survived beneath later
remodelling than one might have thought.

Thomas Bayly was one of Marlborough's most prosperous
citizens; he and John Lawrence both lost more than £2,000 in
the fire, the only people to do so. The house that he rebuilt was
one of the most handsome in the town. It stood near the Market

House, opposite the shambles, at the other end of the High Street from Francis Freeman's house and St Peter's church. As in London after the Great Fire, the old pattern of landownership seems to have been preserved in Marlborough, to the extent that a passage that runs through the Merchant's House to the deep garden behind, where Bayly no doubt grew food for his table and kept the mules that pulled his carts, lies off centre – despite the doorway that ultimately gives access to it being plumb in the middle of the façade. This reflects what must have been a pre-existing layout. In fact it had a practical use: after Bayly's death in 1670, the two properties he had merged were divided. However, his housewright – we do not know who he was – had so far absorbed the new ideas of Inigo Jones – put on parade at Lodge Park – as to make the outside of Bayly's house balanced and symmetrical regardless of what lay behind it.

One would hardly, at first sight, call it classical. Classicism is based on the principles of post-and-beam construction, a dialogue between vertical and horizontal elements. The three peaked gables of the Merchant's House belong to the vernacular tradition of timber building and are like the gables of John Shakespeare's house at Stratford, built a century earlier. Shakespeare, who did not have much money when he started in business, had followed the convenient Elizabethan practice of building a small house and shop to begin with; it consisted of just one gable. As he prospered, he expanded his accommodation by adding more gables along the street. At the Merchant's House, the three gables of the roofline are echoed in two little ones over the central window – useful for throwing off rain. The way in which the frame of this house was made is not so different from the way that of the Clergy House was constructed. The outside now has a shell of tiles, hung vertically, to protect it from the weather (the tile-hanging is probably of a later date), and above the ground and first floors there is a narrow sloping roof to throw water off the façade altogether, a sort of sloping projection called a pentice. This housewright was taking no chances! Between the slopes are projecting bays completely filled with glass. Despite the small panes, the rooms behind are almost as bright as if they had no walls at all.

The one place where classicism does take a bow is in the colonnade, which stands in front of Bayly's shop and continued along to either side, providing a covered place to walk. This feature is reminiscent of the later covered walk in the Pantiles in Tunbridge Wells. There had been covered arcades before – for example, on the north and east sides of Jones's Covent Garden piazza in London, developed from the 1630s, where the form was based on the Place des Vosges in Paris. (Perhaps there was a distant echo of the arcades that surrounded Roman markets.) The Rows of Chester, created in the Tudor period, are a kind of covered street, higher than ground level, though those with colonnades only acquired them later. Although the Marlborough arrangement was not unique – The Pentice on Winchester High Street is an originally Tudor row of shops whose first floors project forward onto columns, allowing shoppers to walk underneath – it nevertheless made an impression on the well-travelled Pepys. 'What is most singular,' he wrote, 'is, their houses on one side having their pent-houses supported with pillars, which makes it a good walk.'

This is not the only singular thing about Bayly's house. The main family room, above the shop, contains a charming caprice in the form of a sundial painted onto a window pane. The conventional Latin motto ('*Dum spectas fugio*' – 'While you watch I fly') is reinforced with an ingenious trompe-l'oeil fly, which makes unkind hands itch for a rolled-up newspaper. This is a comfortable room, panelled in what would have been natural oak – and therefore originally quite blonde in colour, bright with the light from what is virtually a wall of leaded panes – with floorboards also of oak (elsewhere they are of elm). When W. H. Smith, the newsagent, owned the shop in the early twentieth century, they turned two rooms into one by removing a partition (the new space served as a lending library). The original smaller room would have been comfortable and à la mode, warmed by a big stone fireplace which is decorated with strapwork, a kind of abstract pattern of interlaced bands, often used in the seventeenth century. Columns stand to either side of the fireplace supporting a cornice and frieze. More classical detail comes in the narrow space left between the fireplace and the ceiling, where the panelling breaks out into niches known as aedicules.

Paint effects are a feature of the Merchant's House, too. The staircase was made to seem more spacious and balanced by painting balusters on the side wall to mirror those on the stair itself. Because the interiors of so many middle-class houses have disappeared, the only comparisons to be made exist in grander surroundings, such as Knole in Kent – its sumptuous interiors created by an aristocratic familiar of Charles II. However, we can be certain that Bayly's house was, like his silks, bright and colourful. Some of the fireplaces were covered in floral tresses, tightly curled in what still looks like a Tudor style; traces of them can still be seen.

But the most singular feature is the so-called Rainbow Room, probably completed in the 1670s by Bayly's son, Thomas Bayly II, named after another painted effect which is completely unexpected in the house of a Puritan. Vibrant stripes, together more than a foot wide, of terracotta, yellow, pink, blue, white and brown alternate with an olive-green background. The stripes mark their way across the walls without any apparent regard for the placing of architec-tural features, flaunting themselves asymmetrically over doorcases, draping themselves askew over fireplaces, barging across window openings. They have no known parallel anywhere in the country. (This is not to say that they were unique, only that nothing to compare with them has survived.) They seem doubly remarkable in the context of sober-sided Marlborough. Although the Baylys talked the talk of Puritans, their decorative schemes show that politics did not affect their colour sense. A picture that is roughly contemorary with the Rainbow Room by the Dutch artist Pieter de Hooch, now in Madrid, shows a room in Amsterdam Town Hall draped with silk patterned with broad stripes. Perhaps Bayly was trying to create a similar look in paint. Other striped schemes of decoration are emerging in two other bedrooms being restored as I write. Nor was this just a private matter; a triangle of wood known as a spandrel – made to disguise one of the shop's timber supports, whose presence must have been regarded as poor taste – is cheerfully painted with a naïve scene of a swan and a servant, perhaps to represent the annual tally of swans on English rivers known as swan upping. Again, only one of these boards survives; originally there would have been others – we cannot say how many.

The house shatters the still prevalent Victorian notion of a Puritan home as being dark and cheerless. By contrast it is a vibarnt example of how light and colour were welcomed into every corner and at the time regarded as entirely consistent with upright living and spiritual grace.

Sadly Marlborough had not seen the last of its fires. Another struck in 1679, and a third in 1690. At last it was realized that the old by-laws, which threatened householders with a fine of £5 for creating a fire risk near thatch, were not enough. An Act of Parliament was passed forbidding the thatching of roofs at Marlborough. London had come to the same conclusion after the Great Fire. However warmly its adherents might have felt about thatched roofs in the country, towns and thatch clearly did not mix.

7. A Baroque Architect's Romantic Caprice
Vanbrugh Castle, Greenwich

A completely new way of looking at architecture – a new way of looking at everything – began to emerge in Engald around 1700. All great architecture seeks to stir the emotions, but before so much as attempting to do so, classicism must satisfy the mind. The new Baroque aesthetic consciously cultivated an emotional response. It stirred the imagination, it evoked memories, it stimulated ideas. Buildings were designed in the styles of other historical periods and other countries. The resulting 'revival' styles evolved out of a painterly vision, which judged scenery – landscape and architecture – according to how far it conformed to the ideals of the best landscape paintings of the time, judged to be those by the Frenchman Claude Lorrain. The overarching idea was to make the English shires correspond as far as possible to the pictures which gentlemen collected on the Grand Tour. This way of seeing, called the Picturesque, was to be profoundly influential long after the world of aristocratic connoisseurs had passed away. In fact its principles are still enshrined in the English planning system today.

The man who opened the door to this aesthetic was Sir John Vanbrugh, one of the most original and multi-talented of people in an age which was rich in inventive personalities. Neighbours living around Greenwich Park, from which the old Tudor palace had recently been cleared in order to make way for Britain's greatest parade of Baroque public buildings, the former Royal Naval Hospital, had reason to know. His house – or rather the series of five houses he built for himself and family members – was certainly very different from other new buildings round about. It may have seemed just the sort of place that a rackety, high-living playwright-turned-herald-turned-architect would have built for himself, as a species of joke. But really Vanbrugh's houses signalled a revolution of taste.

Vanbrugh had already had several careers before he became an architect. The only unsuccessful one had been his first. The son of a Chester linen merchant, his unusual surname reflecting the origins of his family in Flanders, the young John tried his hand at soldiering – in his case, the resort of a twenty-two-year-old who did not have much idea of what to do with himself. He may have come to soldiering by accident, having approached Lord Huntingdon, a kinsman, to see if he would give him a job after being appointed Warden and Chief Justice in Eyre of Royal Forests South of the Trent. As Vanbrugh's biographer Kerry Downes has observed, the young man can hardly have expected that the result of his request would be the offer of a commission as ensign in Huntingdon's newly formed regiment.

Vanbrugh's late twenties were spent languishing in a series of French jails, following his arrest at Calais for lack of the correct papers. France was going to war with Holland, and he appeared to bear a Dutch name. Once incarcerated, the French formed the opinion that he was a valuable property (those noble connections) and sought to trade him for a Frenchman imprisoned in London. But poor Vanbrugh was not, at that stage, of much interest to anyone. He was twenty-nine when he was released. Soon, however, he had written a witty, worldly, to some people scandalous, play called *The Relapse, or Virtue in Danger*. His first attempt for the theatre, he claimed to have written it in six weeks. From the moment the curtain went up on Boxing Day 1696, the London audience relished its urbane saltiness. Vanbrugh was a celebrity. His career as an author continued, his greatest hit being his second play, *The Provok'd Wife* (1697).

Vanbrugh was a wit; he had many friends. In 1699 a fellow-member of the Kit-Cat Club, the 3rd Earl of Carlisle, who happened also to be Vanbrugh's kinsman, asked – or perhaps was persuaded to allow – him to design a house. Not so much a house, perhaps, as a palace. Vanbrugh was in much the same position as Inigo Jones had been when he entered architecture, and about the same age – an architectural virgin. But whereas Jones had studied the works of the ancients and Palladio in Italy, we have no idea how Vanbrugh had prepared himself for his new career. (From his first career as a painter, Jones could at least draw fluently: not so Vanbrugh.) The satirist Jonathan Swift poked fun at this development by writing, 'Van's genius without Thought or Lecture [reading] / Is hugely turned to architecture.' That cannot have been literally true, but there was something in it. It is all the more remarkable, then, that for his first essay Vanbrugh was able to supplant the experienced, though difficult, country-house architect William Talman, who had been Lord Carlisle's first choice. Before long he had got his job as Comptroller of the King's Works, too.

Lord Carlisle's family name was Howard. Castle Howard, the country house that Vanbrugh created for him, was one of many palaces being built by the powerful aristocrats who supported the Glorious Revolution. Vanbrugh, assisted by Nicholas Hawksmoor, was responsible for several of them: Blenheim Palace for the soldier 1st Duke of Marlborough, Kimbolton Castle for the

1st Duke of Manchester, Grimsthorpe Castle for the 1st Duke of
Ancaster. These were exciting buildings, whose architecture
sought to manipulate the visitor's mood. Jones had used the
classical language for rational discourse; Vanbrugh, as you would
expect of a playwright, preferred drama. The skyline of Blenheim
is enriched with stone representations of exploding grenades.
They set the seal on a building which might be characterized
by the modern military doctrine of 'Shock and Awe', here
achieved through movement, contrast, and light and shade. Being
a first attempt, Castle Howard is more conventional, but it is
important to note the name. This palatial dwelling does not look
much like a castle, but it was called one deliberately; there had
been a Roman fort here. The desire to conjure up history was not
unprecedented: the many towers of Henry VIII's Nonsuch Palace
were probably intended to inspire images of the great age of
chivalry, as were the romantic battlements of Bolsover Castle in
Derbyshire, built for a leading cavalier. Nevertheless, it was a
new departure for the eighteenth century; the end of the journey
would be the Gothic Revival.

By 1701 Vanbrugh had become rich enough to build his own
house. While occupying one of the grandest and most prominent
locations in London, the grounds of the old Palace of Whitehall,
it was not particularly big. But it was packed with architecture.
Swift likened Vanbrugh's building to a 'Goose-pie', and it was
known as Goose-pie House ever after. There is some doubt as to
what exactly constituted a goose pie in the first years of the
eighteenth century: the dish was probably known for its curious
shape and ingredients. We can be sure that Swift meant no
compliment. Presumably he was lampooning what seemed to
him the hotchpotch nature of the design, with its recession and
projection, its bold rusticated stonework in the centre contrasting
with plain ashlar to either side, its contrast of height between
wings and centre block. This novelty of a house was, in short,

Baroque: classicism used with a sculptural freedom that would have shocked Jones. Jones was nothing if not chaste; Vanbrugh rather liked to be naughty.

The whimsicality of the Goose-pie can be measured against the norms that had evolved for domestic architecture during the seventeenth century. Smaller houses were being joined together into terraces to save space, the first development of this kind being Covent Garden piazza, on one side of which stood Jones's church of St Paul. For detached houses, Roger Pratt's Coleshill in Berkshire, built during the Commonwealth, had spawned a taste for squarish, Dutch-looking houses, often with walls of red brick sheltering beneath hipped roofs. There would be a cupola on top of the roof, a doorcase with columns and a hood, but few other overt signs of classicism, beyond the proportions. In one of these houses, The Belvedere on Crooms Hill in Greenwich, Pepys dined 'neatly and nobly' with the lawyer Mark Cuttle; they climbed the winding stairs to the 'fine Turret at top' and enjoyed the view of London and the Thames.

It was Greenwich that Vanbrugh would choose as the site of his country house, Vanbrugh Castle, built on Maze Hill. He had become acquainted with the area through the Royal Naval Hospital, to whose board of directors he was appointed in 1703, succeeding Sir Christopher Wren as Surveyor in 1716. Presumably it was the good air and view which attracted him to Maze Hill. Vanbrugh Castle would be just as idiosyncratic as Goose-pie House – but even more of a foretaste of the way in which intellectual currents were beginning to move.

It was not the first time that Vanbrugh's thoughts had turned to a country house. While building Blenheim Palace for the Duke of Marlborough, he set about rehabilitating the old Manor of Wood-stock, which lay in its grounds, as a residence for himself. Since this was done without authority, he found himself having to explain his actions when Marlborough's implacably Vanbrugh-hating

Duchess, Sarah, realized what he was up to. Thinking on his feet, but also exploring a revolutionary aesthetic idea, he wrote a memorandum on the restoration, arguing that old structures should be valued for the associations they aroused in the mind. They 'move more lively and pleasing Reflections (than History without their aid can do) on the Persons who have inhabited them; on the remarkable things which have been transacted in them, or the extraordinary occasions of erecting them'. By forming a pleasing episode in the landscape, one would positively enhance a gentleman's park rather than detract from it.

It is difficult to appreciate the originality of this approach today, conditioned as we are by such pervasive and particularly British responses as the writings of John Ruskin in the nineteenth century and the conservation crusade in the twentieth. Vanbrugh, however, was writing during a period when form seemed everything in architecture. Building was both laborious and expensive; houses were valued for their solidity, opulence and swank, and most people would have seen very little merit in an outmoded, crumbling ruin. Vanbrugh's architecture is, for obvious reasons, often characterized as theatrical, and his appreciation of Woodstock Manor can truly be said to have had an attribute of theatre, since it was based more upon the Manor's ability to move the viewer than, in a conventional sense, to please the eye. At Maze Hill, he had no old manor house to restore; instead he summoned up the 'Castle Air' of his previous commissions and took it further, in the direction of Picturesque asymmetry.

Vanbrugh had already rented a house at Greenwich for a year or two before building his new one. A friend referred to it as his 'country morsell', for Greenwich was still rural in 1717. But it was not isolated: a couple of Vanbrugh's friends already lived nearby, and prosperous houses like The Belvedere had been built in the previous century. As the years went on, they reflected the change that had overcome the area after the Civil War. No longer were the local residents luminaries of the court (by now the Queen's House was more or less all that remained of Greenwich Palace), but, rather, successful merchants, City men and sea captains. Taking the view remained as important as it had been in Pepys's day, and Vanbrugh gave his Castle a roof of lead flats that could be walked upon.

The glass engraver Laurence Whistler, who wrote a biography of Vanbrugh in 1954, evokes the vista that could be enjoyed:

In the middle distance, then, lay London in the hollow of green hills, still cupped like jewellery in the palm of a hand, and more like jewellery than ever before or ever again. For even in the ordinary kind light of this country, the grey and usual, its many new steeples might be told in the smokeless air, with the whitish lantern of St Paul's high above them, as yet unweathered. Closer at hand rose Greenwich Hospital, with only one cupola silhouetted against the shine of the river, crawling with masts, and beyond the grey-green water-meadows, were the inconspicuous hills of Essex. Nothing much moved in that emptiness, except the gulls, and a row of windmills that for much of the year would be turned to receive the west wind, all moving together like toys.

Whistler may have exaggerated the clarity of the air over London, but it is easy to see why the panorama that he describes, with its combination of pastoral landscape and fine architecture, would have delighted Vanbrugh.

In January 1719, at the age of fifty-four, Vanbrugh married, an episode that allowed his contemporaries some humour at his expense. Early in the courtship, when he was but forty-nine, Lady Mary Wortley Montagu had reported from York (Vanbrugh had been staying at Castle Howard) to a friend: 'His Inclination to Ruins has given him a fancy for Mrs Yarborrough. He sighs and ogles that it would do your heart good to see him.' One would hardly know it from this disparaging reference, but 'Mrs Yarborrough' was in fact

unmarried (it was relatively common for women past girlhood to be
styled as 'Mrs') and just the same age as Lady Mary Wortley
Montagu herself – twenty-four. As an old, or oldish, man taking
a much younger wife, and as a writer of mildly improper plays,
Vanbrugh made a particularly satisfying object of ridicule. The
Vanbrughs' domestic contentment seems to have been quite unaffected by it, however. There may have been twenty-five years
between them, but everything suggests that their marriage was a
happy one.

The new house had been begun seven months before the knot
was tied – perhaps even before its builder knew that he would
marry. It still stands on Maze Hill, though the yellow London
stock bricks have darkened to their usual grimy colour, and it is
now hemmed in by other buildings. When Vanbrugh acquired his
lease of 'a Field and other Grounds' – a triangle of twelve acres
carved from the Westcombe estate (once the property of the
antiquarian William Lambard) – it was still country. The Vanbrughs moved into their new home in 1720, and there could be no
doubting that it was a castle in fact as well as in name. From the
Dover Road visitors had first to penetrate a defensive ring of
walls, bastions and gatehouse – a miniature version of the mock
fortifications at Castle Howard. There was another gateway, just
in front of the house, on the Greenwich side. The Castle itself
comprised a four-square keep, with two square towers at the
corners of the south façade (overlooking the field) and a circular
one in the centre. The circular tower gave every floor a bow
window, to take advantage of the view. There were battlements, a
string course and a kind of scalloped corbel table – all very
medieval. The etiolated proportions do not suggest any great
strength, but the relative height (four storeys) gives the place a
fairy-tale character – in the early twenty-first century, reminiscent
of Disney. The windows were, if not quite arrow slits, decidedly
tall and thin. There had been one or two other medievalizing

houses built or restored over the previous century, but they were very few, obscure and unconnected with the world of fashion inhabited by Vanbrugh. Vanbrugh Castle might be called a revival for revival's sake. It is difficult to estimate its influence, but it must have struck contemporaries as unprecedented. It can claim a place at the very beginning of the Gothic Revival that so delighted Horace Walpole and swept Victorian architects off their feet.

Despite its military bearing, this remarkable house is not large, nor are the rooms within it. As Vanbrugh wrote to 'old Jacob' Tonson, the publisher who had also been secretary of the Kit-Cat Club, '. . . one may find a great deal of Pleasure, in building a Palace for another, when one shou'd find very little living in't ones Self.' By 1722 he could report that he was 'now two Boys Strong in the Nursery'. He adored his children, in the way that older fathers do. Their arrival necessitated the building of new wings. Whereas the original castle had been fanciful in style, but symmetrical in form, symmetry was now thrown to the winds in favour of Picturesque irregularity, not something that Vanbrugh ever tried in his larger commissions.

Nor was that all. Very soon after he acquired the lease of Maze Hill, he set about gathering other members of his family around him. Almost as soon as he began his own Castle, work started on another house on the site, probably for his youngest brother, Philip, a captain in the navy and recently widowed. From earliest days, the house was called The Nunnery. In the next century it would have been called a bungalow: a spreading single-storey structure, with a little tower over the middle. Then came the Castellulum Vanbrugiense (Little Vanbrugh Castle) for John's thirty-two-year-old brother Charles, already prosperous from a faintly shady career at sea and subsequent investments. It was called Mince-pie House – an echo of the Goose-pie House at Whitehall. There is not much that is obviously a mince pie about it, but it was a colourful conception, with a square centrepiece of five bays, a rusticated doorcase and circular side towers, again rusticated (on second thought, the crenellated tops do suggest a pie crust). Like Vanbrugh Castle, these sibling mansions were built of London stock brick. Two further houses, the White Towers, were constructed, not for family members, out of the patented white bricks supplied by a Fulham brick-maker to whom Vanbrugh had given financial backing. The five houses were dotted about the site in a thoroughly Picturesque manner.

The effect must have been that of a caprice, with each house expressing a kind of architectural whim. They seem to have delighted Vanbrugh's older son Charles, which may have been part of the point (sadly, the younger of the two boys in the nursery, John, died at the age of one). One imagines that the sensations that stirred the architect's breast as he passed under the gateway included family warmth, amusement at his own whimsy, a sense of entering a self-contained world of his own making, relief after the externally imposed artifice of the town, and pride in his achievement at having done it all. His personality must have inspired the little community there; his letters show that he never tired of the fun of it all.

Nor did other house builders over the next 150 years. Other gentlemen would follow Vanbrugh's example in giving their houses a martial air – for example the house that Sir William Chambers built for Lord Milton next to Milton Abbey in Dorset. In the 1820s Robert Smirke, architect of the austerely neo-classical British Museum in London, built forbidding Eastnor Castle in Herefordshire. The style could not percolate very far down the social scale, because castles are necessarily big – although Charles Dickens imagined the legal clerk Mr Wemmick retiring to a diminutive castle, with moat, drawbridge, battlements and cannon, in *Great Expectations* (1860–61).

Echoes of Maze Hill can also be found in the follies built in Picturesque landscape parks. And indeed the Picturesque way of looking at buildings and landscape became the British aesthetic which survived, via Romanticism, into the nineteenth century; the Arts and Crafts movement, the Garden City and our invincible green suburbs all owe something to it. Our cities are memorable for their parks, not their grand avenues: this is another aspect of the Picturesque heritage. For better or worse, the rebuilding of London after the Second World War took place along what were arguably Picturesque lines, Modernist architects arguing that new would sit happily alongside old on a mix-and-match basis.

Another aspect of Vanbrugh Castle cannot be passed over, although it is not at all military: the house has sash windows. By this date, the sash window had become securely established as the window of choice for polite architecture. Following their first known use at Whitehall Palace around 1670, sashes were quickly taken up by fashionable builders, reaching Dyrham Park in Gloucestershire in 1692. By the early eighteenth century, they had become so ubiquitous among the better sort of houses that they were known as 'common windows'. Casement windows, their small panes of glass held together with lead, had come to seem desperately old-fashioned.

A sash window is made of two wooden frames, or sash lights, filled with glass; they slide up and down along sash boxes installed vertically to either side. Inside one of the sash boxes is a pulley and two counterweights, which allow a sash light, once it has been raised or lowered, to stay in position. Early sash windows had nine panes of glass in each sash light; and the glazing bars were relatively thick. Refinements in joinery allowed the form of 'six over six' to become standard after the mid-eighteenth century; at the same time, glazing bars changed profile, tapering to what was almost a point. Early examples of sash windows set the sash box flush with the external wall surface; in London this practice was banned by the Building Act of 1709, which insisted that wood should be set back from the front of the building to protect against fire. The verticality of the sash window suited classical ideas of proportion. The lights themselves were apt to be square, so that the window as a whole was in the proportion of 1:2, and a pattern of windows could be made to form other ideal proportions.

The glass that filled sash windows was of the type known as crown, from the stamp of a ducal coronet that it bore as a result of its having been made at the Duke of Buckingham's glass house in Southwark in London. Crown glass had been introduced to England in the 1680s. The process began, as with muff glass, by blowing a lump of molten glass into a globe. Now, however, a metal rod was inserted opposite the blowpipe, and the globe was spun so fast that centrifugal force drew it out into a flat disc known as a table. Eventually glass-blowers became so skilled that they could make the table extend to more than 5 feet in diameter. Because the glass did not come into contact with any other material when it was hot, it was perfectly clear, though slightly ribbed from the spinning (the centre was distinguished by a bull's-eye, or 'punty mark'; this part was sold cheaply and used in obscure places where it could not be much seen). It was also very thin. (Since glass becomes more friable over time, special care has to be taken in cleaning old sash windows.) At night, shutters were folded across them and secured with an iron bar.

Sash windows do not belong naturally to the castle style; even with the shutters closed, it would not take very long for a warlike horde to knock them in. What did Vanbrugh care for that? Their presence makes his Castle seem even more of a caprice.

Vanbrugh had only half a dozen years to enjoy his Maze Hill home, before he died in 1726. With his death the heart went out of the quirky assemblage of houses – a family compound, as it would have been called later in the United States. Today only his own house survives.

8. A Georgian House in Town
19 New King Street, Bath

On the evening of 13 March 1781, William Herschel took his seven-foot telescope into the garden of his house in New King Street, Bath. It was a narrow garden, but beyond it lay an orchard. At the end of the orchard, a high wall stood guard against the frequent flooding of the river Avon, whose course ran on the other side of the water meadow known as the King's Mead. Herschel set up the telescope and resumed the systematic review of the heavens which had become the focus of every moment he could snatch from his career as a music teacher and organist. He had focused his attention on the stars around the constellation Gemini, being particularly interested in pairs of stars, in the hope of being able to measure their distances. He noticed one body that seemed to be larger than the rest, and it was moving against the background of fixed stars. He thought, reasonably, that it was a comet. The scientists of the Royal Society, to whom he communicated his discovery, quickly realized that it was a planet, belonging to our solar system but further out than anyone had previously believed possible. Herschel called the planet Georgium Sidius, or more simply The Georgian, in honour of the King. The name did not catch on. 'Minerva' and 'Herschel' were among the alternatives, but by the middle of the next century scientific opinion had settled on Uranus, father of Saturn. It was an epic discovery. As the astronomer Sir Patrick Moore has written, 'So long as humanity lasts, William Herschel will never be forgotten.'

Why did it happen in Bath? In Roman times, a woman came to the steaming spring that seeped from the ground on a site in what is now the centre of the town and threw a ring into the water. It was recovered, along with another ring, in an archaeological dig in 1979–80. The spring was sacred; the woman was making a sacrifice to the goddess Sulis Minerva – a composite of the Roman Minerva and the pre-Roman Sulis, with whom she shared attributes. Bath's career as a spa resort had been launched. The Romans built bath houses, covering an area as big as a football pitch, which must have astounded the local tribespeople. (A nonplussed Celtic chieftain is supposed to have asked a Roman governor why he bathed once every day. Because, replied the Roman sadly, he was too busy to bathe twice a day.) The barrel vaults and central-heating systems decayed, but medieval folk continued to dip themselves in the famed waters, known for their health-giving properties. What would later be known as the King's Bath was, until the Dissolution, part of a monastery, but the monks did little to exploit it. Perhaps that was because the reputation of baths, or bagnios as they were sometimes known, was no better than it should have been, men and women being thrown together in strange circumstances with an excuse to undress. But from the sixteenth century, when the baths at Bath came into the city's hands, they were increasingly seen as a source of health – and wealth. The patronage of Queen Anne, with her disastrous gynaecological history, put a fashionable gloss on the place, and the first Pump Room was built in 1706, under the aegis of the arbiter of elegant behaviour Beau Nash.

Architecturally the town was still a closely packed jumble of wooden structures, some little better than shanties, their decayed condition a consequence of the failure of the weaving industry. Such new buildings as existed were condemned by the antiquary William Stukeley as a 'disgrace to the architects they have there' in 1724. There may have been no more than 250 dwellings altogether.

In 1727, John Wood took the matter in hand by building Queen Square. In doing so he developed an idea that was to revolutionize the appearance of British cities. There was nothing new in building terraces of houses around squares; Wood's innovation was to design a terrace so that it looked like one very grand building rather than a string of individual dwellings joined together. The north side of Queen Square has the appearance of a palace, with a central pediment, end pavilions and giant columns. Few subsequent terraces were as grand as this, until John Nash built those around Regent's Park in London. But the principle that terraces could be composed to architectural effect was profound, giving order and style to streets that would otherwise have been monotonous. Brighton, London's Belgravia and many other Georgian and Victorian developments were beneficiaries.

Wood had been born in Bath. The son of a builder, he had first been apprenticed to a carpenter before cutting his teeth on some speculative buildings in London. He returned to Bath full of grand visions inspired by the third volume of the architect Colen Campbell's review of contemporary British architecture, *Vitruvius Britannicus* (1725), at the age of twenty-one. Although not classically educated, he seems to have been imbued with a strong idea of Bath's history, since Queen Square recreates some of the town's Roman glory. At first sight, you might think that his next development, the King's Circus (now simply known as the Circus), was also inspired by the classical world. Well-travelled contemporaries would immediately have been put in mind of the Colosseum in Rome. This was clearly at the back of Wood's mind, too, given that his original proposals for rebuilding Bath included, as well as 'a grand Place of Assembly to be called the Royal Forum of Bath; another Place, no less magnificent, for the Exhibition of Sports, to be called the Grand Circus'. Wood's Circus turns the Colosseum inside out, by putting the three classical orders of columns on the inside rather than the outside, as in Rome. Wood later claimed that his inspiration was Stonehenge (which in turn seemed to him, as he argued in *The Origin of Building: or the Plagiarism of the Heathens Detected* (1741), to have been based on the Temple of Jerusalem). Because the curative properties of Bath's hot springs had supposedly been discovered by the town's supposed founder, Prince Bladud (he had been cast out for leprosy and found himself temporarily working as a swineherd), the top of the parapet is adorned with stone acorns. These allusions would not have meant anything to people who lived elsewhere than in Bath, and may have been lost even on them; they were reconciled in Wood's mind by involved and unhistorical theories related to freemasonry. But the idea that fashionable urban developments could unfold as a sequence of geometrical spaces profoundly influenced the Georgian town. Despite his sometimes eccentric theories, Wood's aspirations were those of other informed contemporaries. He admired austerity and mathematical proportions, wanting Bath 'to vie with the famous City of Vicenza, in Italy, when in its highest Pitch of Glory, by the excellent Art of the Celebrated Andrea Palladio'.

Wood died in 1754, just as work on the King's Circus was beginning. Its completion was left to his son, John Wood the Younger, who introduced another geometrical form to Georgian building in the shape of the Royal Crescent. Development in Bath had now been pushed away from the low-lying marsh around the springs and up the hill. Wood, responding to the contemporary taste for the Picturesque, used this to his advantage by turning his new crescent towards the view. A leafy park spills down the hillside: whereas Queen Square and the King's Circus were enclosed urban spaces, the Royal Crescent opens itself towards nature. Like other speculative developers before and since, John Wood the Younger was unable to stay ahead of the game, however, and was heavily in debt at the time of his death in 1782.

There were other architects in Bath. The Bristol architect John Strahan made what the elder Wood regarded as 'piratical' raids on the town. Among his contributions is Rosewell House on Kingsmead Square, Bath's one flirtation with the Baroque (the frilly window surrounds appear almost Austrian). Thomas Baldwin became City Surveyor and ushered Bath away from the Woods' stolid Palladianism towards the lighter neo-classical style of the fashionable Adam brothers; he designed the Pump Room and rebuilt the Cross Bath. But it was not just the Woods' vision as architects which gave shape to Bath and stamped it as an elegant destination for an ever-changing cast of affluent visitors. It was also their energy as developers.

The third figure who was instrumental in transforming Bath lived at Prior Park, on a hill to the south-east of the town. Between 1735 and 1748, John Wood built this splendid country house, with an austerely rectangular profile broken by the pediment of a giant portico, for his friend Ralph Allen. Wood had been influenced in the conception by Campbell's designs for Wanstead in Essex which were published in *Vitruvius Britannicus* – a propaganda tool for Palladianism. Whereas Palladio had built his villas as summer retreats, with sheds for farm carts attached, Prior Park was a substantial residence, much of whose character – like that of Bath as a whole – derived from the creamy limestone from which it was built. The quarries from which that stone came lay nearby. Allen bought them with some of the fortune he had made by reorganizing England's postal service. Rails were laid to allow wagons laden with Bath stone to be trundled down to the river. It is a beautiful stone, and the fact that it is used almost everywhere bestows harmony, even to streets that were run up piecemeal and not always to the highest standards.

Allen became the magnifico of Bath, his circle of literary and artistic friends reflecting the cultural life that the town had to offer. Alexander Pope would stay at Prior Park for months at a time, discussing gardens (the situation of the house was regarded as naturally Picturesque) and ordering stone for urns in his own garden at Twickenham (as well as borrowing Allen's mason). Henry Fielding is supposed to have based the character of Squire Allworthy in *Tom Jones* (1749) on Allen. The actor David Garrick's friendship with Allen is revealed in a lengthy correspondence, and the portrait painter Thomas Gainsborough, establishing a Bath reputation before launching himself in London, was a frequent guest. Prior Park was in every sense the sort of place that allowed guests to leave 'the Madness of the Little Town', as Pope called it, beneath them.

In the course of the century, Bath grew in response to the crowds of noblemen, nabobs, ship owners, admirals, merchants, bishops and chancers who came during the Season (like the London Season, it was a winter festival, held during the months when bad weather made it difficult to get around the countryside). Allen died in 1764. Two years later, the author Tobias Smollett, living in Gay Street, drafted *The Expedition of Humphry Clinker* (not published until 1771), in which the gout-stricken Matthew Bramble inveighs against Bath society:

> Clerks and factors from the East Indies, loaded with the spoil of plundered provinces; planters, negro drivers and hucksters, from our American plantations, enriched they know not how; agents, commissaries, and contractors, who have fattened, in two successive wars, on the blood of the nation; usurers, brokers, and jobbers of every kind; men of low birth, and no breeding, have found themselves suddenly translated into a state of affluence, unknown to former ages; and no wonder that their brains should be intoxicated with pride, vanity, and presumption.

The dubious rubbed shoulders with the genteel, the stiff conventions of London were relaxed, and the seducer Willoughby, in *Sense and Sensibility* (1811), could meet the little-supervised Miss Williams.

It was in 1766, the year when Smollett was writing *Humphry Clinker*, that Herschel arrived in Bath. Herschel had been born in Hanover in Germany, the son of an army bandmaster. Having been educated at the garrison school, he had joined his father in the Hanoverian Guards at the age of fourteen, playing the hautboy and violin. The Guards came to England, where the Hanoverian George II was King, but they then became part of the army which was routed by the French at the Battle of Hastenbeck. Wilhelm Herschel, as he was still known, left the scene, only to spend a night in a water-filled ditch; although he returned to the army, musicians were no longer needed, so he made his way, via Hamburg, to London. He kept himself alive by copying music, while hoping to shine as a composer. He arrived in Bath to be organist at the fashionable Octagon Chapel (a proprietary chapel where all the seats were paid for; there were fireplaces in alcoves, and the congregation might be 'packed like seeds in a sunflower' when a bishop was preaching, according to Samuel Johnson's friend, the writer Mrs Thrale). Since the organ was not as yet ready, Herschel became oboist in an orchestra that played in the Pump Room. His sister Caroline came over from Hanover to keep house in 1772.

They did not immediately move into 19 New King Street. Caroline first arrived at No. 7, where her brother was lodging with Mr and Mrs Bulman, friends from a period spent in Leeds. The Bulmans occupied the ground floor, which might otherwise have had a front dining room and back parlour, although one at least must have been turned into a bedroom (it was still, however, called the parlour floor). Caroline lodged in the attic, along with Herschel's brother Alexander. Herschel occupied the first floor, 'which was furnished in the newest and most handsome style'. The front drawing room contained a harpsichord, which

Caroline, in her journals, calls a Clasicent, for his lessons and musical soirées.

William Herschel's advent in Bath coincided with that of a gout-ridden Cornish clergyman, John Penrose. Having put himself under the care of an apothecary, Penrose described his visit in great detail to his family. He and his daughter Fanny took three rooms, namely a parlour and two bedrooms. The parlour was furnished with six mahogany chairs with horsehair seats, 'an Easy-Chair, a Dining Table', a looking glass over the chimneypiece and another between the windows. 'All the Houses here are sashed,' he noted approvingly, Bath being more up to the minute than Cornwall. 'Our Lodging Room,' he continued the next day, 'has a blew and white flowered Linen Bed, Window Curtains of the same, Walnut Chairs with blew Bottoms, Chest of Drawers, Dressing Table, Looking-Glass: Inside, a closet with hanging Press and Shelves. Fanny's Bed white, with all conveniences, and a closet.' They sound pretty rooms; perhaps Herschel's were similar. The Penroses arrived with their own cups, saucers, plates, teapots and 'Pint Bottle for Bath Water'.

Although the Bulmans were supposed to supervise the one servant, shopping for food was Caroline Herschel's responsibility – one that sat heavily on her, as she was 'sent alone', speaking little English, 'among fishwomen, butchers, basket-women, &c.' She found it even more difficult to manage the 'hot-headed old Welsh woman' whom William had employed as the servant, and whose bad habits allowed the iron-bladed knives to go rusty and the heater of the tea urn to be thrown out with the ashes. Not surprisingly Caroline felt home-sick. The Herschels moved to 19 New King Street in 1777.

New King Street was not one of the town's grander streets, but rather one of three terraced ones thrown out to the west, more or less parallel to the Avon and prone to flood. Built around 1764, the house rises through five floors, including the basement, and the street front is given variety by the use of two different kinds of stone: a whitish limestone on the ground floor and the usual honeyed Bath stone above. The ashlar perfection of the surface was only a front. Behind this outer skin – keyed in by means of projecting 'bonding stones' – most of the thickness of the wall was composed of rubble. Not all of Bath's houses were constructed as soundly as they should have been, speculators having built for a quick sale of their leases. Fortunately for the Herschels, 19 New King Street was solidly built. It did not matter that the back was left in a rougher condition, the stone noticeably more shelly than the smooth oolite of the street front.

The larger houses in Bath contain rounded staircase landings to enable sedan chairs, having brought home their infirm passengers, to be easily turned around. The passage of the sedan-chair men through the streets was preceded, after dark, by boys carrying flaming torches, or links; cone-shaped iron link extinguishers can still be seen outside some front doors. New King Street occupied a considerably more modest place in the hierarchy. Not that the *bon ton* neglected it entirely; witness the handsome doorcases at the east end, nearest the Assembly Rooms. Fanny Nelson, 'sea widow' of the future admiral who was then serving as captain of the *Agamemnon*, would take a house in New King Street for three years during the 1790s, although conscious that its watery location was not as socially eligible as newer developments up the hill. (In Bath, she wrote to her husband, 'the higher you go the dearer'; a house in Gay Street cost £160, as opposed to the £90 she was paying for her New King Street residence.)

New King Street was intended less for rich visitors than for people like the Herschels – the tradesmen, artisans, apothecaries, lawyers and other professionals who kept the town functioning. Inside No. 19, the entrance hall was shared with the staircase, a narrow affair onto each of whose steps the builder squeezed three turned balusters, in the by now distinctly outmoded early Georgian manner. A sedan chair would barely have got into the hall, let alone up the stairs. There was a dining room at the front of this floor and a parlour at the back, while the drawing room occupied the front of the first floor; the back first-floor room was William's workroom and possibly bedroom. 19 New King Street was snug rather than opulent, aspiring to elegance rather than – as we shall see – necessarily achieving it. Even so, the Herschels were better off than most of Bath's population, a third of whom were still sub-sisting on handouts of rice in 1801.

By 1764, the flamboyant era of English plasterwork had largely passed. The Elizabethans had managed to suspend heavy bosses from their ceilings, turning what might otherwise have been flat surfaces into inverted relief maps. In the second half of the seventeenth century, plaster garlands around deep panels attempted to emulate those which Grinling Gibbons was carving from walnut – though not always with such finesse; the arrival of Italian 'stuccadores' in the early eighteenth century introduced a new virtuosity, with moulded plaster scenes and figures taking on the smoothness of marble. This suited the decorative taste of the dainty, frivolous style known as the Rococo, which took its name from the French word *rocaille*, or 'pebble'. The Rococo was particularly associated with the grottoes – fancifully decorated with minerals and shells – then being built in the gardens of country houses, though it danced its way through all the decorative arts – carving, plasterwork, ironwork, furniture, silver, porcelain – subverting the serious endeavours of the classicists to create order and balance. Some Rococo craftsmen threw even sym-metry to the winds. This really was the light fantastic; Palladianism seemed stiff-kneed by comparison. Behind some of the Woods' plain Palladian façades, Bath could be fitted out with a degree of Rococo fantasy – not too much of it, generally, because the rooms were not intended for the permanent occupation of a family, but to be rented out during the Season. But in 19 New King Street, the plaster cornice of garlands and lion masks in the staircase hall is thin. Furthermore, despite the decoratively promising elements of which it is composed, it attempts no caprice. Style had moved on. The sculptural skills of the stuccadore were being replaced by repeating motifs pressed from moulds, perhaps using a material known as *compo*, or possibly *carton pierre* (papier mâché). The effect aimed at by the lion masks, however modest, was Roman dignity.

The Herschel family had always been anxious to get on. As soon as Caroline arrived in England, William began to give her lessons in English, singing and arithmetic. This was not entirely disinterested of him, as he wanted Caroline to sing in his concerts and oratorios, to keep house, and to help with his great hobby: astronomy. She showed signs of becoming a successful singer in her own right, but abandoned her solo career in favour of training William's choir and generally supporting her brother. Too poor to buy a new telescope of sufficiently impressive magnification, Herschel set about making his own, having analysed a discarded example he was able to acquire from one of his neighbours. Caroline made the pasteboard tubes, beginning with one four feet in length. This gave a magnification of forty. Herschel was soon dissatisfied: he went on to make twelve-foot, fifteen-foot and thirty-foot telescopes. He heard about a man in Bath who polished mirrors and bought his tools to make reflectors. By 1775, 'every leisure moment was eagerly snatched at for resuming some work which was in progress, without taking time for changing dress, and many a lace ruffle (which were then worn) was torn or bespattered by molten pitch, &c.' Herschel would spend whole days turning the handle of his polishing machine, during which Caroline would put food into his mouth to save him having to stop. Astronomy was altogether getting the better of them. The actor John Bernard, who took music lessons there, remembered 19 New King Street in his *Retrospections of the Stage* (1830): 'His lodgings resembled an astronomer's much more than a musician's, being heaped up with globes, maps, telescopes, reflectors, &c., under which his piano was hid, and the violoncello, like a discarded favourite, skulked away in a corner.'

It is thanks to astronomy, however, that we have a rare, albeit hardly characteristic, glimpse below stairs in this Georgian house. Caroline would prepare food in the kitchen, with its spit and bread oven, helped by one of the succession of unsatisfactory servants. Next door, William had his workshop. Not only did he polish his lenses, but he cast them as well. To this end he built a furnace and smelting oven. His tour de force was to be the mirror for his thirty-foot telescope, cast in a mould made out of finely ground horse dung (Caroline, needless to say, was pressed into work grinding the dung). Eventually the mould was ready, and over five hundred pounds of the alloy known as speculum was poured into it. But it leaked onto the stone flags – 'and both my brothers and the caster with his men were obliged to run out at opposite doors, for the stone flooring (which ought to have been taken up) flew about in all directions, as high as the ceiling. My poor brother fell, exhausted with heat and exertion, on a heap of brickbats.' Herschel was able to achieve powers of magnification which astounded his scientific contemporaries. But the ever-larger telescopes were unwieldy, and, ironically, Uranus was discovered using a seven-footer.

Georgium Sidius made Herschel a scientific celebrity. George III wanted demonstrations at Windsor and provided a pension. Herschel hurried off, his sister in tow, to a farmhouse in Slough, to be near the King. The forty-foot telescope that he erected there, although largely impractical, became such a landmark that it was recorded on Ordnance Survey maps.

9. A Curate's Picturesque Garden
The Wakes, Selborne

'**S**et up my first Oil-Jar Vase at the bottom of the Ewel-Close with a pannel only in front: Mount, pedestal, & Vase nine feet high.' This entry, for 14 May 1756, comes from the journal of Gilbert White, curate of Selborne in Hampshire. White would come to be celebrated, at the end of his life and thereafter, as one of the first naturalists to make careful, first-hand observations of the living world. His *Natural History and Antiquities of Selborne*, literally his life's work, has never been out of print since its first publication in 1789. In this respect he was a pioneer, taking advantage of his seclusion in Selborne – partly enforced by his financial circumstances, partly the choice of a home-loving bachelor, partly the result of the extreme travel sickness that he suffered in carriages – to observe the habits of cuckoos and nightjars, hedgehogs and eels. But he was also a man of his time.

Educated at Oxford, he had absorbed the attitude to nature expressed in the landscape parks being created by 'Capability' Brown for gentlemen up and down the country. On his narrow income, White could not afford to employ a professional garden designer. A rich man would have erected a classical urn to terminate a view; White substituted a terracotta oil jar on a wooden base. His garden interprets fashionable ideas on the modest, domestic scale that he could afford. His journals and letters paint a picture of home, and what it meant to a clergyman of refined taste, in the mid-eighteenth century.

White had been born in Selborne, where his grandfather, also Gilbert, had been vicar. His father, John, failed to make much of a way in the world, and in 1720 was still living, with his wife, in the vicarage, which stands next to the church. The Wakes, which would become Gilbert the naturalist's home, lies only a hundred yards away from it, across a space of green called the Plestor. (White delighted in the derivation of this unusual word: like Plaistow, it comes from the Saxon for 'pleasure ground'.) His grandfather had bought the little house as a place for his widow to live when he died, at which moment a new vicar would move into the vicarage. Until then it had been occupied by a family called Wake, who bequeathed it their name.

The Wakes had started life around 1500 as a house of three bays, comprising a hall, parlour and service rooms. It was built of what looks like blocks of chalk, with brick quoins and window sur-rounds, but chalk would have washed away if it had not been covered. The material is in fact malmstone, a kind of white (calcareous) sandstone which makes good soil (it was a source of chagrin to White that the soil in his part of the parish was not good). The house had grown – and would continue to grow into the twentieth century. Some time during the 1500s, a fireplace had been installed in the parlour; then, about 1600, a ceiling was put into the hall to divide it into two floors. (Perhaps some of my forebears would have seen it. I am told that the village was full of Aslets at this time, not a very usual name.) Some 125 years later, a solar wing was built across the end of the house; although it was the second quarter of the eighteenth century, the medieval term *solar* was retained, and was used by White. This wing contained a kitchen and scullery on the ground floor. Since White appears to have used the words *kitchen* and *dining room* to refer to the same place, this was presumably where he normally ate. The Wakes was not, as yet, by any means a big place.

If White had gone to Magdalen College, Oxford, like his grandfather, he might have become vicar of Selborne, since the living was in Magdalen's gift. Instead, not knowing that Selborne would become his home for more than sixty years, he followed his Uncle Charles to Oriel. In due course he became a Fellow, and eventually acquired the modest Oriel living of Moreton Pinkney in Northamptonshire, which he rarely visited. Once he had settled back into Selborne as curate, he did not put himself out to improve his lot by obtaining a better living from his college. For a year he went back to Oxford to serve in the somewhat unglamorous role of Junior Proctor (responsible for policing the behaviour of undergraduates). But the pull of Selborne was too strong for him not to return. There were mutterings in Oriel that, as a non-resident with a College living, he should have resigned his Fellowship, particularly after the death of his father, when it was assumed that he had come into property; but the inheritance was scant and he felt too poor to do so. Occasionally he travelled to see family in London and elsewhere. For the most part, however, he remained sealed up in his parish – quite literally, in winter, when snow drifts blocked the sunken lanes which were the only means of reaching the village. At the best of times, Selborne, though only fifty miles from London, was so inaccessible that strangers could not find it without a guide.

Within Selborne, White's intellectual circle may have been limited, but he brought with him the store of ideas he had acquired at Oxford. On one occasion, he had met no less a figure than Alexander Pope, who gave him a copy of his six-volume translation of the *Iliad*. As White would have known, Pope was one of the foremost advocates of the new Picturesque attitude to gardening and landscape. In his 'Epistle to Burlington' (1731), Pope codified its ideals in the famous lines:

> In all, let Nature never be forgot . . .
> Consult the Genius of the Place in all
> That tells the water or to rise, or fall . . .
> Paints as you plant, and as you work, Designs.

Previously, gardeners had sought to impose order on their surroundings by means of geometrical parterres and radiating avenues. Now, Pope urged, the yew hedges and topiary were to be cut down, in order to create naturalistic effects.

Pope had not coined the term 'Genius of the Place'; it had been in circulation since 1709, when the 3rd Earl of Shaftesbury had written 'The Moralists, a Philosophical Rhapsody', endorsing 'the passion growing in me for Things of a *natural* kind'. Elsewhere he wrote of the new taste as a specially national phenomenon. While few ideas could hope to gain an English following in the eighteenth century if they were thought to be foreign, the truth is that this one was a self-conscious import. Memories of the Grand Tour were mixed with allusions to the classical world, making Stowe in Buckinghamshire – which Lord Percival regarded as the 'finest seat in England' when he visited in 1724 – as 'near as an approach to Elysium as English soil and climate will permit' (in the words of Pope). But Stowe's owner Lord Cobham also made the place into an allegory of the British constitution and politics, and the Italian and even Chinese garden influences became naturalized. By 1750 the French were using the phrase '*le jardin anglais*' to describe gardens with lawns, lakes, woods and waterfalls. The love of nature that they expressed seemed particularly British, as did the landowners' love of country life.

It was extremely piquant to try to turn your own estate into one of these half-real, half-imaginary landscapes; you might even choose to look at the result in a mirrored Claude glass, which had the effect of instantly varnishing nature with a golden glow – the rays of the long afternoon sun being all too often absent from Hampshire, according to White's meteorological records. By the third quarter of the eighteenth century, Walpole could exclaim that 'every journey is made through a succession of pictures.' Some of these 'pictures' had been created by human hands moving hills, damming up streams to form lakes and planting clumps of trees, which were also good for the foxes that were now hunted.

Nature itself, especially in what was thought of as the wild and romantic scenery of Wales and the Lake District, could also be regarded as a series of painterly views. It was less a question, for some writers, of paintings being judged according to their fidelity to the natural world, than of nature corresponding to an artistic ideal: a curious inversion of values to which Gilbert White was not immune. He describes the 'very grotesque and wild appearances' of the sunken lanes near Selborne, eighteen feet deep in places, their sides a mass of tangled roots which hang with icicles in winter, in terms that recall the exaggeratedly terrifying landscapes of the Italian painter Salvator Rosa. (The aesthetic theorist and politician Edmund Burke called the fright that such scenes gave viewers – once they had got their breath back – a sensation of pleasure: the 'Sublime'.) Woods were no longer regarded as frightening places, as they had been during the fourteenth century. 'Perhaps of all species of landscape, there is none, which so universally captivates mankind, as forest-scenery,' wrote the Picturesque theorist William Gilpin. In the same spirit White regarded the October beech woods at Selborne as 'very engaging to the eye, & imagination . . . These scenes are worthy the pencil of a Reubens [sic].' As a naturalist and local patriot, he more often thought that nature surpassed the efforts of human imitators: 'Sunday 26, 1783. If a masterly landscape painter was to take our hanging woods in their autumnal colours, persons unacquainted with the country would object to the strength & deepness of the tints, & would pronounce, at an exhibition, that they were heightened & shaded beyond nature.' On other occasions this otherwise rational man gave his imagination a loose rein. For example, on 3 December 1789 he recorded: 'Beautiful picturesque, partial fogs along the vales, representing rivers, islands, & arms of the sea!'

White would have been particularly susceptible to the Picturesque because, as the title of his great book indicates, he was not only a naturalist but an antiquarian. Antiquarianism as a learned hobby had become something of a craze for educated gentlemen of his stamp, probing into the past from the comfort of their country-house libraries. It encouraged an appreciation of ruins and other kinds of architecture that were remote in time or place from Georgian England. This had been part and parcel of the Picturesque movement from the beginning. Ultimately these ideas would have a profound influence on the way houses were designed. There would also develop a cult of the ruin, as otherwise sensibly conducted ladies and gentlemen permitted themselves a cold shiver in response to a crumbling building's mustiness and gloom. Jane Austen would satirize the taste in *Northanger Abbey* (1818) but, as a connoisseur of landscape, was not entirely insensible to it. 'Nothing,' she wrote in *The History of England by a Partial, Prejudiced and Ignorant Historian* (1791), could pardon the crimes of Henry VIII 'but that his abolishing Religious Houses and leaving them to the ruinous depredations of Time has been of infinite use to the Landscape of England'. Presumably White did not wholly share this enthusiasm; there is no Gothic ruin at The Wakes. But like Austen he enjoyed the associations that buildings, judiciously placed in gardens or landscapes, aroused in his mind.

The first eighteenth-century gardeners to show a taste for informality did so on the authority of the Chinese. Very few English people had actually seen the gardens of China, but travellers' engravings indicated grottoes, wildernesses, serpentine paths and an absence of topiary. Chinese influence can be seen in the wriggling paths of the garden Lord Burlington laid out at Chiswick, probably designed with the help of Charles Bridgeman, but whose painterly effects were contributed by the architect and decorator William Kent. Follies also played an essential part.

We have seen how White created an urn-effect using a humble oil jar; he put up a second one on the rise in the fields known as Baker's Hill – next to five firs planted like the dots on a die to form a quincunx – so that one oil jar could be seen from the other. Economy was the mother of invention. Some of White's caprices – like those of the poet William Shenstone, landscaping on a budget at his Warwickshire *ferme ornée* called The Leasowes – were more ingenious than those of many gentlemen who spent more money on their parks. Particularly striking must have been the vista of six farm gates, lined up so that, with the effect of perspective, they seemed to fit one into another like a Chinese box. (White's fellow-Oriel cleric and lifelong friend John Mulso wrote that 'Missy [presumably his horse] desires me to tell You that She is charmed with this happy Circumstance; a Six Bar Gate in the Country being One of her favourite Coups d'Oeils; but to have Six at once ye happiness of a Century.') The view ended in a twelve-foot figure of Hercules, not in the form of a three-dimensional statue, but as a wooden cutout painted in trompe l'oeil.

After the oil jars, the surprise is not that White chose to economize so much as his choice of Hercules in his lion skin as a subject – hardly the alter ego of a stay-at-home bachelor clergyman, one would have thought. However, there is a horticultural allusion; this is a Hesperian Hercules – the hero is shown clutching the golden apples of the Hesperides. Winning them was a Labour, just as growing melons was to Gardener White. Even more original was the seat that White put up on a mound in his meadow; it was created out of an old wine pipe or barrel, and could be swivelled to follow – or avoid – the sun. A classically trained mind would have immediately spotted a reference to Greek philosopher Diogenes. Perhaps White found the perch useful for birdwatching.

While White could not afford a Heathen Temple – which, in the case of a curate, might have been even more inappropriate than the Hercules – he erected a wooden alcove, flanked by pilasters, at the end of a terrace, and 'nailed-up a Greek, & an Italian inscription' above it. That was in 1788; twenty-four years earlier, shortly after he had finally inherited The Wakes, he had 'got a stone-mason to fix the stone with my name & the date of the wall in the middle of the fruit-wall', noting with typical interest in practicalities: 'When the mason came to chizzel a hole for the stone he found the wall perfectly sound, dry, & hard.' Up on the Hanger, the whaleback of beech-covered hill that rises above White's garden and fields, he had another construction, this time of a conventionally fashionable although apt nature: a hermitage. Hermitages evoked the contemplative pleasures of the solitary, prayerful life – a fitting parallel to White's own existence. Very rich men sometimes employed hermits to occupy their follies, though rarely with any lasting success (they tended not to live up to their ascetic image, and at least one was dismissed for drunkenness). White of course was not in that league, but in June 1763 persuaded his thirty-year-old brother Harry to dress up as an Old Hermit, to great effect, when a party of young ladies walked up from the vicarage for tea. 'His appearance made me start,' wrote Miss Catherine Battie in her diary. 'After tea we went into the woods, return'd to the hermitage to see it by lamplight, it look'd sweetly indeed.' White built a second hermitage on the Hanger in the 1770s.

Naturally, the approach to the Hanger had been created on Picturesque principles although White did not actually own this land; a steep path that hairpins tightly up the cliff had been dug while he had been serving as Junior Proctor in Oxford, largely by his brother John, then attempting to work his way back into family favour, having left Oxford with debts. The path was known as the

Zig-Zag. The Hanger was so important to White that, as infirmity prevented him from making the ascent, another, more gently sloping path was cut, named (using a local word) the Bostal.

The moving of a forty-foot barn to the upper end of White's orchard was more of a technical than an aesthetic achievement. His journal entry for 26 April 1766 describes the process:

> It began to move on Thursday the 17, & went with great ease by the assistance of about 8 men for that little way that it went in a straight line: but in general it moved in a curve, & was turned once quite round, & half way round again. When it came to the pitch of the Hill it required 20 hands; & particularly when it wanted to be shoved into its place side ways, parallel with Collins's hedge. Near one day of the time was taken-up in making new sills, one of which was broken in two by skrewing it round sideways.

The ha-ha – a fence sunk in a ditch or, as at Selborne, just a ditch with one sheer side – was a different matter. Such features were thrown round the grounds immediately surrounding a house, to prevent cattle or sheep from munching their way through flower beds or poaching immaculate turf. The name derived from the exclamation of surprise uninitiated visitors made when, unawares, they came upon the trick. For the ha-ha was invisible except close to; looking out from a house, there appeared to be no division between the parkland beyond it and the grounds within. Originating in France, the ha-ha had crossed the Channel in about 1710; White built his in 1761, an early date for a small garden. The labour involved was emphasized by Long, White's mason, who said that the feature contained 'double the Quantity of stone usual in such walls'. Parts were nearly 6 feet tall. The earth that was removed from the ditch formed the mound for White's wine-barrel seat.

White began his journal in the guise, not of a naturalist, but of a market gardener. His first love was his vegetables, and they remained a preoccupation. It is easy to understand why: the produce that found its way into the kitchen-cum-dining room was largely raised on his own land, so the failure of his apricot trees to fruit or the destruction of the fish in the fish ponds by hard frost was deeply felt. Cabbages had to be guarded against caterpillars, celery against hares, and cherry trees against bullfinches (White had no compunction about having miscreants shot). Boys were paid for destroying wasps' nests, as many as twenty-six in a summer. White planted on an exceptional scale, five hundred or a thousand Savoy cabbages at a time. Some vegetables were sent to relatives; one imagines some were sold. There would have been gluts in summer, but a restricted choice during the winter months. Entries such as 'Eat my last grapes' in November 1764 have a melancholy ring.

In season, White could enjoy cucumbers, kidney beans, wood strawberries, cultivated strawberries ('not finely flavoured' in 1786; '. . . the season has been too dry'), currants, raspberries (which could be turned into jam), cherries (which could be bottled), walnuts (which could be pickled), cos lettuce, peas, mushrooms, gooseberries, plums, pears, peaches, nectarines, endive, 'spinage', onions, parsnips, radishes, asparagus, apples and (after the 1787 harvest) 'prodigious' quantities of potatoes. He was an adventurous plantsman. Dr Celia Fisher of the Royal Botanic Gardens at Kew has identified recent introductions as being cauliflower, rhubarb, maize, capsicums, wild rice from Canada, sea kale (being piloted by the botanist William Curtis), as well as mazagon beans, 'never planted in England', and 'small beans from Oxford never sowed but once in England'. A special place in White's heart was occupied by the melon. Like cucumbers and out-of-season salads, melons flourished only in the warmth generated by smoking-hot beds of fresh horse dung, which a local farmer would deliver in quantities of as much as twenty cartloads at a time. (It was only loaned to White; once the dung had rotted down, the farmer collected it again, to spread on his fields.) Maintaining the right temperature was a constant anxiety. No wonder that, when White had smallpox in 1748, an Oriel friend, John Scrope, wrote a somewhat less than kind poem for his convalescence, 'Metamorphosis', which imagined him being turned into a melon. While not great verse, the lines 'Anxious and stooping o'er his treasure, low / Poring he kneels, and thinks he sees it grow' conjure up a convincing picture of the fussing horticulturalist.

It is noticeable that when White went to London he recorded the sea fish he saw in the shops. Thus in 1769 (Wednesday, 26 April): 'Herrings lately abound, & are the usual forerunners of mackrels.' (Thursday, 27 April): 'Dutch plaise abound. Turbots.' (Friday, 28 April): 'Some mackrels.' (Sunday, 30 April): 'Fresh ling. Hallibut.' (Thursday, 4 May): 'Crayfish in high season. Smelts in season.' At home, there was no fishmonger because Selborne, in the days before refrigeration, lay too far from the sea, so White had to content himself with salt fish of variable quality. He kept pigs, which he turned into the Hanger in November to eat the beech mast; once slaughtered, their meat would be trodden into a tub of salt, smoked in Mr Etty's smoke loft or hung in a paper bag in White's own chimney. One of the daily blessings of White's life at The Wakes was the well, never running dry, always providing sweet water, albeit mysteriously host to freshwater shrimps in the summer of 1790.

In addition to his landscaping and gardening works, White made an architectural contribution to his residence. Although he was to become famous for his observations of nature, written up in a little room overlooking the butcher's (he planted four lime trees to shield his eyes from the 'Blood & filth'), he was also a gentleman, albeit a poor one, who enjoyed conversation and entertaining. He was therefore in need of a parlour. We can track its progress through the journals. Work began in June 1777 and was sufficiently advanced by October for White to begin lighting fires in the room, with the aim of drying it out. The next month the plasterers were applying the first coat of plaster, mixed with horsehair, to the wooden 'battin-work', or laths, on the wall, and to the ceiling. The cornice was finished three days before Christmas. In January, fires were again being lit to dry the room. White was in despair when he found that the plaster turned clammy in damp weather, accusing the plasterer of mixing wood ash with the mortar. Fortunately, in April he could record, 'The great parlor dries very fast.'

The result was a handsome room on which the otherwise parsimonious White expended considerable sums in decoration. The chimneypiece was made of veined white marble from Italy. At £5 17s 11d, the cost even of this extravagance was exceeded by the looking glass, which cost £9 19s. 'Flock sattin' wallpaper in light brown with a coloured border was complemented by a 'fine stout large Turkey carpet'. Tall sash windows looked out over the landscape that White had augmented with circular flower beds, rows of vegetables and classical allusions. The air teemed with his favourite house martins and swallows. Now in his late fifties, White was finally in a position to enjoy the 'Arcady' which his friend Mulso had teased him with wishing to create when he was but twenty-four.

10. A Home for Mill Workers
10 North Street, Cromford

'Below Matlock a new creation of Sr Rd Arkwright's is started up, which has crouded the village of Cromford with cottages, supported by his three magnificent cotton mills,' observed Viscount Torrington in his diary when he visited Cromford in Derbyshire in 1789. 'There is so much water, so much rock, so much population, and so much wood that it looks like a Chinese town.' This is a whimsical picture, evoking the contrast that the busy cotton spinners made with the wild Derbyshire scenery amid which their industry took place.

Craggy Derbyshire was a destination for connoisseurs of Picturesque scenery, and Matlock, next door to Cromford, was building its fortune on it. But Torrington's account hardly seems a vivid depiction of North Street, a terrace of the 'cottages' with which the village had supposedly become crammed. Built out of the tough, pinkish local stone – gritstone – and regular in layout, its front doors hinting that they would like to be finished off with classical surrounds, it does not strike one as remotely Chinese. This is perhaps the earliest industrial housing in England. Belonging firmly to its time and place, it does not try to be anything different.

Before opening the front door of No. 10, now owned by the Landmark Trust, let us shake hands with the man who built it. Richard Arkwright, born in 1732, came from nowhere. Even now, surprisingly little, considering his importance in establishing the factory system, is known about his beginnings. He started off as a barber, at one time trying to run a public house; by the time of his death he had been knighted, lived in a mansion overlooking his works, and had been made High Sheriff of Derbyshire. A portrait by Joseph Wright of Derby (now in the Derby Museum and Art Gallery) shows an alert, confident man, his great dome of a stomach displayed to advantage in a striped waistcoat, his heavy cheeks suggestive of much chewing. The wig, as you would expect of a former barber, is crisply curled. This is a portrait of misleading elegance, given that Arkwright did not normally favour shoes and silk stockings, preferring his robust working clothes on all occasions. He does not look like the sort of person who cared much for other people's tender feelings if they got in his way, and by all accounts, he wasn't. Contemporaries thought him unreasonably tight with his money. He was, however, shrewd. He realized that his enterprise needed workers, and that to attract them to a remote spot in a wilderness of rocky outcrops and torrents he had to lay on attractions: good houses and a sense of communal life.

Undoubtedly Arkwright was a genius of organization, as the scale and rapid development of Cromford show; he may have been – though here the jury is still out – an inventor of genius as well. A pivotal moment came in 1767. He had graduated from hair-cutting to making wigs, and was travelling the country in search of the human hair that went into them. In Warrington he encountered a clockmaker called Richard Kay. Kay did some work for him, and they went off for a glass of wine. Arkwright, typically brass-necked, asked if Kay made good money from his work. On being told it was only 14s a week, he bragged that he did better from his wigs. The conversation turned to spinning. Weaving by this date had been improved by the invention of John Kay's flying shuttle. As a result, spinners, whose productivity was limited, were in high demand; the weavers needed more thread to keep busy. Arkwright thought that spinning could not be mechanized, because a number of entrepreneurs had tried to do so and failed. Kay was not so sure. Arkwright encouraged him to make a model, which he then took away and found individuals to back. The result was a spinning frame, which drew out the thread between rollers turning at different speeds. Arkwright opened his first mill in Nottingham, then the centre of the stocking trade, using horses to power the frames. Although the Nottingham mill grew to be a four-storey building, the decision was quickly taken to move the base of operations to Cromford in Derbyshire, where Arkwright built his first mill in 1771.

Why Cromford? Like other aspects of Arkwright's life, there is an element of mystery about the choice. Such a wild location had obvious drawbacks. Raw cotton had to be brought in by packhorse, spun cotton sent out by the same means. (The Cromford Canal was not built until 1789.) However, the place teemed with fast-flowing streams; they were manageable and, if not large, that did not matter initially, since the thousand looms of Arkwright's first mill required little motive force to drive them. The area was also a centre of lead mining. Waste water from the mines drained into Cromford Sough, supplying a source that for some reason never froze. Workers could be recruited from among the mining families.

Arkwright set his first mill next to a working corn mill, taking advantage of the existing watercourse. Stone for it came from a house called Steephill Grange which he bought and pulled down for the purpose. Work had progressed sufficiently by 10 December 1771 for an advertisement to be placed in the *Derby Mercury* for 'two journey men and Clock-Makers, or others that understand Tooth and Pinion well', as well as a smith and two wood turners, to construct the machinery. 'Weavers residing at the Mill, may have good work,' it continued. 'There is Employment at the above Place, for Women, Children, &c. and good wages.' In March of the next year Arkwright wrote to one of his partners expressing satisfaction in the machinery, each hand being capable of spinning up to a thousand hanks a day.

Within five years another, larger mill was built on the east side of the courtyard; a third was constructed next to the second in 1789. The 1780s also saw the construction of Masson Mill on the Derwent, built out of mottled orange brick with stone dressings, with tiers of Palladian and segmental windows in the centre block to give a sense of class. Water for the Cromford mills had to be controlled by a clever arrangement of dams and sluices, channelling it to whichever millpond needed it most. The Sough was taken through a conduit, running partly beneath the gardens around North Street.

When Arkwright arrived, Cromford was no more than a scattered hamlet with no skilled workforce. Whereas other mills – Styal in Cheshire, for example – used apprenticed labour, which could be lodged in dormitory-style apprentice houses, the Cromford system depended upon families. Ideally the head of the family would be a skilled man – an overseer or craftsman – while the mother and children, with their sharp eyesight and nimble hands, would watch the frames in the mills. These people generally had to be tempted from other places, and North Street might well have appealed to them. The priority that Arkwright gave to accommodation can be judged from its having been constructed within a few years of his arrival at Cromford, around 1776.

There is a hint of dignity about North Street, an embryonic classicism trying to make its presence felt around the front doors (they have a rudimentary structure of base, column, capital and lintel in blocks of stone). The ground and first-floor windows have old-fashioned stone mullions, one side fixed, the other opened, curiously, by means of the more à la mode sashes. Beneath the attics are rows of four small, closely spaced windows. These have only one opening pane: Derbyshire summers are rarely stifling.

The front door of each house opens directly into the parlour. On the left is the narrow staircase, again rising directly out of the room; on the opposite wall, beneath a massive stone lintel, stands the cooking range. It is not a large room, about fifteen feet square, but everything that was not sleep or work happened here. People cooked, they ate, they sat, they talked. Not that there was much time for the last; parents and children alike were expected to work a thirteen-hour day. They must have been grateful to climb the steep staircase that leads to the one bedroom on the floor above. It was heated by a little fireplace let directly into the wall without any surround, not even a mantelshelf. There could be no waste of space in a room which had to make do for all the family. The notion that different generations were expected to sleep in the same space would have shocked Victorian improvers. Presumably children in large families would have been found beds of one kind or another – beds that folded away to save space were common in poor households – in the parlour as well.

An even steeper staircase, its turning treads leaving barely enough space to place adult feet, leads up into what now seems to be the best room in the house, lit by the four-light window at the front and another window mirroring it at the back. It gave fine views of Cromford and the craggy landscape surrounding it for anyone with the leisure to spend time looking at it. More to the point, fine light for working by. It was in this room that the family kept its loom. Weaving gave a source of extra income. While Arkwright had succeeded in mechanizing spinning, it was still a cottage industry. No doubt this room provided another place for makeshift beds as well.

North Street was the forerunner of hundreds of modest streets, built to house industrial workers across northern England over the next century. By later standards the accommodation was generous. Some terraces were only one storey tall. Elsewhere space was saved by butting one terrace up to another, leaving no yard or back windows. Before the end of the nineteenth century, these back-to-backs had come to be regarded as notoriously unhealthy, due to the lack of ventilation. The absence of any space at the back meant that washing lines and outside lavatories had to be erected at the front. Whatever they were like when first occupied, they in time became slums, and were so unpopular that nearly all of them have now been destroyed; indeed such is their extreme rarity that one in Birmingham has been acquired by the National Trust.

The problem for the Victorian city was growth. The population of Britain as a whole rose by sixty per cent in the first forty years of the nineteenth century. That was nothing to the rate at which some industrial cities swelled; the number of people living in Manchester, for example, increased sixfold in the sixty years after 1771. Mill workers were forced into what the poet Robert Southey, visiting in 1808, called 'narrow streets and lanes, blocked up from light and air, crowded together because every inch of land is of such value that room for light and air cannot be afforded them'. Writing *The Condition of the Working Class in England* in 1842, Friedrich Engels painted an even fouler picture, describing one court in which inhabitants could only pass in and out by wading through stagnant pools of excreta from a doorless privy. 'And it is not the buildings surviving from the old times of Manchester which are to blame for this; the confusion has only recently reached its height when every scrap of space left by the old way of building has been filled up and patched over until not a foot of land is left to be further occupied.' Slum buildings were thrown up, and quite often tumbled down again. 'Twice, lately, there has been a crash, and a cloud of dust, like the springing of a mine, in Tom-all-Alone's,' Dickens wrote of a

London slum, or rookery, in *Bleak House*, 'and, each time, a house has fallen.' A clergyman in London's Saffron Hill investigated living conditions in his parish in the early 1850s. The first house he came to had eight rooms. It was inhabited by fifty-three people. Four of the rooms 'were without chair, table, stool, or bedstead of any kind'.

Cromford belongs to a different, paradoxically arcadian, phase of the Industrial Revolution. Immediately outside it lay the idyllic scenery evoked by Alison Uttley in *The Country Child* (1931). 10 North Street backs onto a paddock: originally there would have been fields for the whole length of the terrace. To incentivize good workers, Arkwright at one point gave twenty-seven of them 'fine Milch Cows, worth from 8*l*. to 10*l*. each, for the Service of their respective Families'.

In the manner of the later, Victorian paternalists Titus Salt of Saltaire, Edward Ackroyd of Ackroydon and George Cadbury of Bournville, Arkwright wanted Cromford to develop into a community. But unlike many successful industrialists with a conscience, he was not a Dissenter, but an Anglican, and seemingly a Tory Anglican at that. Building a church was not his first priority, though he did build St Mary's church near his mills, and was himself ultimately buried there. It was not his happiest undertaking in architecture, combining a classical pediment and Gothic windows. Unpretentious North Street is altogether more satisfactory.

The heart of Cromford was not the church, but the market which Arkwright established after acquiring the lordship of the manor in 1789. The marketplace straddled the principal road. At that time the latter was nothing more than a rough lane, but overlooking it was the handsome Greyhound Inn, built some years earlier. Arkwright had been behind this building, too, presumably to provide somewhere suitably imposing to put up clients. There were permanent shops, a small row of which survives next to the Greyhound (it was originally mirrored by another row, further back, which was demolished early this century). In addition, stallholders set up in the market. Critics claimed that Arkwright's object in establishing the market was self-interest: paying out such large sums to his workforce every week, he liked to see some of it retained in the neighbourhood. Be that as it may, he shrewdly encouraged a high standard of produce by offering, according to Lord Torrington, 'a Grand Assortment of Prizes . . . to be given at the year's end to such Bakers, Butchers, etc. as shall have best furnished the Market. How this will be peaceably settled I cannot tell!!'

The whole 'colony' was a hierarchy, expressed, not least, through the homes Arkwright provided, with North Street representing the lowest rung. More substantial dwellings were built around the marketplace for tradesmen and the professions. In the adjoining village of Scarthin are three-storey, semi-detached houses for mill foremen and better-off craftsmen. A solid, square detached house, with steps up to the front door, was occupied by the mill manager. Above this building lived Arkwright himself, in the aptly named Rock House, perched on a crag and literally overlooking his mills. As Arkwright rose in society, his domestic ideas became grander, and he employed the London architect William Thomas, author of *Original Designs in Architecture* (1783), to build an imposing new mansion, Willersley Castle. What a long way mock fortifications had come since Vanbrugh's playful castle at Greenwich! Willersley Castle seems further evidence of Arkwright's Toryism, evoking power, tradition and the established order of things, not social change. Picturesquely sited on a rise, the mansion was thought too high and too near the mills, 'within and without, an effort of inconvenient ill taste'; '. . . the approach is dangerous, the ceilings are of gew-gaw fret work; the small circular staircase . . . is so dark and narrow, that people cannot pass each other . . .' Arkwright never saw it completed. Fire gutted the house in 1791, and he was dead before Thomas Gardner, a Staffordshire architect, could finish it.

Arkwright, for all his supposed meanness, spent openly on festivities that would generate the sense he wished to engender among his workforce. The celebrations to mark his becoming High Sheriff were prodigal. Very much in the Victorian paternalist manner – but without the example of the Middle Ages to inspire him – he introduced a parade known as 'candlelighting', which became a Cromford tradition, held every September from the mid-1770s. All the workers and children from the mills – five hundred or more of them – followed a band round the village, then repaired to the mills for music and dancing. The candlelightings merged with one of the two balls that Arkwright threw at the Greyhound every year. Hundreds of mill hands and visitors from Matlock sang praises to the founder of the feast:

> Our number we count seven Hundred or more,
> All cloathed and fed from his bountiful Store,
> Then envy don't flout us, nor say any's poor,
> *At the Cotton Mills now at Cromford.*
> *The famous renown'd Cotton Mills.*

Did the family who first lived at 10 North Street open its throats in joyful gratitude? Presumably. Alas, we do not know anything about them, even their names.

Not everyone was happy all the time in Cromford, however. There were riots in 1779 which must have given Arkwright special reason to spend generously on housing and entertainments. The conditions in which children worked (from the age of seven) seem exploitative today. Breakfast was served in the mills, and allocated half an hour; those who got their food first had longer to eat it. Richard Arkwright II claimed that, in the afternoon, not all children chose to eat their tea – surely a surprising state of affairs, if true. They were in other respects normal children, whom he could see from Willesley Castle 'playing in groups in summertime until it is dark'. In Cromford they could at least aspire to a glimmering of education at the Sunday school, which as many as two hundred of them attended each week. It was only during the Regency that childhood came to be valued as a state in itself. Of course it helped when the children's parents were dukes.

11. A Duke's Flight of Fancy
Endsleigh Cottage

By the Regency period, the Picturesque had been taken up a notch. Gilbert White, with his oil jars and cut-out Hercules, wanted to embellish his fields with follies in emulation of fashionable gardens of the time. He did not expect his new dining room to contribute to the effect, nor, on the whole, did aristocrats adjust the style of their mansions to the mood of their parks. But in time the house itself became a player in the game that had previously been restricted to gardens and landscapes. Battlements were adopted by gentlemen who wanted their neatly proportioned, many-windowed houses to evoke castles. Antiquarian, or 'Gothick', taste sought to entice the imagination with shadows, stained glass and the effects of age, its showplace being Horace Walpole's Strawberry Hill. At Endsleigh Cottage in Devon – another exceptional essay in taste – house and landscape were conceived as one.

The word *cottage* is significant here. As regards the scale of the place, Endsleigh is not, by normal standards, a cottage or anything like one. But to the aristocratic couple who built it – the 6th Duke of Bedford and his young wife – the mood they wished to evoke was one of rustic simplicity, representing, so far as the Duke was concerned, 'ultra-retirement'. Whereas most houses are designed to make the most of themselves, to impress by their size, the idea behind Endsleigh was that it should look smaller than it really is. The plan was folded around a courtyard, with the two wings at a 45-degree angle to the main block. As you walk around the building, you only see a small part at any one time. There are cottagey bargeboards to the eaves and Tudor drip moulds over the windows. Rusticity abounds on the verandah: tree trunks hold up the roof, and the floor has been laid with little lumpy things that turn out, on close inspection, to be the knuckle bones of dead sheep. Endsleigh may not literally be a cottage, but the Bedfords were certainly making an effort.

They were not alone in doing so. The Picturesque movement had stimulated a feeling for the countryside, one which motivates British people even today. Literature, as it had done since Virgil, sang the praises of a pastoral idyll, in contrast to the evils of the town. As George Crabbe exclaimed, presenting a comforting picture of the farm labourer as happy in his self-sufficiency:

> Behold the Cot! where thrives th'industrious swain,
> Source of his pride, his pleasure and his gain;
> Screen'd from the winter's wind, the sun's last ray
> Smiles on the window and prolongs the day;
> Projecting thatch the woodbine's branches stop,
> And turn their blossoms to the casement's top:
> All need requires is in that cot contain'd
> And much that taste untaught and unrestrain'd
> Surveys delighted . . .

Towards the end of the eighteenth century and particularly during the Regency, when fashionable life was becoming more and more artificial, complicated and luxurious, the simple life as depicted by Crabbe and others looked deliciously refreshing to jaded palates. Never mind that the real life of labourers was often brutal. For the first time, the English house fell victim to inverted snobbery: it became voguish for houses to ape the appearance of dwellings towards the bottom of the social scale, rather than at the top.

A practical approach to improving the accommodation of farm labourers (then still called 'peasants') was presented in the reports of the Board of Agriculture from 1797–1818. In comparison to these genuine cottages, a *cottage orné* such as Endsleigh was a kind of stage version – the dwelling of someone who liked, in the manner of Marie Antoinette in her *hameau* at Versailles, to pretend that her tastes were simple and rustic when they might, in fact, be very sophisticated indeed.

When T. D. W. Dearn published 'A design for a cottage orné' in *Sketches in Architecture* (1807), he explained the popularity of the form in terms of necessity. During the Napoleonic Wars, 'when many sacrifices [had to] be made and many privations endured', economy became a consideration, even to people who had been previously well off: 'There are many who, without the most rigid attention, must stoop from that happy state of independence in which their lives have hitherto been passed, and depend for daily food on their daily exertions.' To Dearn, the *cottage orné* seemed appropriate to the national mood, and he noted approvingly that 'under the sanction of fashion, we have seen royalty itself become the inmate and inhabitant of a cottage.' George III's wife, Queen Charlotte, led the way, perhaps herself taking a hand in the design of her elaborately thatched cottage at Kew. For her son, the Prince Regent, John Nash built Adelaide Cottage, or the 'Thatched Palace', in Windsor Great Park. Visitors to the Duke of Kent's Castle Hill Lodge at Ealing were greeted by six footmen at the door, accompanied, if the guests were very grand, by the elderly French steward. Castle Hill Lodge was full of musical novelties:

cages of singing birds, organs with dancing horses, musical clocks. *Cottages ornés* attracted gimmicks.

Through association with the Prince Regent and his circle, they were also in danger of acquiring a raffish reputation. One was owned by the decorator Walsh Porter, a friend of the Prince's, who decorated the Throne Room in Buckingham Palace. Situated in Fulham, it was called Craven Cottage after the Margravine of Anspach, who had built it when she was Countess of Craven. It contained only three rooms, but those were extremely elaborate. The 'principal saloon' was Egyptian in theme, 'supported by large palm-trees of considerable size, exceedingly well executed, with their drooping foliage at the top supporting the cornice and architraves of the room . . . The furniture comprised a lion's skin for a hearth-rug, for a sofa the back of a tiger, the supports of the tables in most instances were four twisted serpents or hydras.' The room gave onto a large Gothic dining room, while the third room was a semicircular library.

'Retirement' – if not ultra-retirement – was one of the qualities that was most associated with the *cottage orné*. The businessman who ended his career 'without the attainment of affluence yet not entirely destitute of success' was here 'free from the noise and bustle to which he has hitherto been accustomed', as the architectural writer T. F. Hunt described a design in the 1820s. Or the *cottage orné* might simply be a place of tranquillity. The Isle of Wight, literally detached from the everyday life of the mainland, was a *locus classicus*. *Cottages ornés* were often built by the seaside.

Devon attracted more than its fair share of the genre; there was a colony of *cottages ornés* at Lynmouth, which Southey described enthusiastically as the finest spot he ever saw except for Cintra and the Arrabida in Portugal. The whimsical A-la-Ronde, decorated with lady's work and curios by two much-travelled maiden ladies, the Misses Parminter, can be found outside Exmouth. (Despite the name, the building is not so much circular as sixteen-sided, after the inspiration of the octagonal church of San Vitale in Ravenna, Italy.) Another favourite location – as at Endsleigh – was amid romantic wooded scenery which heightened the piquancy of the cottage image. Because the *cottage orné* was essentially a gentleman's residence in fancy dress, it was often filled with beguiling novelties to save space, like mirrors that slid up to cover windows cunningly placed over fireplaces, transforming a small room into an elegant drawing room. Endsleigh, being quite large inside, had no need of them.

Irregularity, both of plan and design, was made into a virtue. James Malton's *An Essay on British Cottage Architecture* (1797), for instance, was subtitled 'being an attempt to perpetuate on Principle that peculiar mode of building, which was originally the effect of Chance'. Mrs Dashwood of Jane Austen's *Sense and Sensibility* would have approved. She found Barton Cottage 'small, comfortable and compact', but not sufficiently Picturesque: '. . . as a cottage it was defective, for the building was regular, the roof was tiled, the window shutters were not painted green, nor were the walls covered with honeysuckles.' She would surely have approved of Endsleigh's tree-trunk columns: even the most sober of writers advocated them.

John, the 6th Duke of Bedford, had not expected to inherit. His brother Francis, the 5th Duke, had been one of the great agricultural reformers of the age, a founder-member of the Board of Agriculture and first president of the Smithfield Club who was famous for the annual Sheep Shearings – forerunners of agricultural shows – that he held at Woburn. A friend of the Prince of Wales, Francis had also employed the Prince's architect, Henry Holland, to remodel the south front of Woburn in Bedfordshire, creating a suite of rooms in the smartest neo-classical taste, flooded with light from tall windows. He also built a Sculpture Gallery, Riding School, Tennis Court and Chinese Dairy. There was as yet no chatelaine at Woburn, only mistresses in the park (or rather Marylebone, where three of the five women who received annuities after his death were to be found), but as the Duke passed the age of thirty-five he began to look for a wife. One was provided for him by that indefatigable Tory matchmaker the Duchess of Gordon in the shape of her youngest daughter, Georgina: the Bedfords may have been Whigs, but they were still dukes. Death intervened. Playing tennis in 1802, the Duke suffered a strangulated hernia and underwent an agonizing operation with great fortitude, but quickly died. Georgina was taken to Paris to recover her spirits. The 6th Duke, whose first wife had died six months before, undertook to deliver the lock of hair Francis had left to her as a keepsake. A new romance blossomed. The Duchess of Gordon had pulled off another coup.

The Bedfords began married life by bringing Woburn further up to date, installing the French furniture and bibelots which they had bought in Paris, and employing Humphry Repton to embellish the grounds. The 6th Duke was, as Charles Greville commented in 1839, 'a complete sensualist' who did not allow himself to be 'ruffled by the slightest self-denial'. Within a few weeks of inheriting, he wrote to the agriculturalist Arthur Young to ask him to help carry through his brother's wishes for improving agriculture on the estate. But when Young visited, his judgement was severe: 'This poor Duke of Bedford, whose nominal income is so enormous, will, I fear, involve himself with the same imprudence [as his brother] . . . An extravagant duchess, Paris toys, a great farm, little economy and immense debts, will prove a canker in all the rosebuds of his garden of life.' In the end, the 6th Duke did not fulfil his brother's intention of turning the park at Woburn into a farm, though Repton did improve its beauties. The Red Book of watercolours, its well-known flaps providing before and after views, was the biggest he produced for any job.

Georgina, having married aged twenty-one, was fifteen years younger than her husband. She had inherited her mother's animal high spirits, and house parties would echo with her romping games, during which candles and oranges might be thrown and exquisite furniture overturned. According to the Duke, she liked nothing better than to make others happy and comfortable. But there was only so much that could be done to enliven their vast and formal house, which they came to regard as 'a mausoleum'. Endsleigh was to be their escape.

They hit upon the site in 1809 in Devon; the Russell family owned a large chunk of the county, although they had no substantial house there. Endsleigh was to be built on one of the steep sides of an inaccessible valley, at the bottom of which brawls the river Tamar: the natural beauty of the scene would present Repton with 'the most picturesque subjects on which I have ever been professionally consulted'. To the Duchess, the 'rapid' Tavy, which runs through the estate, was 'as bright as any Scotch stream'. Georgina had grown up in Scotland. However grand they may have been in London, the Gordons threw off their formality in sporting lodges, ducal 'cottages' and turf-roofed shooting huts – and Georgina never lost her taste for them. (Later she would inspire her young lover, Edwin 'Monarch of the Glen' Landseer, in his appetite for things Scottish.) Endsleigh offers the nearest approach to a glen that it is possible to find south of the border. The Duchess was a fisherwoman; the Duke laid down pheasants. While at Woburn he 'was anxious to have a quantity of game killed that should maintain the reputation of the Abbey, for the first sporting-ground in Great Britain'; at Endsleigh he shot for pleasure. Only intimate friends were allowed there. Rather than on French porcelain as at Woburn, dinner at Endsleigh was served on a specially commissioned service of china made into the shapes of cauliflowers, bunches of asparagus and other vegetables.

Initially Repton and his sons were called upon to make proposals for a house, but their efforts were rejected. Instead the Duke turned to Jeffry Wyatt, square-jawed, no-nonsense and still speaking with the burr of Burton-on-Trent where he had grown up (their 'ryal eyenesses' is how the Duke of Devonshire remembered him speaking of the royal family). Two of Jeffry's uncles – Samuel and the more famous, if notoriously slapdash, James – were architects, and he worked for both of them. A commission to remodel Windsor Castle, during the building of which he adopted the medievalizing surname Wyatville and was awarded an even more aggrandizing knighthood, lay in the future. Wyatt was to become extremely successful. When the Bedfords commissioned him, he had already built a *cottage orné* – small by the standards of Endsleigh – on the Longleat estate, and that had also required working with Repton.

The bluff Wyatt was never a creature of quivering aesthetic sensibility, and on close inspection the detail of Endsleigh is rather crude. But the plan is interesting, not being four-square but informally following a sinuous line dictated by the site. The curve created what the Edwardians would call a 'sun-trap' effect, associating it with good health and fresh air. At Endsleigh, the virtue of the sweep was that it allowed different rooms to enjoy different views. 'The woodbine, the ivy and honeysuckle grow along the walls and form natural festoons above the windows,' reads the description in John Preston Neale's *Views of Seats* (1818); '. . . under the shelter of these plants birds build their nests and cheer the scene with their notes.'

The foundation stone was laid by the Duchess and her four eldest sons (but not the children of the Duke's first marriage) in September 1810, according to an inscription above a fountain in the stable court. Thereafter the progress of building work can be followed in the accounts in the Devon Record Office at Exeter. It did not go quickly at first; the mason was not used to buildings of this scale, and, according to a report made to the agent William Bray in July 1811, '. . . a great many men are imployed [*sic*], and very little work done, and a great deal of money expended.' Little interruption, however, was caused by the Napoleonic Wars, then raging. Nor did they prevent the Duke and Duchess, with an entourage of nineteen and a cow to provide fresh milk for the children, leaving England for a two-year tour of the Continent in 1813. In the course of it they visited Napoleon, in exile on Elba, and bought the *Three Graces* from Antonio Canova – a hymn to the female bottom, whose distilled neo-classicism is about as far removed in taste as it is possible to imagine from a *cottage orné* in Devon. Endsleigh was still being finished in the month of Waterloo, June 1815.

Meanwhile, Repton had met Wyatt on site in April 1814; given the rivalry, it is not surprising that he should have found him, as he wrote to the Duke's lawyer William Adam, 'grown as much out of all due proportion for a bodkin as either yourself or me' (a little cryptic perhaps, but the meaning is clear). But the relationship between Repton and Adam was good, and the letters between them record the landscape in less formal terms than Repton used in his Red Book and his published *Fragments on the Theory and Practice of Landscape Gardening* (1816). By now, the gardener was in his sixties and racked by pains that meant he could 'neither stand 5 minutes nor walk 5 yards uphill, or upstairs'. On 17 July 1814 he wrote: 'Any exertion brings on the most alarming Spasms in my Chest – I thought it water, but it turns out to be fire – and I believe it is Angina Pectoria – in short the Harpoon seems fix'd & my length of line is very precarious, but I will not give in while I can flounder.' When consulted at Bath, Dr Parry advised Repton to leave off the 'locomotive part of my profession', and indeed there was nothing else for it. As he laments in the Red Book of 1814, 'I could only become acquainted with [Endsleigh's] recondite beauties, by being carried to places otherwise inaccessible to a cripple.'

Near the Cottage were a number of terraces for admiring the scenery. Two of them were called the Upper and Lower Georgies, after the Duchess. The rose walk gave Repton particular pause; he provided foreground detail through a series of ironwork arches, entwined with roses and honeysuckle, and pots planted with flowers. The object, as he told Adam, was 'to make a greater contrast with the Grandeur of the Landscape, in that with the latter I can do so little, that I must only turn frame maker instead of Landscape Gardener'. This walk ends in a grotto decorated with local minerals and fossils.

Across the river, a boatman's cottage supplied Endsleigh's greatest note of Picturesque artifice: a fire that was lit whether or not anyone was living there, because a wisp of wood smoke added to the appeal of the landscape. Hidden in the woods the thatched model dairy and a Swiss Cottage can still be found. These were playthings for adults; elsewhere the needs of children were paramount. Georgina was remarkable for a woman of her station in breastfeeding her many babies. As they grew up, they continued to occupy a prominent position in the Bedfords' life. The Duke adored them: 'The merry girls, and jumping, sporting boys, / Make the old Abbey echo with their noise,' as he wrote in a poem addressed to Georgina. The part that the Russell children played in their parents' life is expressed in Endsleigh's plan: while the nursery may have been placed at some distance from the main house, it gave onto a children's lawn which was overlooked by the Duke and Duchess's rooms. At the edge of the garden was a rill for sailing model boats. 'At this enchanting Retreat the most pleasing attention has been paid to the Comforts of Infancy and Youth,' Repton wrote in his Red Book. Advocating the planting of raised beds to allow people such as himself, who could not stoop down, to study rock plants closely, he continued, 'Let the same attention be extended to solace the infirmities of Age.'

Repton was especially proud of his work at Endsleigh. As he told Adam, 'I will confess I never [was] so well pleased myself – but we are apt to make a favorite [*sic*] of the youngest child – especially after a difficult Labour & being l'Enfant de la Vieillesse – & you saw me on my last legs in Devonshire.' It was no less popular with the Bedfords. Although they continued to ornament Woburn,

Endsleigh was their favourite home. They usually came in the spring or early summer. Outings included boat trips to Plymouth; the evenings were spent making music or playing cards. The Duke was happy there. 'As a locale I know no place so gay, and we are occupied and interested from morning till night,' he wrote on one occasion.

For such a sybarite, the comforts of life needed maintaining, as they did in any nineteenth-century house. Servants came at the ring of a bell. In his lodgings in London's Adelphi, Dickens's David Copperfield would summon his landlady from the basement, though that is not to say that she came willingly, if at all. In the country, it would hardly have been possible for houses to develop their sprawling plans if it had not been for the elaborate network of wires and pulleys that linked every room with the line of bells outside the servants' hall. At Endsleigh, the bell-hanger arrived in September 1816 and spent twenty-three days at his task. Equally, the supply of fresh produce was minutely considered. Repton not only planted the hundreds of trees which can now be seen in their mature glory, but a large number of fruit trees of different kinds and varieties, the object being to extend the season as long as possible. His shopping list for the trees in the kitchen garden ran to two figs, two mulberries, two medlars, four quinces, forty-four peaches, apricots and nectarines, sixty-two cherries and plums, and eighty-five apples.

It was at Endsleigh that the 6th Duke suffered the stroke that froze part of his face in July 1822. During the 1830s, with the Duchess occupied with Landseer and the Duke restless, their domestic lives became even more complex. 'The Duke is now leading the wandering life he loves so much,' complained the Marquess of Tavistock, the future 7th Duke. 'He has left the Duchess and the children in Scotland, and both seem to prefer any place to Woburn.' Nevertheless, the 6th Duke did not neglect Woburn and its beauties entirely. Although his sons despaired of his profligacy, to the

botanist W. J. Hooker he was virtue incarnate. 'To have seen him,'
Hooker wrote after his death, 'regardless of his elevated station
condescending to enter with the heartiest zeal into whatever concerned the park, the gardens, the marbles, the pictures, the library
and the other treasures of that princely seat, was one of those
gratifications that are justly accounted privileges.' The Duke was
particularly proud of the new London entrance drive, which he
emphatically claimed to have been his achievement, 'assisted' by
Repton. As he declared to Lord George William Russell on 29
August 1836, 'I will place you at the London Entrance and defy
you to construct a better approach to the West front than I have
done. Repton was a Coxcomb, but he had infinitely more *Genius*
than one half of his critics and detractors.' The other half of the
Endsleigh team, Wyatt, now Sir Jeffry Wyatville, built a glass
Botanical House in 1838; it was 282 feet long. After a violent hailstorm
in 1843, the 6th Duke's successor, the sternly moralistic and cost-
conscious 7th Duke, computed the damage to this horticultural
establishment as 10,686 broken panes in the botanical range, 20,646
in the Camellia House, 3,080 in the heathery, 2,820 in the Orchidaäe,
and over 2,000 in the propagating pits. The inspiration of the
Botanical House was evidently the Great Stove built at Chatsworth
by the 6th Duke's old friend, the Duke of Devonshire. In the centre
was a palm house with a glazed roof supported on cast-iron columns.
But unlike Joseph Paxton's building, it was triumphantly classical
and conservative. 'What do you think Old John Bedford has been at;
why, making an Arboretum this winter in imitation of the one at
Chatsworth,' exclaimed Paxton to his wife after a visit.

It will be a miserable failure. This is not all; the old codger has had Sir
Jeffry Wyatville from London to plan a stove! I suppose they are jealous
of us; their stove will be on a par with their Arboretum. John wanted a
stove like our new one. Sir Jeffry said it would not answer, so they have
persuaded the poor old man to have one of the old kind.

In 1833, the Duke built a Chinese temple in the maze of the Pleasure Grounds at Woburn, surprisingly, at this date, based closely on a plate in a much earlier book, Sir William Chambers's *Designs of Chinese Buildings, Furniture, Dresses, Machines and Utensils* (1757). The Duke was not specially fussed about keeping up with architectural fashion. On the other hand, the last follies that he constructed, shortly before his death in 1839, are Victorian both in date and feeling, though they developed themes that had been tried at Endsleigh more than twenty years before. The Log Cabin was, according to an album of watercolours by the topographical artist J. C. Bourne, 'constructed in imitation of the buildings erected by the immigrants to Canada, in the backwoods of America'. (In fact it was modelled on a 'bathing house' at Barronscourt in Ireland.) It is a simple three-room cottage, the walls built of tree trunks on a stone plinth and the doors decorated with split twigs. No sheep's knuckle bones, but a step further in rusticity than Endsleigh. Although staked out in the summer of 1838, it had not been roofed by November of that year, when the Duke, who (albeit from a distance) took a minute interest in his buildings, wrote that the shingles need not necessarily be oak, but could be deal with two or three coats of linseed oil.

In the last year of his life, the Duke built a grotto at Woburn, originally entered by an enchanting rose pergola. An improvement on the grotto at Endsleigh, the interior was encrusted with geological specimens from Devon and Cornwall, about which the Duke fussed a good deal in May 1839. Two cases of specimens were due to leave Plymouth on 27 May: 'It will be very necessary that great care should be taken in transshipping the cases from the steam packet to the Canal Boat, for if they are roughly handled, the crystalizations may probably be broken or otherwise injured.' The floor of pebbles, now obscured by a wishing well, was divided into compartments by bands of different-coloured Devonshire marbles.

After the Duke's death a jeweller called Urquhart was paid for polishing the stones.

The Duke's building projects at Woburn have something neurotic about them; they are like an elevated kind of shopping, a displacement activity to stave off boredom. Endsleigh remained the Bedfords' favourite home. After the Duke's death, the Duchess wrote to her stepson, the 7th Duke, after hearing that he had visited Endsleigh: 'Your father and I created it together, every walk, every plant and most of the trees, for years and years we watched their growth – and such another place I do not believe is to be found – I shall often follow you in thought along my favourite haunts.'

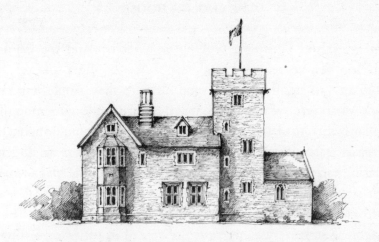

12. Pugin's House by the Sea
The Grange, Ramsgate

While the Duke and Duchess of Bedford were holidaying at Endsleigh, other sorts of people were making their less aristocratic way to the newly established spa of Ramsgate. Ramsgate lies at the extreme south-eastern point of England, a snub nose permanently turned up towards France. The town has had reason to feel the proximity more than once. Photographs in the library at nearby Margate – Ramsgate's own pretty library burned down in 2004 – show a policeman in white sleeves calmly directing traffic during the Second World War above a notice which reads 'Enemy Shelling in Progress'. In an earlier period, Ramsgate was a port from which soldiers embarked for the Napoleonic Wars; Jane Austen's brother Frank was stationed there. In order to maintain secrecy, a tunnel was cut through the chalk cliff.

So much military activity was a spur to development. Work was carried out in the flush of patriotic triumphalism that followed 1815. Developers gave their new terraces flagrantly opportunistic names, such as Nelson Crescent, Wellington Crescent and the Plains of Waterloo. These terraces tend not to be of the po-faced mid-Georgian variety, flat-fronted and austere; they ripple with bow windows and ironwork verandahs, the former allowing more light into the house, the latter a place on which the air could be taken, and the passing scene surveyed. There was a good square (Spencer Square), various Lawns (Liverpool Lawn, Guildford Lawn: the lawn, more or less a field, was a unique attribute of Ramsgate), and, developers not being given to understatement, a street called the Paragon. Ramsgate was, as *Punch* observed in July 1842, a town of cannibals; the inhabitants fed off 'lodgers caught in the season. Hence half-a-dozen single men are found quite sufficient to feed a widow and a child or two for a year, if subsisting in a moderate way; whilst the more luxurious eaters – the owners of drawing and sitting-rooms – require husbands, wives and families.' Welcome to the seaside.

Seaside towns, like inland spas, lived or died by their reputations for *bon ton*. Offering little else to induce people of quality to visit them, they made a particular effort to keep up appearances. The former fishing village of Brighthelmstone broke out into a lather of white-fronted crescents, terraces and squares following the advent of the Prince of Wales, later George IV, and his Pavilion in the 1780s (this very obvious bestowal of royal patronage in another quarter marked the beginning of Bath's decline into stiff-necked, no longer ultra-fashionable gentility). In its less spectacular way, Ramsgate followed suit.

Brighton owed its reinvention to Dr Richard Russell's *Dissertation Concerning the Use of Sea Water in Diseases of the Glands*, published in Latin in 1750 and in English three years later. Similarly, Ramsgate had a medical champion in Dr Thomas Reid, who published his *Directions for Warm and Cold Sea-bathing; with Observations on their Application and Effects in Different Diseases* (1798). Jane Austen's relation by marriage, Mrs Edward Bridges, was among the professed invalids who sought to recoup their strength at Ramsgate. Jane, however, was having none of it, declaring that Mrs Bridges was 'a poor Honey – the sort of woman who gives me the idea of being determined never to be well – and who likes her spasms and nervousness and the consequences they give her, better than anything else'.

Like Bath, Ramsgate also had its master of ceremonies, if not quite on the epic scale of Beau Nash. This was James Townley, known only for having written a doggerel encomium, 'To my good horse, Hamlet', in 1800. Townley presided over the assembly rooms which stood near the harbour, ensuring that only properly dressed company (no boots or swords for any but military gentlemen on ball nights) were admitted, and that ladies did not push themselves forward in the dances.

We have seen that the ashlar perfection of Bath was, in some streets, only a front, and that regular façades might hide all manner of shoddy workmanship. Ramsgate is even flimsier; many houses are covered in a plaster coating that was originally used to ape the effect of ashlar but that could also, in unscrupulous hands, cover up a multitude of sins. 'In an evil hour *stucco* was invented,' thundered one disapproving Victorian,

and thenceforth, wherever it was employed, good and bad work was reduced, in the eyes of the general public, to one common level. It mattered little whether brick or rubble, English or Flemish bond were used; whether the courses exceeded their proper height by a dangerous preponderance of mortar; whether the openings were really arched over or only spanned by a fictitious lintel. What signified such considerations as these when the whole front was to be enveloped in a fair and specious mask of cement?

Dickens knew Ramsgate; the paddle steamers of the General Steam Navigation Company and the Commercial Steam Packet Company stopped there (at one point the companies were in such furious competition that the fare from London, one hundred miles away by sea, was only a shilling). But he did not have much of an opinion of it, or its lodgings; perhaps it was too genteel for his more boisterous taste. It is gentility that draws the Tuggs family, Southwark grocers who come into money, to Ramsgate, in *The Tuggs's at Ramsgate* by Boz (1836). They are welcomed to their accommodation with the grace that would typify the seaside landlady for 150 years, their horse-drawn fly stopping before

> a dusty house, with a bay window, from which you could obtain a beautiful glimpse of the sea – if you thrust half your body out of it, at the imminent peril of falling into the area. Mrs. Tuggs alighted. One ground-floor sitting-room, and three cells with beds in them up stairs – a double house – family on the opposite side – five children milk-and-watering in the parlour, and one dear little boy expelled for bad behaviour, screaming on his back in the passage . . .
>
> 'Five guineas a week, Ma'am, *with* attendance,' replied the lodging-house keeper. (Attendance means the privilege of ringing the bell as often as you like, for your own personal amusement.)

Predictably, gentility and Ramsgate get the better of the Tuggses, but their fate – to be relieved of a large sum of money by three designing characters – did not put off others from coming. 'All London quits London,' wrote the anonymous author of *All About Ramsgate and Broadstairs* (good enough to be Dickens) in 1865;

> . . . the old broken case remains, but the works and moving figures are taken out. Russell Square sends its plate to the banker's, and, leaving word that it is on the Continent, bargains for a first-floor and double-bedded rooms at Ramsgate; Cadogan Place buys itself big-brimmed hats, and commences bathing at Broadstairs; and Camden Town and Kennington rush off to shrimp teas at Margate.

The seaside community began its migration to other quarters, vacating the best rooms in their houses for visitors:

> Those virtuous elderly spinsters who have lived the long winter months in their deserted houses, solitary as spiders in their webs, wake up from their torpidity and grow lively with the summer heat. They take from the linen-closet the clean blinds for the bedroom windows and the net curtains for the handsome drawing rooms and 'neat parlours'; the faded chintz sofa-coverings are washed and ironed, and, buying a bottle of furniture polish, they make their poor arms ache with rubbing up the dull tables and sideboards into a waxy lustre.

Lumbering wooden bathing machines with a deep canvas hood at one end and a horse at the other would be trundled into the water and turned around. Drivers and horses splashed back to the beach; bathers issued from beneath the canvas hood, which reached down to the sea. It was not foolproof as regards privacy. From the waterside it was 'just possible to catch a sly glance at the forms in dark dresses "bobbing around" and splashing each other, and to hear them giggling, as if they were up to all sorts of imaginable mischief'. Men had only the sea to preserve modesty. Scandalous, thought Dr Spenser Thomson, author of *Health Resorts of Britain and How to Profit by Them* (1860), and quite unnecessary, given that in other countries 'male bathers are compelled to wear some sort of decent covering, such as short drawers, which do not in the least impede the movements of the body.' Out of the water, there were telescopes, donkey rides, German bands and all the activities crowding William Powell Frith's painting *Ramsgate Sands*, now owned by HM The Queen, to distract the visitor. Until nightfall, that is, when Mr Fuller's 'famed marine library' came into its own – not only a repository of books but a music hall, a bazaar and a very mild kind of casino, where a shilling stake might win you a cake of soap, a bottle of hair oil or a wooden spade.

Queen Victoria was to have happy memories of her childhood holidays at Ramsgate (no doubt why she bought *Ramsgate Sands*), but the truth must out: she also contracted typhoid there in 1835. (She could have caught typhoid anywhere; bad drains were generally the problem. Drains were to be a Victorian preoccupation, and understandably so.) Yet there were other things about Ramsgate that might not have struck her as completely right. When Elizabeth Grant, then a schoolgirl, visited with her sick mother in 1812, she found that the next-door house on the East Cliff was occupied by the wife of one of Queen Victoria's uncles, the Duke of Sussex. However, since the Duke had not obtained the King and the Privy Council's permission for the union, it was recognized in Italy, where it had been contracted, and everywhere else in the world except Britain, despite the fact that the ceremony had been performed for a second time in St George's, Hanover Square. She was known by the title Baroness d'Ameland. At the age of sixteen, her son Augustus was given the name d'Este, one of the royal surnames but nevertheless not Sussex. He was to spend his life trying to assert his legitimacy, only to die bitter and disappointed. It left an unsatisfactory memory of Regency carryings-on, but the seaside was like that.

The presence of Samuel Taylor Coleridge, who came regularly after 1819, can only have added to the raffish tone; by now in middle age and addicted to opium, he arrived with the family of the doctor with whom he had boarded at Highgate. The author Wilkie Collins was even less reputable; a member of the yacht club, he kept his boat in the harbour and from 1870 came to recuperate from the illnesses brought on by excessive dosing with laudanum. Collins set *The Fallen Leaves* (1879) in Ramsgate, with an adulterous plot.

It wouldn't do. Morals were getting caught up with everything, including health. Hear Dr Thomson inveigh against the 'almost heathen indecency of our bathing-places', with their shocking absence of privacy and no bathing-trunks:

> How is it that, amid the well-bred visitors of Ramsgate . . . both modesty and manners seem to be left at their lodgings, so that bathers on the one hand, and the line of lookers-on on the other hand, some with opera-glasses or telescopes, seem to have no more sense of decency than so many South-Sea Islanders?

How indeed. But the world was changing. Architecturally, this happened more slowly at Ramsgate than elsewhere; what seem to be Regency terraces such as Guildford Lawn were still being built in the 1840s. But in the course of that decade an architect of a far from frivolous stamp chose to make Ramsgate, of all places, his centre of operations. It was a typically combative decision. The end for bow-fronted houses and jaunty verandahs had come.

One of the places where the German band played in Ramsgate was the Parade, at what was then the extreme west end of the town. In the late 1840s, audiences who stood with their backs to the sea faced a startling new house which was quite unlike anything that had yet been built in the town, or anywhere else in Britain for that matter. Behind garden walls of knapped flint – a traditional building material in a county where flints are found on the surface in fields and on beaches – it was built of yellow brick, with a pointed gable on one side and a stout tower on the other. There was no stucco, no parapet, no portico with columns, no symmetry. It was called by a monastic name, The Grange – and in time a monastery would arise on the other side of the road. But for the time being, the man who was responsible for it was still frantically at work, building not only The Grange but also a church next to it, and earning the money for both projects from designs for other people. He was well known around Ramsgate from his rolling sailor's gait, his robust way of

speaking (some contemporaries thought it coarse), his curious
indifference to what he wore so long as it was weatherproof,
and his passionate temperament. He made up his mind instantly
and always spoke with conviction. As an architect he was certain
that his preferred style of Gothic was morally right and ought to
replace all others in the country.

A. W. N. Pugin's early life had not been easy. He had designed
scenery for London theatres. He had gone to sea and been ship-
wrecked. His first wife, heavily pregnant before they married, had
died, leaving him with a daughter, before he was twenty years old.
Even now he supplemented his income by watching for wrecks
from the tower of his house, and rowing out through the wild night
to rescue sailors and claim the cargo. (Just offshore lay the trea-
cherous Goodwin Sands.) He would also sail his lugger *The
Caroline* to France and Belgium to pick up medieval antiquities,
which he studied and displayed in his house, or sometimes sold.
Bullish, unwhiskered, a magnet whom friends and admirers found
irresistibly attractive, but from whom a large measure of Victorian
society was forcibly repelled, this was the great controversialist and
inspiration of the Gothic Revival.

It was typical of Pugin that he should have chosen Ramsgate as
the location of his home. Architecturally, the new terraces represented everything he most loathed about the modern world.
Ramsgate was a challenge. In 1836 he published one of the greatest
works of propaganda in the English language: *Contrasts; or,
A Parallel Between the Noble Edifices of the Fourteenth and
Fifteenth Centuries, and Similar Buildings of the Present Day . . .*
The work juxtaposed engravings of contemporary buildings with
examples of their supposed equivalents from the great age of faith,
when England still acknowledged the Pope and the Reformation
had not been thought of. The modern era was made to look
meagre, ungodly, mean and squalid ('the masses of brick and
composition which have been erected in what are termed

watering-places' were specially excoriated), whereas an idealized Middle Ages shone forth as charitable, supportive, architecturally glorious and devout. Everything had been right until Henry VIII had changed the national religion; everything had gone wrong ever since. Pugin reached this conclusion through his response to Gothic architecture. The year before *Contrasts* was published, he had brought his spiritual life into line with his aesthetic deductions and converted to Roman Catholicism. It was a typically brave act; at a stroke he became an object of suspicion and put himself out of contention for any work in the mainstream of church architecture. For someone with Pugin's ambition – at Ramsgate he was determined to build a church out of his own income – this was a sacrifice indeed. In 1841 came *The True Principles of Pointed or Christian Architecture*, a Gothic Revival manifesto which sought to justify his aesthetic preference in terms of absolute values. To Pugin, classicism was a style of extraneous ornament and deceit; Gothic, by contrast, expressed the logic of its construction. Stucco, which sought to imitate something it was not (stone ashlar) and disguised an inferior material (brick), symbolized the iniquities of the age. 'Our good old St Martin's, St John's, St Peter's, and St Mary's streets, are becoming Bellevue Places, Adelaide Rows, Apollo Terraces, Regent Squares, and Royal Circuses,' Pugin moaned. If anywhere typified the Regency descent into fashionable terraces and squares, it was Ramsgate.

Pugin's choice of Ramsgate illustrates something of the personality of the man, and the personality of the man illuminates his remarkable – and influential – house. Born in 1812, he had grown up against a Regency background of money troubles and visual taste. His father, Auguste Charles Pugin, had left Revolutionary France in the late 1790s and was making his living as a draughtsman. He managed to give the impression he was the comte de Pugin, which his son Augustus believed; perhaps the aristocratic

air helped land Auguste a job in the office of John Nash, who may
have recognized a mixture of talent, high living and expediency
similar to his own. Auguste also taught drawing, Augustus
naturally becoming one of his pupils. Eventually, Auguste began
to make his own way by contributing to the series of coloured
views of the capital published by Rudolph Ackermann as *Micro-cosm of London* (1808–10) – images that were to determine how
successive generations pictured the London of the Prince Regent.
Augustus would grow up to help his father, imbibing Gothic
detail at its fountainhead during the 1820s, when Auguste
published two books of medieval crockets, corbels and roof
bosses: *Specimens of Gothic Architecture* and *Examples of Gothic
Architecture*. A generation whose historical sense had been
awoken by the novels of Sir Walter Scott, with their photogra-phically particular descriptions of places and things, was no
longer satisfied by the generalized Gothic references – a parapet
here, a pointed arch there – which had been enough for Sir
Richard Arkwright. *Specimens* and *Examples* gave a vocabulary
to what would emerge as the Gothic Revival. The younger Pugin
learned it by heart. At the age of fourteen he was given the
responsibility of drawing Rochester Cathedral for publication;
the next year he had the job of designing Gothic furniture for
Windsor Castle. It was a lot to expect of a fifteen-year-old; in
Paris at Notre Dame he collapsed from overwork.

Naturally, as soon as Augustus could take control of his own
affairs, he threw over the hard work, the result being the theatre
and his first marriage. To the supposed comte de Pugin this must
have been a disappointment. When the wife died, the family
remembered that Augustus had an aunt, Selina Welby, living at
Rose Cottage in Ramsgate, one of the uncomplaining legion of
nineteenth-century spinsters whose existence was forgotten until
they had some duty of care to fulfil, in this case helping to bring
up Pugin's daughter while he established his career. That career

was given new focus by the death, in devastatingly quick succession, of both his father and his mother.

Pugin took lodgings near the Norman church of St Lawrence – the original nucleus of Ramsgate – in a small house 'with a magnificent view of the channel' which he filled with 'antiquities of various sorts from William the Conqueror to Henry 8'. Before long he was married to Louisa, his second wife, and five more children arrived. The first son, Edward, who would also become an architect and finish some of his father's commissions, was baptized in St Lawrence's. Ramsgate, whatever its personal shortcomings, had the advantage, for an increasingly fanatical medievalist, of being near Canterbury Cathedral and other great churches. It was thought that St Augustine, who had brought Christianity from Rome, had landed at Ebbsfleet a little outside the town. But just as Pugin seemed to be experiencing a period of stability, his aunt, who had been a second mother to his growing family, died. However, she left him a legacy of £3,000 with which he was able to transfer the family to Salisbury, and build his first house, St Marie's Grange.

But St Marie's Grange did not suit. For once in his life Pugin was let down by the scale of his ambition; he built it too small. The Pugins transferred to Cheyne Walk, Chelsea, near the Thames in London. But a river was no real substitute for the sea; Ramsgate reasserted its pull, with Pugin making visits to sail and work. *True Principles* was published there, and in 1843, he bought the site of The Grange. He drew a sketch of a house almost exactly as it would be built. But before it was finished, another tragedy blighted his life: Louisa died. Pugin gave up Cheyne Walk and moved his family into the uncompleted Grange. Before long the widower was looking around for a new wife; Pugin needed to love and be loved and, working at a furious pace, relied on the support of women to succour him and his children. There was an engagement, broken at the last minute when the would-be bride's relations dissuaded her

from marrying a Roman Catholic. Pugin responded in characteristic fashion, by publishing a pamphlet. The hurt was soon assuaged
by his third marriage, to Jane Knill. Two more children joined the
family. All too soon Jane was nursing her husband through illness
and dementia, probably brought on by doses of mercury he took
for his inflamed eyes. Pugin died in 1852, aged forty-one. Before
his death his doctor told him that he had done a hundred years'
work in forty.

But for the time being the German band plays on. If we
approach The Grange and look in through a window, we can
see – perhaps to our surprise, given the austerity and conviction
of Pugin's personality – that the effect is rich and luxurious.
Pugin worked in his library, the heart of the house, its walls
papered with an assertive, diagonally barred pattern, incorporating the martlet of his coat of arms and the motto 'En avant' –
Forward! It is a paper that he specially designed for The Grange
and he would not allow it to be used anywhere else. Around the
cornice are the names of his most important clients and some best
friends. He worked, as many architects did, standing up. There is
no door to separate this room from the adjacent drawing room,
only a curtain. A door would have always been banging, Pugin
believed. To keep up his extraordinary rate of production, he
needed quiet.

Pugin's heavy front door is exceptionally strong. This is not just
for effect, although no doubt the symbolism of a stout door
shutting out the perils of the world was appealing. Pugin had a
fear of robbers. As a Catholic he and his family were also vulnerable. Ramsgate was a low-church town, whose inhabitants still
harboured the primitive prejudices of their Georgian forebears.
Disturbances followed the reintroduction of the Catholic hierarchy
in 1850. The young Pugins were abused on the street; excrement was
smeared on the walls of The Grange; the Pope was burned in effigy
on 5 November, the crowd only being prevented from parading the

figure past The Grange by the police. Pugin of course wrote a pamphlet. He also kept the doors locked.

When John Hardman Powell arrived shortly before Christmas 1844 – he had been sent by his uncle, the Birmingham metalworker and stained-glass maker John Hardman, to be Pugin's one and only pupil in the desperate period after Louisa's death – he found the greeting was bluff but short: 'Compline at 8, supper at 9, bed at 10.' Religion permeated the house, co-existing and intermingling with Pugin's other passions. 'In the Hall was a large figure of the Blessed Virgin niched in oak with folding doors,' Powell remembered, 'and a rack of favourite Telescopes, Souwesters, and Tarpaulins.' The floor was laid with tessellated tiles, waterproof and resistant to hobnailed boots. A strongly diagonal staircase rail – more of the coat of arms – served also to prevent small children from falling off the corridor above. The panelling was simple matchboard, perhaps out of economy, more probably because, for all his exuberance, Pugin preferred trimness and simplicity to unnecessary opulence. All the rooms in his day had big stone fireplaces, painted stone colour: they were redecorated by his son Edward to reflect the later Victorian taste for polychromy (but returned to their original colour by the Landmark Trust).

According to Powell, Pugin set himself to illustrate *True Principles* in the life of his household: 'Reverence, order, simplicity, Holy Mass in the chapel whenever he could get a priest friend to stay, then plenty of work, good food and exercise, the Church Festivals being the holidays in both senses'. Pugin liked to have a priest resident in the house, although it could be a trial, particularly during the era of Dr Acquaroni, who had no feeling for Gothic. Everyone was expected to help out during services. Mrs Greaves, who looked after the children, acted as organist, as did Pugin's eldest daughter, Anne; young Pugins and stained-glass workers from Hardman's sang in the choir (woe betide them if they were out of tune); Pugin himself, with his rich baritone voice, enjoyed 'going into choir as Cantor and singing the Mass from his big Gregorian books at the lectern, giving his most sonorous notes at the Credo'. However overwhelming the piety, it must have been enormous fun. When Ramsgate laughed at the family for trooping into church wearing hoods, saying that they looked like monks, he replied, 'Yes, United Augustinians.' The Grange embodied a vision of community, based on family. The house itself, with its extreme wallpapers and vibrant colours, throbbed with vitality.

There were appetites to be fed. The dining room was the most elaborately decorated of the reception rooms, with pine linenfold panelling stained to resemble mahogany – Pugin could compromise his edict against imitation when he wanted to. The 'En avant' paper was hung in colours of pink, red and white. The fireplace incorporates a figure of St Augustine as bishop and a Latin text from the *Magnificat*. Here Pugin would entertain his friends in state. But most family meals were eaten, extraordinarily for the period, in the kitchen, in front of the cooking range. The window framed a view of the church. Pugin ate heartily, the larder being 'well stocked with fine hams, cheese and butter, home baked bread'. He drank only filtered water that was kept cold in a refrigerator during the summer; he never smoked. Guests who insisted on their cigars had to consume them outside.

Like a true sailor, Pugin kept the inside of his house ship-shape; he insisted on tidiness. His working habits followed the same principle. He answered letters immediately and then burned them, only keeping copies on the rare occasions that he feared later unpleasantness. Drawings streamed from his table, seemingly without corrections, but he cared nothing for their preservation. He worked by himself, with no clerk and, except for young Powell, no assistant.

The work pressed on, and gradually his community arose. First came the schoolhouse, which doubled in the early years as a church. Then a house for a priest, and the church itself. It never achieved the spire that Pugin hoped for, but the flagpole, held up by guy ropes, withstood the strain of tempests, and Pugin finally gave the building to the diocese. It was a triumph mitigated only by the energy of some Ramsgate neighbours who set up their own school in opposition to his; better funded, it prospered, whereas the Puginian enterprise – attracting the roughest children – closed down.

The Grange is not an easy house to appreciate; Pugin was not an easy person. It makes no external claim to prettiness. In the course of the nineteenth century, other thinkers – John Ruskin, William Morris, the apostles of the Arts and Crafts movement – tried to establish communities, generally more secular than religious; Pugin can be glimpsed at the back of them, driving them on. They did not, however, try to emulate the architectural style of The Grange. Pugin was influential as a propagandist; by example he showed what could be done. He injected moral fervour into the Gothic Revival, demonstrating through his own life that Gothic architecture was not merely a decorative style, but part of a complete view of the world, dependent upon faith. The Grange was the built embodiment of that conception. If it did not influence his contemporaries directly, it was integral to the Puginian vision which shaped much High Victorian architecture. It was the precursor to a thousand parsonage houses and north Oxford villas.

In departing Ramsgate, let us take our leave of Pugin at Christmas, the festival which Dickens had done so much to package for Victorian susceptibilities. (Not that Dickens is thought to have cared for Pugin much. He was suspicious of anyone who told other people how to live. It is even said that elements of Pugin were incorporated into the hypocritical architect Seth Pecksmith in *Martin Chuzzlewit*). Every year Pugin had a Christmas tree, even if this was without medieval

precedent. But the greatest celebration took place on Twelfth
Night. There was a huge cake with St George and the Dragon
fighting on top of it. Guests came and were given characters to
act, the whole evening being kept afloat by Pugin's boisterous
hospitality. But it did not go on beyond 10.30. Then it was
'douse the glims and clear decks' to make the house shipshape
again. Not a remnant of the festivity was left for morning.

13. High Farming in Cumbria
Mechi Farm

William Lawson, born in 1836, did not pretend to have been a diligent student. The son of Sir Wilfrid Lawson, a Cumberland baronet, he was educated at home, on religious principles, with lessons in Latin, Greek and other subjects, but, as he frankly said, he 'learnt as little as possible'. While his elder brother became a temperance campaigner and long-bearded MP, he was packed off abroad. Before he was eighteen, William had travelled widely in Europe and the Middle East, without picking up much knowledge of business or anything else; at home he distinguished himself only as a sportsman, 'trained as a shooter of animals, a hunter of Cumberland beasts with hounds, and a trapper of vermin' and master of his brother's foxhounds. But by the age of twenty-five he had turned against field sports as 'barbarous cruelties'. Although hardly trained for the purpose, he was determined to think for himself, and became a vegetarian. In 1862 he embarked on a project, inspired by the utopian mill owner Robert Owen at New Lanark, to reconstruct an estate that he bought at Blennerhasset in Cumbria on the most progressive lines. Part of this would involve building a farmhouse and cottages for his employees.

Until the Victorian conscience got to work, rural labourers' cottages were likely to be damp, poorly maintained, dark, crowded and verminous. In earlier centuries, it could be difficult for country people to find homes at all. Landowners who saw more money in sheep than the mixed farming practised on medieval manors did not need so many people on the land. A foretaste of many later struggles came in 1607, when a Northamptonshire magnate, Sir Thomas Tresham, bought some forest land from the Crown. Peasants had been living in the woods for years, if not generations; they did not want to leave the homes they had built there. Sir Thomas began felling trees, digging draining ditches and putting up fences; the squatters responded by filling in the ditches and pulling down the fences. The result was a pitched battle, with as many as a thousand Levellers (the name was to resonate in Oliver Cromwell's army) carrying sticks faced by Sir Thomas and a well-armed militia. Several dozen of the Levellers were killed and the rest driven off.

There would be hundreds of other disputes between country folk and enclosing landlords over the next two centuries. Poor people who wanted to build cottages could find it next to impossible to squeeze sites out of local landowners. When John Butcher applied to occupy a disused cottage in Middle Claydon in Buckinghamshire in 1660, Sir Ralph Verney of Claydon Hall responded by ordering his bailiff to remove the roof and floorboards and demolish the chimney, thus rendering it uninhabitable. Housing of some kind was essential to Butcher's marriage plans. After three years he announced that his betrothed was pregnant. They set up home in a barn, and Verney, albeit furious, was compelled to house them. But, perhaps not surprisingly, they do not seem to have prospered; there would have been few openings for them in Verney's new way of farming, based on fattening cattle. The Butchers were still receiving charity twenty years later. At one point while still unhoused, they had proposed that Verney should help them emigrate to the colonies as vagrants; that might have been a better course for everyone concerned.

In the game being played between landowners and the rural poor, the landowners held most of the cards. They were the principal employers, and controlled poor relief and charity; they were magistrates; they might have the power of appointing the parish priest. In *Tom Jones*, Henry Fielding describes a countryside in which squires might eat mountains of beef at a sitting, wash it down with several bottles of wine, and feast off game that was preserved by draconian laws, while the family of 'Black George' Seagrim, the dismissed gamekeeper, could live in 'cold, hunger and nakedness' (albeit Fielding turns the squalor of the Seagrims' cottage to comic effect, when Tom climbs up to Molly's bedroom in the attic; not much privacy there, particularly since another lover is hiding behind a rug pinned up to conceal some hanging clothes). While conditions in the factory and mining towns that began to grow in the eighteenth century were often miserable – Arkwright's solidly built terraces at Cromford being the exception – most rural housing was as bad. It was unsanitary and unsightly.

The latter, as much as the former, quality would influence the landscape improvers of the Picturesque movement. Ever since the age of Boothby Pagnell, country-house owners had lived in close proximity to the people who worked their land; as often as not, the village clustered at the hem of the country seat. Under the dispensation of 'Capability' Brown, such mean dwellings could not be allowed to obtrude themselves into the Picturesque Arcadia, so some villages were demolished and rebuilt. Lord Milton, for example, expelled the inhabitants of the market town that flourished inconveniently near the skirts of his new country seat, Milton Abbey in Dorset, and rehoused some of them in a village of neat boxes under thatched roofs at Milton Abbas. (Not everyone was grateful for the exchange, and a local solicitor is supposed only to have moved after a stream was diverted through his house.) Oliver Goldsmith had the likes of Lord Milton in mind when he wrote of the 'tyrant's power' and 'spoiler's hand' driving England's 'bold peasantry' into exile in *The Deserted Village* (1770).

James Malton was an architect who specialized in providing what he called 'peasant huts' for Picturesque landowners. The important thing was what they looked like in the landscape and the associations that they inspired in the mind of the educated visitor. 'When mention is made of the kind of dwelling called a Cottage,' he wrote in *An Essay on British Cottage Architecture* (1798),

I figure in my imagination a small house in the country; of odd, irregular form, with various, harmonious colouring, the effect of weather, time, and accident; the whole environed with smiling verdure, having a contented, cheerful, inviting aspect, and door on the latch, ready to receive the gossip neighbour, or weary, exhausted traveller.

He quoted the Picturesque landowner Richard Payne Knight's description of a cottage in his poem 'The Landscape' with approval:

Its roof, with reeds and mosses cover'd o'er,
And honey-suckles climbing round the door,
While mantling vines along its walls are spread,
And clust'ring ivy decks the chimney's head!

The charm lay partly in the appearance of being tumble-down. It would not do for the Victorians. It certainly did not do for some of the people whose houses were being pulled down for the sake of the Picturesque cause.

At Endsleigh, the Regency Duke of Bedford enjoyed the pretence of cottage life; his Victorian son was made of another fibre. His interest in cottages was their improvement. This ought to have been the duty and 'truest pleasure' of every landlord: affording labourers 'the means of greater cleanliness, health, and comfort in their own homes; to extend education, and thus raise the social and moral habits of those most valuable members of the community'. Social responsibility of this kind was not entirely without self-interest; there were 'undeniable advantages of making the rural population content with their condition'. Well housed, workers would work harder and grumble less; with proper sanitation they would fall ill less often. Health was a theme that obsessed landlords, architects, householders and writers about domestic life throughout the Victorian period, and with good reason. A Scottish doctor was quoted by the Poor Law Commissioners in their Report on the Sanitary Condition of the Labouring Population made to the House of Lords in 1842; he remembered attending a young father who was dying of typhus in a single-room cottage where 'the horse stood at the back of the bed. The stench was dreadful.'

In 1864 Henry Julian Hunter published his *Inquiry into the State of the Dwellings of Rural Labourers*. In the course of his researches, he visited the 'extraordinarily shabby village' of Warter, where the inhabitants 'put up with mossy, mouldy thatch, with bulging walls, uneven floors, windows that will not open and doors that will not shut. They have to sleep in windowless, chimneyless lofts.' This was not remarkable. Hunter found that most rural workers around Britain lived in slums like this, many of them built of mud. Warter's villagers certainly paid high rents to their landlord, Lord Muncaster of Warter Priory. The criticism stung. Lord Muncaster, who had already begun building new cottages, hurried on with his improvements, and by the end of the century – after a change of ownership, following a picturesque episode during which Muncaster was captured by brigands in Greece – Warter had been completely rebuilt. There were hundreds of other Warters across Britain. In George Eliot's *Middlemarch* (1872), Dorothea Brooke sees it as

her Christian duty to promote the building of model cottages.
Many Victorian landlords would have shared this belief.
(Although early in the next century the vicar of Geddington
in Northamptonshire was still complaining to the Duke of
Buccleuch's agent that His Grace housed his workers worse
than his cattle.)

John Claudius Loudon, an extraordinarily hard-working and
humourless Scot who began his career as a gardener, caught the
beginnings of the moral tide. His *Encyclopaedia of Cottage, Farm
and Villa Architecture* (1833) showed two thousand drawings of
rural buildings, some designed by himself, many by other architects. The cottages proposed for emulation were solid, brick-built
affairs, sheltered by slate roofs and lit by iron casement windows.
Loudon's approach, however, was that of the omnivore. By the
time J. Bailey Denton published *The Farm Homesteads of England*
in 1864, greater science was being applied to the question. Outrage at
the hovels into which large families were still being crowded had led
to the conclusion that 'no cottages are suitable unless they contain
five rooms, of which three are bed-rooms, of prescribed dimen-
sions, with minor offices.' The idea that different generations and
different sexes could share bedrooms – acceptable when Arkwright
built 10 North Street in Cromford – was now considered to be
morally horrific. Denton made a speciality of farm and estate
buildings; it was a sign of the growing importance of this branch
of architecture that he could do so.

John Birch was another practitioner of experience. In the same
year that Denton's book was published, Birch won an award from
the Society of Arts for a design for a pair of agricultural labourers'
cottages, which, as he announced to the public in *Country
Architecture, a Work Designed for the use of the Nobility and
Country Gentlemen* (1874), came to be built under his supervision
in Berkshire, Carmarthenshire, Cheshire, Derbyshire, Essex,
Hertfordshire, Herefordshire, Huntingdonshire, Hampshire,

Leicestershire, Northamptonshire, Surrey, Sussex, Shropshire, Warwick-shire, Wiltshire and Worcestershire. His clients included Earl Spencer at Althorp, the Marquess of Ailesbury at Great Bedwyn and – a sign of the times – the Salisbury and Yeovil Railway Company. Comfort and serviceability were watchwords, the plans that he published 'having been prepared with a view to their practical utility rather than having regard solely to external effect'. What a long way architecture has travelled since the painterly considerations of the Picturesque!

In *Middlemarch*, Dorothea's uncle Mr Brooke thinks her plans too expensive, and it is only because Sir James Chettham hopes to marry her that they are realized. Without that romantic incentive, landowners might well have been inclined to agree with Mr Brooke, were it not that the mid-nineteenth century was a boom time for agriculture. The High Victorian period coincided with what was called 'High Farming'. Sir James Chettham was an exponent of it. 'I am reading *Agricultural Chemistry* [by Sir Humphrey Davy],' he told Dorothea, 'because I am going to take one of my farms into my own hands and see if something cannot be done in setting a good pattern of farming among my tenants.' High Farming maximized returns by using the latest scientific and technological advances to increase yields. Fertilizers were applied to the soil. Farm buildings were organized on industrial principles. Steam engines were used to power threshing machines, cattle-cake crushers, chaff cutters, turnip slicers and grain bruisers. Pairs of traction engines were trundled out into the fields to power ploughs. It was a trend that had been foreseen by the ever-industrious Loudon. 'As it is extremely probable that steam will soon be very generally employed for impelling threshing-machines,' he wrote, 'and as nothing disfigures the country more than red brick chimney-shafts, like those common in the manufacturing towns of Lancashire, we would strongly recommend some attention to elegance of form in these very conspicuous parts of a modern farmery.'

It was a time when gentlemen established foreign species of animals in their parks – there was a society specially devoted to encouraging them. Some were valued as four-legged decoration, some seemed likely to improve the British countryside through their superior performance. The grey squirrel, the muntjak and other invaders, now ineradicable, are the legacy. Native wildlife was too commonplace to be protected, and the great bustard was shot out of existence. Farmers' wives were swept up by the enthusiasm. Traditionally they had responsibility for keeping chickens, and in the mid-nineteenth century it was seen that the birds' egg-laying and decorative potential could be increased by the introduction of foreign breeds. Queen Victoria led the way, taking a close interest in the Poultry House that was built at Windsor in 1843. W. B. Dickson's *Poultry* (1838) lists twenty different breeds of chicken, more than double those cited by Bonington Moubray in his breeding manual of 1815. And when the Queen was presented with five pullets and two cockerels of a hitherto unknown type, fresh off a ship from China, it caused a sensation in the poultry-keeping world. The Shanghais, or Cochins, as they came to be called, were published in the *Illustrated London News*, exhibited at agricultural shows and given by the Queen freely as presents.

Like many others, William Lawson saw himself as a 'gentleman farmer', and he used his fortune to develop a new model of rural society. It was based on Owen's democratic concept of 'co-operation', whereby each member of the workforce had an equal say in the direction of the enterprise. Lawson had about a hundred people on his payroll at Blennerhasset. They worked on an estate which was as modern as Lawson could make it – an advertisement for the principles of High Farming. The home farm was named Mechi Farm after the apostle of High Farming, Alderman Mechi of Essex. Blennerhasset lacked for nothing. Farm operations were conducted with the help of a gasometer, a smithy on the scale of a small foundry, an immense hydraulic engine for irrigation, a chemical laboratory, a plant for making manure, an underground water turbine, washing machines, a flour mill, lathes, tramways with turntables and trucks for feeding the cattle, and a flax-starching mill. The social provision included a school, a library with seven hundred books, a lecture hall, a music hall and a banqueting hall. The glory of the estate were the steam ploughs. First came a Fowler's number 95 traction engine, causing astonishment at the railway station when it was seen to move away on its own without horses. A local man burst into poetry to celebrate its advent:

> The porter lads with vigor ran;
> The whistle shrieked aloud;
> Sir Wilfrid was in ecstasies,
> And so were all the crowd.
>
> And still we shrieked, and still we ran;
> Throughout the livelong day;
> Through loam and sand, through mire and mud,
> Through stones and heavy clay.

One of the tenets of High Farming was that the land should be ploughed deep. The steam plough made light work of doing so. But this pioneering engine proved unreliable. Far from abandoning the experiment, Lawson bought two others, known by the biblical names of Cain and Abel. They could plough seven grand furrows apiece and were hugely popular with the Blennerhasset community. Their virtue was also appreciated by a wider circle, for they could be contracted to plough for neighbouring farmers. But the sort of vagaries which had afflicted the Fowler 95 came to plague them, too. Leaky boilers, broken clutches and other breakdowns necessitated expensive repairs. Their fate was decided on the best principles of co-operation, at one of the daily after-dinner 'Parliaments'. Lawson, who provided all the capital for the estate, argued strongly that they should be got rid of; everyone else voted to keep them, cheering loudly when they saw the forest of pro-Cain and -Abel hands. It can be no surprise that the Blennerhasset enterprise never paid, nor that Lawson could not keep farm managers, who objected that their professional judgements were overturned, in the words of one of them, by a 'motley mixture of boys, girls, women, and men of all trades and no trade or profession, indiscriminately drawn together into a council-chamber for the purpose of discussing and deciding upon the most important subjects regarding farming operations, though nineteen-twentieths of them were quite ignorant and inexperienced' in such matters.

Lawson was an enthusiast but not a leader; he was often absent in Australia, did not care much for detail, and, in his eagerness to try out every form of farm innovation at Blennerhasset, had too many irons in the fire at once. It would be easy to make fun of the result, and indeed Lawson himself, writing an account of his experience under the title *Ten Years of Gentleman Farming at Blennerhasset with Co-operative Objects* (1874), invites us to do so. The vegetarian Christmas dinner served in 1866 was so revolting that, next day, not even the pigs would eat it. The hundreds of guests went home hungry, and 'for miles around, the farm and cotters' houses were cleared of every thing eatable.' The Blennerhasset banquets cannot have been improved by the talks on diet which preceded them, professors expounding at length on the virtues of the 'hygienic' meal – sans milk, sans eggs, sans salt, sans pepper, sans sugar, all of which were considered to have depraved the 'nerves of taste'. Nevertheless, one has to note that the Christmas celebrations came to be thronged with merrymakers from around the county – so many that tickets had to be issued. The co-operators must have been convivial company. The mighty Cain, splendidly decked out, served as a gigantic tea kettle.

There is one respect in which Lawson's experiment cannot be judged a failure: his buildings. The home farm still stands as a massive tribute to his investment. The grey, buff and pink rubble walls, finished with red-sandstone quoins and lintels, look as solid as a cathedral. There are round-headed windows beneath the gable ends. Although the clock mechanism has disappeared from the campanile-like clock tower, only the stumps of iron brackets remain of the gas lamps, and little remains of the turnip pulper, straw cutter and grinding mill that were state of the art in the 1860s, the barns are still in use (with only minor adaptations, such as the raising of door heights to allow tractors to enter). The farmhouse, built of the same materials as the barns, is L-shaped. The main part, three windows across, provided accommodation for the farm manager; the wing attached to it at right angles was equipped with an outside staircase, its sandstone treads showing the wear of innumerable agricultural boots. This led up to an attic dormitory for the unmarried hands. A further terrace of cottages for Lawson's workers was built in the village.

By 1872, Lawson had to conclude that 'gentleman farming', at least as he conducted it, was a lost cause. Having paid £45,410 for land, buildings and farm machinery in 1862, he sold up a decade later for £38,113 – his total loss (including the losses made through selling farm produce at less than the cost of growing it) being £13,525. As an American reviewer of his book commented wryly, 'The wonder is, not that his scheme of "gentleman farming" proved a losing investment, but that he could have invested so much and so variously, leaving every thing to the care of others while he studied co-operation and model farming pretty much all over the planet, and not have lost infinitely more.' As it was, the High Farming moment was about to pass, with the coming of bad harvests, refrigerated ships from the Antipodes and South America, and an agricultural recession that lasted beyond 1900. For the look of the countryside, this may have been just as well. Too many Cains and

Abels at work would have required bigger fields, with the sort of consequences for hedgerows that would be seen when scientific farming was again in the ascendancy after the Second World War. The farming slump paid an architectural dividend in the form of the Settled Land Acts, which enabled the owners of traditional estates, whose income from farming had collapsed, to sell ancient and decrepit manor houses like East Barsham Manor to enthusiastic, romantically minded restorers. But improvers like Lawson had established the principle that country people, like their counterparts in the industrial cities, deserved to be properly housed.

14. Artistic London at Home
18 Stafford Terrace, Kensington

The Aslets' house in Pimlico has forgotten much of its history; the lives of the early owners remain shadowy. There is, however, one house in London that is not wholly dissimilar, which survives much as its Victorian family knew it, and where we can reconstruct what went on from diaries. This is 18 Stafford Terrace, built in 1871, some twenty years after 154 Tachbrook Street, and on a more expansive scale. Pimlico would have looked up to Kensington, where Stafford Terrace is to be found; it still does. In the intervening twenty years house façades had broken out into bay windows whose extra panes might have provided more light had they not been obscured by heavy draperies. Stafford Terrace first resisted stucco, being unashamed of naked yellow stock brick, and then went overboard for it, hiding the whole of its front behind an all-enveloping white sheet. Nevertheless, the plans of the Tachbrook Street and Stafford Terrace houses are about the same. In this they are like thousands of others, built in the years when, in the opinion of a French visitor, London ceased 'to be a town, and was becoming a vast province'.

In general, Stafford Terrace was occupied by barristers, senior civil servants, retired officers and successful tradesmen. But the Sambournes, at No. 18, were different. Linley Sambourne was an artist. With middle-class money entering the picture market, and people of all kinds buying the prints that were made after paintings shown at the Royal Academy, artists in Victorian England could do very well. The most prosperous built studio houses, with tall, north-facing windows lighting large rooms specially dedicated to their art. There were a number of these very near Stafford Terrace, including the great Frederic, Lord Leighton's house of art in Holland Park; some of these Academicians, such as Marcus Stone and Luke Fildes, were Sambourne's friends. But Sambourne himself was not in this league. He was an illustrator for the weekly humorous magazine *Punch*, occupying, for most of his working life, the position of Second Cartoon. (The First Cartoon, Sir John Tenniel, did not retire until he was eighty, in 1901; when Sambourne finally stepped into his shoes he was a few days short of fifty-seven.) The job was not extravagantly well paid, and the suspicion is that the money to buy the lease of 18 Stafford Terrace, acquired after the death of the first resident, came from Sambourne's wife Marion Herapath's family; Mr Herapath was a stockbroker who had done well out of South American railways. The Sambournes moved in in 1874, the year after their marriage. He was thirty-one, she twenty-three.

Mr and Mrs Herapath lived round the corner from Stafford Terrace at Upper Phillimore Gardens, making it easy for Marion to visit them. She paid most of her social calls by foot. Very occasionally her parents would order up their carriage as a favour, but this was exceptional: even when Marion had access to a vehicle, she did not always choose to use it, as harnessing the horses was too much of a fuss. The Herapaths also had a house called Westwood

Lodge, outside a resort which has already made its appearance in these pages: Ramsgate. Every autumn, the Sambournes would decamp to Ramsgate – eventually occupying rented houses in the town – and stay there through the winter. There was a *Punch* as well as a family connection: Frank Burnand, the editor, had a house in Royal Crescent. ('Very jolly evening at Burnands,' reads a typical entry from Marion's diary.) But the Sambournes may have done it to save money. They could keep a smaller establishment at Ramsgate, they did not entertain, and there were no West End shops. By métier and way of life, Sambourne was a bohemian, never flush, invariably late in settling bills (to the extent that a Broadway piano took twenty years to pay off). The decoration of their house was nonetheless à la mode. Conventional ideas about decorating at this period were typified by massive solidity and self-evidently expensive ornament – so much so that, as Dickens observed apropos of Mr Podsnap in *Our Mutual Friend* (1864–5), the very concept of sophisticated 'taste' was in some quarters suspect:

> Mr. Podsnap could tolerate taste in a mushroom man who stood in need of that sort of thing, but was far above it himself. Hideous stolidity was the characteristic of the Podsnap plate. Everything was made to look as heavy as it could, and to take up as much room as possible. Everything said boastfully, 'Here you have as much of me in my ugliness as if I were only lead; but I am so many ounces of precious metal worth so much an ounce; – wouldn't you like to melt me down?'

The Sambournes – more particularly Linley – tended towards the progressive art-for-art's-sake Aesthetic movement, as popularized in Charles Eastlake's *Hints on Household Taste* (1868). It is easy to imagine them reading Eastlake aloud to one another and nodding in agreement, for 18 Stafford Terrace exemplifies many Eastlakian principles. But it may also be that they never opened the book, probably not needing books to find inspiration. After all, they had their artistic friends to keep them up to the minute, and they followed their own – that is to say, Linley's – taste. It ran to a profusion of pattern and an abhorrence of vacuum that left every wall surface covered and every floor space crowded with furniture. Was it typically Victorian? In some ways. It was also what they happened to like, particularly what Linley liked. Sometimes it drove Marion mad.

Sambourne was by no means a typical follower of Aesthetic fashion. He looked less like Dante Gabriel Rossetti or Oscar Wilde (whom he satirized in his work) than like a portly country squire, and it was an impression he fostered. He shot, he fished, he sailed. He was fond of riding his horses – a mare called Dolly, or Blondin (named after a famous tight-rope walker), whose hoof is preserved in the drawing room – and he leased stables in Phillimore Mews and kept a groom. On the top floor was a speaking tube and whistle directly communicating with the stables. Seven hunting scenes by John Leach, illustrator of R. S. Surtees, hung on the stairs. As an artist Sambourne was more or less self-taught, having been first apprenticed as a draughtsman in a marine-engineering works. Nor did Aesthetic movement tea gowns tempt Marion, however much she chastised herself over extravagance at the dressmaker's; photographs generally show her wearing sensible tailor-mades. It was Sambourne who took the lead; Marion loyally celebrated her husband's talent, and seems to have been content to have faded into the richly decorated, closely hung background, prone to mysterious ailments that kept her in bed until noon. For most of the time she put up uncomplainingly with her husband's regime, with its weekly *Punch* dinners and evenings at the Garrick Club.

Though Marion was the one who was often alone in the house, it was probably Sambourne who decorated it. The decor had been a lot simpler when they arrived. The previous occupant had put up William Morris wallpapers, but it was the Sambournes who introduced the dado and cornice rails, dividing each wall into three fields. Each field was papered differently. The ceiling was also wallpapered, sometimes with one of the patterns on the wall but in a different colourway. Ceiling roses were bronzed and picked out (in the dining room) in turquoise. The skirting board was marbled. The mantelpiece was hung with a tasselled velvet valance. Sambourne personally painted pots of flowers onto the panels of the door to the dining room. Nowadays the impression inside 18 Stafford Terrace is sumptuous and treacly, as though one has strayed into some dark, secret hideaway in a wood. But allowance has to be made for 130 years of bottle age which has tended to make the colours more sombre than they were originally. When the interiors were new, the effect must have been rich and vibrant, the opulent moss greens and burgundy reds set off with glittering brass and silver ornaments, most of which have now gone.

The wallpapers were expensive. Nevertheless, the Sambournes chose to cover them with a dense hanging of pictures, so closely packed that their frames almost touch. Sambourne, as we shall see, was fascinated by photography, and furthermore not in a position to buy many original works of art. So instead of the fashionable conversation pieces shown at the Royal Academy he bought photographic prints of them. They all show people, generally in historical scenes – forming a parallel with his own work for *Punch*.

'We live in an age of Omnium Gatherum,' commented the architect Robert Kerr in *The English Gentleman's House* (1864); '. . . all the world's a museum, and men and women are its students.' At first sight, the furniture at 18 Stafford Terrace looks as though it is a collection assembled over many years. Antiques were coming into vogue for the first time, and here we have Sheraton rubbing shoulders with the French eighteenth century, neo-Gothic and Chinese lacquer, as well as Victorian mahogany. Sambourne was unable to enter a shop without making a purchase. Close inspection shows that many of the pieces are reproductions, and they were not assembled over a long period, since an inventory of 1877 indicates that many had arrived by that date. The house filled up very quickly. There were already sixty-six upright chairs by 1877, ten of which were in the best bedroom, with another ten in the day nursery. From the start, a stout man such as Sambourne would have had to take care as he edged between the armchairs and the cabinets, the palms and the bronzes. They trembled when Sambourne's son Roy played blind man's buff. Navigation was not made easier by the subdued light, strained through the stained glass of which the Sambournes were particularly fond; it often incorporates their armorial bearings or initials. (They were not really entitled to the coat of arms, but used it with growing confidence as time went on. It appears on metal panels on doors, in the stained glass, even on the cover of that expensive piano with its long-outstanding bill.) The crowding only got worse. 'Dear Lin worried with bills,' laments Marion in 1884, 'wish he could be less extravagant, so difficult to make him understand *absolute* necessity.' Although to a modern eye the house seems over-furnished, about a third of the pieces mentioned in the 1877 inventory are no longer there.

The layout of 18 Stafford Terrace is much the same as any other London house of the period: narrow hall, staircase, two rooms on the ground floor, two on the floor above; on the floor above that, a bedroom for Mr and Mrs Sambourne, a bedroom for Roy – and space found somewhere or other for Roy's sister Maud. To the Danish architect Steen Rasmussen, writing in 1937, the wonder of the London house (let alone the even more elaborately planned country house) was its separation of function: 'The house itself is a small community no less specialized than the town where it lies. Each member has his own course marked out, and when he sticks to it he can live at his ease and the different members need not interfere with each other's affairs.' This was a trend that had developed since the Georgian period, when householders, even quite grand ones, had been prepared to muddle through in an almost medieval way. 'In a really distinguished house,' wrote

Rasmussen, reflecting a pattern of life that had become established in the Victorian age,

> there are now a number of bed-rooms and plenty of spare rooms. The children have their own drawing-room, their *day nursery*. There is a *breakfast-room* and a *dining-room*, there is a *library* and a billiard-room, there is the drawing-room for the mistress of the house where no smoking is allowed and where the ladies retire when the gentlemen remain over the wine and walnuts, there is the sitting-room of the master of the house and so forth.

The domestic system was divided into separate spheres, revolving around the master and mistress, their children and their servants, which followed their own orbits and should, in the well-regulated universe, rarely if ever collide. This was the ideal to which the Sambournes aspired.

At 18 Stafford Terrace, the builder had left the first floor as one L-shaped room, though with the necessary door that would have allowed it to be separated easily into two rooms if required. The Sambournes preferred to retain it as a single drawing room. But it was not only a drawing room. While the houses of the most prosperous artists had separate studio entrances to prevent the artists' wives encountering socially dubious models on the stairs, Linley Sambourne was not quite in this league. For most of his life he did not have a studio as such, only an extension of the drawing room, created in the 1880s, which contained his easel; it was a considerable relief to Marion when he devised new working space in the old attic bedrooms, after their daughter had left home – but that was not until the 1920s. As the Saturday-morning deadline for delivering the woodblocks to the engravers loomed, Sambourne would work furiously; dinner would be left to shrivel on the kitchen range, as sometimes he did not finish until the small hours. Working in black and white, he was not constrained by daylight hours; a portable gas lamp and a glass engraver's globe, concentrating a beam of light onto the page, boosted the light level. In the murk of London this would sometimes have been necessary during the day, even if it had not been for the stained glass introduced into all the back windows to hide domestic activities in the yard.

Sambourne did not work directly from live models. Instead he filled chests of drawers with thousands of reference photographs, filed by subject. Anything that he needed to sketch – from a newborn baby to one of the fashionable young ladies wittily filed under 'Zoological studies' – had its reference, which could be pulled out during his Friday-afternoon scramble to meet his deadline. Models were posed in attitudes that were likely to come in useful, and then followed faithfully in the resulting cartoon. Sambourne posed his friends, his wife, his children, his brothers-in-law, or would even put himself – curtseying in an apron, or grimacing theatrically – in front of the camera. Professional models were photographed nude and clothed: Sambourne took his art seriously. He also had an eye for a pretty girl. A favourite seems to have been called Maud Easton. The nude photography sessions took place when Marion was in Ramsgate, the servants having been given the day off. Not all of Maud Easton's poses were suitable for *Punch*. Perhaps not surprisingly, Marion came to feel that the photography had gone too far. 'Lin at those everlasting photos,' she would exclaim. Or, 'More of those photos. Lin wastes time, late with work.' One session might yield eighty photographs. The negatives were developed in a steep-sided, coffin-shaped marble bath, designed by Sambourne himself; there was a folding shelf at the side for setting out bottles and paper.

The first-floor drawing room was, in London houses, a standard arrangement, separating the principal room of entertainment from the noises of the basement, and providing a sense of occasion when company descended, arm in arm, to dinner. Going down to dinner – it was usually down – was a ritual of Victorian life: the grander the house, the more elaborate the route of parade. As foreign residents, used to living horizontally in apartments, frequently observe, London houses are tall, so bells, calling servants from remote regions, were as important in London as at Endsleigh. In the dining room at 18 Stafford Terrace, there was additionally a speaking tube to allow direct communication with the kitchen below. 'Home dinner. Very good. They did not stay so late as usual,' Sambourne noted in his diary for 31 May 1895. 'Took some carbonate of soda at 12.15 when going to Bed. All went off well.' On that occasion, the meal had started rather late, because he did not get home until 8.35, after a day trip to Calais; usually it was hoped that 'home dinners' would start about 8.00. The octagonal table normally limited the numbers to eight, although occasionally there were a couple more, in which case Roy would sit by himself at a side table or even in the next room. The Sambournes usually hired a waiter or waitress for these dinner parties, if possible from the Royal Academy, because it was always preferable to have someone you knew. (On 13 March 1897, when Luke Fildes and his wife were in the party, a 'strange waitress muddled the wines'.) These home dinners were state occasions taking place two or three times a year.

Sambourne, like others of his generation, does not seem to have noticed the finer points of food, but for an exceptionally grand dinner of twelve on 25 July 1899 he was moved to write down the menu. It started with caviar and Château-d'Yquem, moved on to sole and champagne, and finished – after courses of tongue, lamb and chicken, washed down with old wines – with raspberry purée, a savory of whiting and forty-eight-year-old Courvoisier brandy. Next day he got up late at 8.45, walked the dogs, gave an old woman 3d and came home: 'Slight head on,' he noted unsurprisingly. He set himself up with a Turkish bath and a haircut. Ordinary fare might include fresh fish, and there would be a joint of beef once a week, but the staple was mutton in all its forms – roast, boiled, hashed, stewed and curried.

During the day, the Sambournes could enjoy a fernery in a glass box that still occupies the dining-room window, projecting out over the sill towards the street. This was the sort of thing that, in Charles Eastlake's opinion, represented the only means of giving personality to an otherwise dreary London façade. Another glass box on the stairs combined a miniature conservatory with an aquarium. Winter gardens were all the rage; these were the best that the Sambournes, with little outside space, could manage. In a nod to science, they displayed minerals and shells acquired at Ramsgate in the aquarium. It was not, however, a highly scientific arrangement; the fish always died.

The dining room was separated from the morning room – Mrs Sambourne's preserve – by a heavy *portière*. *Portières* were valued as a defence against draughts, which were hated as a possible threat to health; in other contexts they also helped preserve the privacy that was the holy grail of the decorous, but overcrowded, Victorian household. The morning room was, and is, the only room hung with oil paintings rather than photographs or line drawings. It was from here that Marion ran the household.

There were three indoor servants at 18 Stafford Terrace: house-maid, parlourmaid and cook. Although the Sambournes lived to the limit of their income and perhaps beyond it, three servants was not a large staff; furthermore, they were all 'female servants' – like those of John Ruskin's parents, who, unlike the Sambournes, 'lived with strict economy' on Herne Hill in south London. Servants were a constant presence in the lives of their employers, and domestic order could not be maintained without them. With an expanding population, Britain did not, as yet, suffer from a shortage of young girls entering service (that would come in the Edwardian age); we have seen the poverty that existed in the countryside, where it was difficult to support a large family on an agricultural wage and there was little work for women. Many of the Sambournes' housemaids came from Norfolk. They were extremely young, on average twelve years old though sometimes as young as ten. This was not unusual. Once in London, these young country girls would have had little choice but to stay in service: there were few alternative occupations except prostitution.

The housemaid had all the cleaning to do. She was a foot soldier in the Victorian household's constant war against grime, made more difficult by the elaboration of the decor, with its *portières*, deep fringes and superabundance of furniture. Carrying coal, lighting fires and blacking grates were important duties; another was disposing of the dust, not to mention cleaning away the smuts of soot from other people's fires that were apt to float in through the windows. Since Britain's first gasworks had opened in 1813 (in Westminster, as it happens), by 1850 it was no longer necessary to put out and trim the oil lamps that had been in standard use during the Regency. Nevertheless, the dirt borne by the air encouraged the Victorian love of rich colours. As the century wore on, writers increasingly castigated the ornament of the mid-Victorian interior as likely to gather dust, which was associated with disease. Dusting the overfilled rooms of 18 Stafford Terrace must have been a particular chore. Fortunately, dusting and washing delicate ornaments were activities that Marion herself quite enjoyed.

Water had to be carried upstairs. Linley's bathroom, with plumbed-in cold water and lavatory, was regarded as his preserve. Bathrooms were thought to save labour, not to improve comfort. Marion used chamber pots and took her bath in front of the fire. Even the hot water for the bathroom had to be carried. As a result, the stairs and many of the floors that were not on public view were laid with linoleum. A stair carpet stretched as far as the drawing room; it could easily have been rolled up.

The parlourmaid had more responsibility than the housemaid; the distinction was recognized by the use of her surname rather than her first name. She also waited at table. During a fit of economy, Marion tried to manage with a second housemaid, rather than a parlourmaid, but it did not answer. These young girls – housemaid and parlourmaid – shared the same narrow metal bed, sleeping head to toe. One hopes they slept soundly (typically Sambourne photographed at least one of them while doing so).

Highest in the below hierarchy was the cook, usually honoured by the courtesy title of 'Mrs'. Cooking at a Victorian range was a long, hot business, and cooks were famously bad-tempered and thirsty (that is to say, drunk). A good cook was worth keeping. The Sambournes, who had plenty of experience of employing grumpy, impertinent, lazy ones, had a treasure called Emma who stayed with them, on and off, for a quarter of a century. They bore with the storms of her drunken husband, who kicked doors and smashed windows. The cook slept on a fold-out bed in the kitchen.

Marion's sphere was a narrow one, in comparison to her con-vivial husband. Mostly she put a brave face on it, only once letting the mask slip when her brother Spencer went bankrupt. The strain compounded what must have been a nagging dissatisfaction with her domestic lot. 'Feel awfully done up,' she sighed shortly before Christmas 1888. 'Often think it a pity Lin ever married – only cares for his home as a sort of warehouse for surplus furniture – our lives drifting apart.' The next day she felt worse, wondering if Lin would notice for more than an hour if she died, but before long she had rallied.

Maud Sambourne did well for herself, going on a round of country-house visits ('Oh my goodness what a place!!!!!!! You never saw anything to equal it under the sun – no never because I never have !!!!!!!' she wrote to Marion during a visit to Buscot Park) and eventually marrying a rich young banker, Leonard Messel. It was her affection for the house, and his money, transmitted to her daughter Anne, Countess of Rosse, that ensured that 18 Stafford Terrace remained as she knew it when growing up.

Preservation has made this house very remarkable, yet in its architectural bones and domestic regime it was recognizably akin to all other London terraced houses of the period, whatever their status. In the late 1880s – just as Marion was despairing, temporarily, of her marriage – Sambourne's *Punch* colleagues George and Weedon Grossmith were writing the column which would in time be published as *The Diary of a Nobody*, recording the life of the fictional Charles Pooter at the Laurels, Brickfield Terrace, in the newly built suburb of Holloway. As a City clerk, Mr Pooter would have thought bohemianism best avoided; nevertheless, his domestic arrangements sought to emulate those of families like the Sambournes. The Grossmiths knew Holloway well, having been brought up nearby. The Laurels is of course much smaller than 18 Stafford Terrace, but the Italianate detail (pediment over window, rudimentary classical doorcase) comes from the same architectural family. There are steps up to the front door, which Mr Pooter wants to keep clean (a perfectly white front step, washed and scrubbed with pumice, was regarded as a badge of domestic virtue in the Victorian age); for this reason, the door itself is never used, leaving visitors to arrive through the side door in the basement. Here the door is opened – to a stream of delivery boys and tradesmen, but also to Mr Pooter's guests – by the Pooters' one maid, Sarah. Sarah is demonstrably harassed. This is not the way to keep up appearances.

Mr Pooter is a domestic animal. He gives much thought to ornamenting his house with decorative fans, plaster stags' heads, enlarged and tinted photographs with Liberty silk bows at the corners, and a quantity of red enamel which he disastrously applies to the bath. The Pooters also hang framed photographs rather than paintings. On one red-letter day, they hire a waiter, neighbours and friends assemble in the first-floor drawing room, and the evening begins with music around the piano. They go down to dinner at 10 o'clock. Mr Pooter's wife, Carrie, has been 'busy all day, making little cakes and open jam puffs and jellies'. These are put on the dining table with sandwiches, cold chicken and ham, and some sweet dishes, while there are cold beef and tongue on a sideboard. Characteristically, Mr Pooter is alarmed by how much some of his guests eat and drink. After dinner, Lupin Pooter, the go-ahead son, performs musical turns with his friends. There is nothing left to eat or drink when Mr Pooter's boss, Mr Perkupp, arrives, in the middle of the faintly indecorous music-hall antics.

I suspect that the Sambournes would have enjoyed the music-hall turns, and would have recognized the social ideal that they were comically failing to live up to. Caviar and old brandy were not on offer in Brickfield Terrace, but the organization of the terraced house, and the social forms that went with it, permeated the respectable classes.

15. An Antidote to Industrialism
Brantwood

There are three Victorian sages whose houses have come down to us, thus transmitting an intimate understanding of their domestic personalities: Carlyle in Cheyne Row, Chelsea; Darwin at Down House near Biggin Hill, at the point where Kent collides with London; and Ruskin at Brantwood in the Lake District. For architecture, Ruskin is the most important of the trio. His writings – voluminous as they were – conditioned the way his contemporaries saw the world, and their influence is felt through the philosophy of planning and the care of old buildings today. Ruskin thought deeply about how people should live. But how did he live himself?

There were several Ruskins – the aesthete, the thinker, the social campaigner, the painter. His vision of the world grew out of his first love, geology. He studied rocks and learned to paint them. When rocks assemble together on a sufficiently large scale, they of course become a landscape. Landscape painting became a cause. To begin with, Ruskin championed the Pre-Raphaelites, whose meticulous, close-focused observation of nature appealed to his quasi-scientific interest. Then he became propagandist-in-chief for England's greatest artist, Turner; among Ruskin's treasures at Brantwood was the gold ring set with an antique intaglio that Turner habitually wore. He was a man of strong passions and beliefs, though his ardent nature did not find an expression in physical love. After a brief disaster of a marriage, his wife ran off with the painter Millais. Ruskin seemed barely to notice.

He turned his energy to fulminations against the industrial city, which seemed to leave no place for beauty in the lives of its drones. In Ruskin's view, labour was the thing to redeem society. Book-worms ought to be prepared to spend a portion of every day in hard physical work, perhaps mending the road. Manufacturers should close down their factories and let their workers produce as much as possible by hand. Handwork allowed for some individual expression; this made each stone of a medieval buidling unique, which is why Ruskin was furious when he saw restorers replacing old stones with new. Craft skill gave meaning to the life of the worker: factories robbed him of his humanity. It is not surprising that, holding these radical views, which were so much in opposition to the prevailing currents of the age, Ruskin suffered bouts of madness towards the end of his life. To this highly strung man, Brantwood was the antidote to the ugliness and grind of much of Victorian life that kept him, for a time at least, sane.

Brought up in the claustrophobic dullness of a house in south London, Ruskin had been taken to the Lakes by his parents – his father was a sherry merchant and had to visit his customers. He had played near the future site of Brantwood when he was seven. In Herne Hill, the most exciting event of the day was the arrival of the dustcart; not surprisingly the expansiveness of nature that the little boy experienced in the Lake District made a heady impression. Being taken to the brow of Friar's Crag on Derwentwater by his nurse formed his first important memories, and – as he recalled in

Modern Painters (1843) – the 'intense joy' that he took in the mossy roots he saw explains his subsequent love of twining roots and trees. The Picturesque movement, in which landscapes were created for human enjoyment, had been overtaken by Romanticism, for whose poets mountains were an epic force, capable (as Wordsworth revealed in 'The Prelude') of shaping tje human personality, particularly in youth.

As an adult, Ruskin sketched what would become the 'principal feature' in the view from his study window – an old stone house with conical chimneys, called Coniston Hall – from a boat in the middle of the lake, using the drawings as an illustration in an early article in *Architectural Magazine*, as well as in *The Poetry of Architecture* (1893). It was because he knew the all-important view that Ruskin did not need to see Brantwood before buying it, after his first serious illness, in 1871. In December of the next year he described the landscape in one of many admiring passages to his cousin Joan Severn. Despite 'the loss in foliage', it was even more thrilling in winter than in summer: 'The sun coming down among the thin woods is like enchanted light, and the ivy and walls and waters are all as perfect as ever – so that I never yet had a walk among the lakes so lovely, and few in Italy.' This view, he wrote in the preface to the rearranged edition of *Modern Painters* (1883), was not so much classically beautiful as 'entirely pastoral and pure'. If so much as the tip of an ironworks chimney had appeared over the hills, its value for Ruskin, with his hatred of industrial exploitation, would have been completely destroyed.

Mountain scenery, wildflowers, geology (the crag below the garden was of a formation he knew from Bonneville and Annecy in the Alps), remoteness from the rest of Victorian England – these were the things Ruskin knew he could expect from his new home. If he also hoped to find a pretty house, he was to be disappointed. Brantwood, built at the end of the previous century, was not much to look at and, despite becoming home to Victorian England's great apostle of beauty, never would be. At first he required no more than a cottage. But even as a cottage, Brantwood was not of the soundest – 'a mere shed of rotten timber and loose stone' that cost £1,500, he remembered in an 1877 instalment of his monthly *Fors Clavigera*. During his first visit in September 1871, he sketched it for Mrs Severn, who with her husband – the artist Arthur Severn – and children would live in the house with him.

Since 1853 Brantwood had been lived in by the wood engraver and printer W. J. Linton, a radical who had left London when his political views made work hard to find. From Brantwood he issued a series of radical publications including a paper called *The English Republic*. 'Only an enthusiast,' wrote Linton's sympathizer W. E. Adams, 'would have thought of setting up a printing office in a remote quarter of the Lake District miles away from the nearest railway station.' To house the press, a rough shed, its walls scratched with the slogans 'God and the People', 'Light more Light' and '*Laborare est orare*', was built beside the cottage.

From the start the Coniston tradespeople had been suspicious of Linton's solvency, and their doubts had been realized when he emigrated, following his republican beliefs, to America. Brantwood had to be sold to pay debts. In May 1871 he wrote to Ruskin, whom he had met, to ask if the writer could suggest a buyer. It was an opportune moment. During the summer, when he had been critically ill, Ruskin had been thinking specially of Coniston Water as a place to recover. When he bought Brantwood he was anxious that Linton's debts in the neighbourhood should be cleared, and therefore waived the conveyancing fee. Ruskin wanted to get the house into order quickly. There had been a fate in buying it, he wrote to Mrs Severn, especially as *The English Republic* might be compared to his own *Fors*.

The house was originally two bays across; to this a one-bay extension had been added in the 1830s. Linton had turned the centre window on the ground floor into a bay which let extra light into the library, while the ground-floor window to the left of it lit the drawing room. The house was roughcast, later washed a pale yellow colour. Clearly it would not do as it was, and by the spring of 1872 Ruskin was at work on improvements. These included building a lodge and a coach house at the foot of the short, steep drive and adding a corner turret to the house itself. Although not ambitious for a man of his fortune (he had inherited over £150,000 during the previous six years) or passion for architecture, they are an intriguing example of Ruskinian theory put into effect, for Ruskin was here (for the only time in his life) his own architect.

The first thing one looks for is the influence of Venice, but it is scarcely to be seen. Only the long mullioned window to the new dining room, which was added in 1878–9 – the seven lights of the window said, implausibly, to symbolize the Seven Lamps of Architecture – strikes a faintly Venetian note. The porch is a modest classical affair. What Brantwood shows is Ruskin's increasing commitment to local styles, prefiguring the Arts and Crafts movement, and his pleasure in rough and rugged buildings – smooth finishes had become all too easy to achieve thanks to the hated mechanization. Such was the state of society and the building trades that roughness was not easy to obtain. It required constant supervision to see that the local builder, George Usher, built the lodge of a traditional material – Coniston slate – in the traditional, unelaborate way. 'If I ever left him alone for a day,' Ruskin wrote in a note on a Fine Art Society exhibition in 1879–80, 'some corner stone was sure to be sent from Bath or Portland, and the ledges I had left to invite stonecrop and swallows, trimmed away in the advanced style of the railway station at Carnforth.' Finally the builder acquiesced and was pleased with the result, while observing doubtfully, 'Everybody who sees it, cracks about it.'

The lodge was larger than Ruskin had intended since the couple who were to live in it, his valet Frederick Crawley and his wife, had three children. The accommodation was still not over-generous, and became tighter when one of the Severn girls took over a bedroom as a studio, requiring a new staircase (since removed) to be built outside. There were two front rooms on the ground floor with a dividing wall between. To his great disappointment the wall came exactly where Ruskin had hoped to put the front door. 'I was annoyed because the plan of the house inside did not admit of a door to the front,' he wrote to Mrs Severn on 4 March 1872. 'So I gave up my door – but we will have a creeping tree instead and manage to make it all pretty.' The lodge is entered by a door at the side.

The lodge also has turrets to either side. The turret erected on the main house is similar, more elaborate and polygonal in form, the object being to give a panoramic view of the lake from its windows. The turrets may look somewhat Germanic, but that was not what Ruskin had in mind. 'Before the glass was in, it looked just like a bit of Kenilworth Castle, the window mullions seen against dark . . . but even now, it is very pretty, and does me credit.' The parallel would hardly strike one today, but it appealed to the intense romanticism of Ruskin's nature, fired by his reading of Sir Walter Scott. 'And at this day, though I have kind invitations enough to visit America,' he wrote in *Praeterita*, 'I could not, even for a couple of months, live in a country so miserable as to possess no castles.' In about 1878 he added the new dining room to the house, along with the seven-light window already mentioned. Ruskin planned the roof so that it would shelter bees, which it did – although he was surprised afterwards to hear from the builder that 'he would not like me to put flowerpots on it'.

Ruskin believed that it was right for all classes of society to share in manual labour and had made this an unwritten tenet of the Guild of St George, which he had founded in 1871. Brantwood was an opportunity to put the principles of the Guild into practice, although what was achieved here, as on the Guild's other land, was disappointing. After his illness of 1871, he was helped to recover his health by 'setting to work in the lovely little work garden where the bee-house is'. Soon the Oxford disciples who visited him at Brantwood found their hours of exercise consigned to a project equivalent to digging the Hinksey Road: building a harbour on the lake.

Ruskin was a good oarsman, and his boat, the *Jumping Jenny*, is still at the house. A little harbour – there had been one before, but it was 'bad' – was necessary to give shelter from the lake waves in stormy weather. Work began on 18 February 1873, Ruskin's chief assistants being his future biographer, the artist and antiquarian W. G. Collingwood, and Alexander Wedderburn, who had come north to translate Xenophon's *Economist* for an edition for use by people joining the Guild of St George. 'The harbour *will* be a beauty,' opined Ruskin on 20 April, 'but will take me . . . till the year 1880, before it is done.' The walls were less than waist height, but, as in so many of Ruskin's enterprises, he was amused to discover that zeal and theory were no equals to practical experience: a waller in the shape of a local farmer's son had to be called in to ensure that they would not collapse. 'My own better acquaintance with the laws of gravity and of statistics,' he told an Oxford lecture audience, 'did not enable me, myself, to build six inches of dyke that would stand.' It was a lesson in life which confirmed Ruskin in his utopian belief in the dignity of labour.

An ambition of the Guild of St George had been to obtain land for husbandry by reclaiming waste ground. At Brantwood Ruskin attempted to bring a section of moor into cultivation by stripping the earth to stone, turning it and terracing it down the hillside. Corn was tried without success; however, the land was found able to bear fruit trees. In a similar spirit Ruskin encouraged local industries, especially the making of 'Ruskin lace', and a blacksmith began a line in the 'Ruskin shovel' for the hearth.

Another aspect of Ruskin's practical work was the garden. Collingwood recalled that, as they stood by the porch, visitors might glimpse through the window the writer's soft hat, thick gloves and stout knife – evidence that he had lately returned from woodcutting. When Ruskin came to Brantwood he found it surrounded by, in his phrase, 'uncommon green evergreens', and set about clearing paths through the bush. He was his own landscape gardener as he was his own architect, to considerable effect.

'The visitor to Brantwood who went for an afternoon ramble with his host would be taken, if in spring time, through a mist of wild hyacinths, to a clearing in the wood, where, at "Fairfield Seat", a view of the lake and mountains bursts open,' wrote E. T. Cook and Wedderburn in their introduction to the *Love's Meine* and *Proserpina* volume of the library edition of Ruskin's *Works*, 'or, if in autumn, up to the moor, bright with heather and bracken, and rich in wild raspberries and strawberries.' He took pleasure in diverting streams and making waterfalls, and beside one waterfall had erected a monumental seat made from sheets of slate. Ruskin's neighbour at The Thwaite, Susanna Beever, sent her gardener to build it.

During Ruskin's ownership, the estate around Brantwood grew from five acres to over five hundred. The cottage also expanded piecemeal into a fairly large country house. In later years, the impulse to build was more the Severns' than Ruskin's. Both in London – where Ruskin had given them the lease of his parents' house on their marriage – and at Brantwood, as well as on some of Ruskin's numerous travels, they lived a shared existence. When they were separated, Ruskin almost always wrote to Mrs Severn once if not twice a day – often in the infuriating 'tabby talk' inspired by their joint love of cats.

As the Severn family grew, Brantwood grew with it. More bedrooms were built over an archway and then a large studio, commensurate with Severn's role as a successful artist. A roof strut in the studio is signed *William Deney Painter Coniston and C* and dated 1892. After Ruskin's death in 1900, the drawing room was enlarged; the Severns had a position in the county to maintain, which would have been of little interest to Ruskin.

It pleased Ruskin, though, that a campaign of building undertaken in 1882–3 made Mrs Severn happy. But one can surely detect a note of ruefulness beneath the old-fashioned courtesy with which he thanked Mr Marshall, the architect, for what he described as 'the new house'. The enlarged Brantwood was, he wrote, 'a complete delight to all who live in it and a sight for all the neighbours; nor am I annoyed with it in general effect in the landscape myself, though it has destroyed all my claims to humility of Cottage life!'

By growing piecemeal, Brantwood evolved into a sometimes awkward house, lacking in unity of impact and at first sight curiously muddled for the dwelling of such a sage. But its long evolution was a fulfilment of Picturesque doctrine, which held that a building should expand as changing needs dictated. Furthermore the idea of the cottage had a peculiar place in Ruskin's thought. Thirty-five years before buying Brantwood, he had advocated the 'cottage-villa' as a desirable building type for country mansions in *The Poetry of Architecture*. 'Buildings of a very large size,' he had written, 'are decidedly destructive of effect among the English lakes.' The broken mass of the cottage-villa suited a landscape on a less majestic scale than the Alps. He also had a special feeling for the simple rural cottage, because of its natural harmony with its surroundings. 'Not that we have any idea of living in a cottage, as a comfortable thing,' he wrote, concluding the section on The Cottage, 'not that we prefer mud to marble, or deal to mahogany; but that, with it, we leave much of what is most beautiful of earth, the low and bee-inhabited scenery, which is full of quiet and prideless emotion, of such calmness as we can imagine prevailing over our earth when it was new in heaven.' Calmness to Ruskin – sensitive, tormented, often sunk in depression as he contemplated the ugliness of industrialization – became increasingly elusive. But the beauties of the Lake District lifted his spirit, and Brantwood can only be understood in the context of the landscape that so much thrilled its owner.

The challenge of Brantwood is to understand why, in some respects, it was so ordinary. Ruskin was not only an art critic who held his age enthralled, but a painter of exquisite delicacy. He had an unrivalled collection of works by J. M. W. Turner. The wallpaper in the study at Brantwood was specially made to a design copied from the priest's embroidered sleeve in Marco Marziale's *The Circumcision of Christ* in the National Gallery, London. Yet Ruskin's white-and-gold coffee service was conspicuously run-of-the-mill – not plain in an Arts and Crafts sense, just typical of middle-class taste. The same goes for much of the furniture, such as the mahogany dining chairs. One would have expected him to patronize Morris and Company or the Kendal cabinetmaker Arthur Simpson, who knew Morris and was favoured by W. G. Collingwood. Instead, he bought from Snell of Albemarle Street, who had furnished his parents' house.

'What often surprised me very much was his not caring what colours went together,' wrote Arthur Severn in his memoir of the professor. Ruskin noticed beautiful things, but 'he wouldn't mind a room in execrable taste as long as there was a comfortable chair to sit in.' An explanation for the furnishing of Brantwood lies partly in Ruskin's innate conservatism. 'I am, and my father was before me, a violent Tory of the old school,' he began *Praeterita*, '– Walter Scott's school, that is to say, and Homer's.' Old associations were important. The objects of Ruskin's piety towards the past sat side by side with those acquired through his highly developed love of beauty, whether art or rocks and flowers. As a result, when you walk through the house you are constantly brought up sharp by the contrast between the majestic and the banal.

The heart of the house is Ruskin's study, in the old cottage part, facing south-east over Coniston Water. It stands between the drawing room and the dining room (these, apart from the hall and Arthur Severn's studio, are all the principal spaces). 'You will jump and squeak, I am sure, when you see the study again,' Ruskin wrote to Joan Severn on 19 January 1873. 'It is another room. When Pussie's away, The mice will play. I've got my great Turner Geneva over the chimneypiece. And all four beautiful Hunts over the sofa! . . . and the Turner Aosta beside the door.' There was a cabinet for watercolours with upright sliding shelves in the base. Each of the four bookcases in the room had names such as 'Geology' and 'Botany' – although the Botany bookcase, for instance, did not contain only botany books, nor were all the botany books in the house to be found there. Ruskin was a keen buyer of books, but as he was almost as active as a giver, his library was not enormous.

Although Ruskin possessed an astonishing range of books – on history, architecture, the fine arts, botany, geology and other subjects – and some of the books were rare, he could not be called a bibliophile. He did not hesitate to saw off the top and bottom of a tome that did not fit into its allotted shelf, and manuscript leaves were frequently given away to students whom he thought would learn a lesson in art from them. Other books were put in his bedroom. 'The new bookcases make my room quite lovely and finished,' he wrote to Mrs Severn in January 1873, 'and I've got the Encyclopaedia! looking *so* nice, and all the *profane* books – none of the religious ones – that I sent upstairs.' There were also books in the drawing room: Lady Burne-Jones remembered how Ruskin played with her daughter Margaret, at jumping over piles of them.

The most precise description of the study comes from Ruskin himself. In 1881 he provided a careful inventory to complement a drawing made by A. Macdonald. Scattered about on the tables and desks were a medieval lectionary, a missal and various rocks on which Ruskin was working at the time. Propped against the wall were the framed leaves of a psalter, leaning against the desk Ruskin's own last sketch of porches at St Mark's, Venice. Two 'bran-new globes' had arrived in the 1870s, but, as Ruskin commented in *Deucalion*, '. . . there's so much in them that I can see nothing. The names are too many on the earth, and the stars too crowded in the heaven.'

When the new dining room, with its view of the lake, was added in 1878–9, the old dining room, so small that the servants had difficulty squeezing between the chairs and the wall as they served, was made into an overflow for books. The mahogany table and chairs in the new room came from Snell, while over the fireplace hung Catena's portrait of Doge Andrea Gritti, then thought to be by Titian. Other pictures and 'eighty pretty pieces of china' added to the decor.

Ruskin's day would begin shortly after dawn, so that by the time a breakfast with local strawberries and cream was served, he had already got in several hours' writing – and could regale his guests with a reading of the results. This would be followed by a passage from a novel by Scott, some of whose manuscripts Ruskin owned. After dinner the company would again assemble in the drawing room – some of the men having meanwhile sneaked off for a cigarette by the lake, as Ruskin detested the smell of tobacco smoke. They would play chess, which he enjoyed and at which he was 'not unskilful', or they would talk.

Ruskin's bedroom was where his most loved paintings were hung. 'When I die,' he said of the Turners around his bed, 'I hope that they may be the last things my eyes will rest on in this world.' His first bedroom had a turret, designed for views over the lake. But the hallucinations he experienced during his first attack of madness remained too vivid for him to stay there when he recovered, and his bed was moved next door, to the room where he died. Like all the paintings in the house, the Turners were constantly being rearranged and rehung.

Ruskin at Brantwood – trying hopelessly to fry a sole and happy in arranging his teacups – is a different figure from the one suggested by the more pontifical of his works. Overwork made him tired, however, and he frequently complained of feeling 'misby' (as he put it in the cat talk he spoke with Mrs Severn), especially when he was on his own for long periods. 'The relief to me is very great,' he wrote of a visit by the artist William Holman Hunt and his wife in May 1873, 'for when I am alone the shadow of the past and future is always heavy on me, but somehow the human presences take it away.' He had many visitors, including Charles Darwin, and the beauty of the Lakes was an unfailing source of joy. The last era of his life was spent increasingly at Brantwood, and after his death he was buried in Coniston churchyard.

16. The Triumph of Local Materials
Marsh Court

On the hills above the Test Valley in Hampshire stands one of the most remarkable houses in Britain, with completely white walls that make it shimmer like a vision from *The Fairy Queen*. The walls are built from clunch, a kind of chalk: it comes from the lower beds, which are harder than the upper ones, but even so makes an unlikely building material. If you lean against one of the arches in the broad entrance passage, your shoulder will be dusted in white. This is Marsh Court, begun in 1899. Clunch had been used for building before this: you sometimes see blocks of it used to make a chequerwork pattern on façades around Hampshire and Wiltshire. An example is Lake House in Wiltshire, where the other squares are knapped flint; flint, another rock made from the shells of sea creatures, is often found in conjunction with chalk. In the Vale of the White Horse in Wiltshire, where the White Horse itself is formed of chalk, many of the old cottages are built from clunch. But it is unprecedented to find a clunch house of the scale of Marsh

Court. The architect, the impish genius Edwin Lutyens, is supposed to have built it for a bet.

Marsh Court makes a small bow towards the chequerwork tradition of Lake House: a narrow pattern of small flint squares runs across the bottom of the entrance front, like a policeman's cap band. Other little episodes of flint and tile seem to bubble to the surface of the chalk, these occasional, irregular dots breaking what might otherwise have been the overpowering purity of the white. Most intriguing of all are the cases where knobbly flints can be seen poking out of the beautifully squared blocks. These are flints which have occurred naturally in the chalk. Lutyens could have discarded the blocks which were compromised by their appearance; instead, he kept them and made a virtue of it. This is evidence of a profound change of mood which overcame architecture towards the end of the nineteenth century. With the advent of the railways, the Steam Age had shattered distance, making it possible for industrially produced materials – bricks from Bedfordshire, glazed tiles from Staffordshire, limestone from Portland – to be sent all over the country. Victorian tools allowed builders to achieve a mechanically regular finish which seemed close to perfection. At Marsh Court, Lutyens used the improbable material of clunch precisely because it was local to an area famous for its chalk streams. He rejoiced in the imperfections made by the flints. The oddity would have appealed to him as a joke (he was an irrepressible joker), but there was a serious point, too. Lutyens belonged to a generation of architects who wanted to capture the virtues of the traditional England they saw disappearing before their eyes. A sometimes exaggerated use of local materials was part of their fight against uniformity.

Lutyens shared his love of local materials with the architects of the Arts and Crafts movement. The great engine of this movement had been William Morris. Brawny, gregarious, red-haired, Morris threw himself at the task of improving his contemporaries' lives and taste. When he was not writing epic poetry, he was weaving textiles; when he was not weaving textiles, he was delivering lectures on his romantic brand of socialism; when he was not lecturing, he was writing utopian tracts, or founding the Society for the Protection of Ancient Buildings, or designing wallpaper. The nail which stabilized this fizzing Catherine wheel of energy was the home. Morris had an idealized concept of it, reinforced by his vision of the Middle Ages. Naturally his own homes were important to him.

The first was Red House at Bexleyheath in Kent, begun in 1859 by a twenty-five-year-old Morris, newly married to a beautiful young wife. Designed by his austere young architect friend Philip Webb, the idiom was that of a Gothic Revival parsonage, combining red brick, pointed arches and sash windows. But for Morris it breathed romance through turrets that had been first conceived during an architectural tour of the Seine valley in France. There was a porch that Morris pictured as a resting place for pilgrims en route to Canterbury, the road to which passed nearby. Artist friends who stayed with the Morrises were pressed into service painting murals and decorating furniture on Arthurian themes, designing stained-glass windows and making tiles. Everything in the house was thought out from first principles. The result was not always comfortable, but the ebullience of Morris's personality – he was a prodigious host – made up for it.

It was the need to furnish Red House which inspired Morris to found his own decorating firm of Morris and Company, with offices in London. As time went on, the demands of London increased and he could spend fewer days among his apple trees in Kent. Besides, his investments were doing badly. Though not very large, Red House, with its stables, was expensive to run. It was – and is – penetratingly cold in winter, and roasting during the summer: a more experienced architect than the previously untried Webb might not have made the main rooms face north. And the house had never fulfilled all Morris's dreams for it. So he and his wife moved on, eventually coming to rest in a stone-built Elizabethan manor house outside Lechlade in Gloucestershire, called Kelmscott Manor.

Kelmscott was the Arts and Crafts ideal, a house so organic that it seemed (in Morris's words) to 'grow out of the soil'. It was also in what became an epicentre of Arts and Crafts activity, the Cotswolds. The area began to attract artistic interest in the 1880s, when the painter John Singer Sargent, the novelist Henry James and others formed a summer colony at Broadway. With its old-fashioned villages, their grey stone streets dignified by classical doorcases, their churches still redolent of the wealth of the medieval wool trade, the Cotswolds were far from London, pre-industrial and cheap. Ernest Gimson and the Barnsley brothers, Ernest and Sidney, established themselves at Sapperton, to make furniture with their own hands. Gimson was an architect as well as a craftsman: his father had known Morris, and he was one of the band of young architects on the committee of the Society for the Protection of Ancient Buildings, studying 'the common facts of traditional buildings in scores and hundreds of examples' under the tutelage of Philip Webb. Detmar Blow, whom Ruskin had taken up after discovering him sketching in Abbeville Cathedral in France, was the clerk of works for a cottage called Stoneywell which Gimson built in Leicestershire: a house that seems even more organic than Kelmscott, emerging from an outcrop of rock.

It was a busy time for domestic architects. Blow eventually established a practice building beautiful country houses, often in Wiltshire, for the gilded aesthetes and intellectuals known as the Souls. C. R. Voysey specialized in somewhat puritanical houses, generally in the Home Counties, with whitewashed walls, low ceilings and woodwork with hearts cut out of it – Voysey designed every detail, down to the door knockers. M. H. Baillie Scott had a more decorative taste; his sensuous designs were enthusiastically received on the Continent, where Art Nouveau had stimulated an appetite for colour and pattern. No success, however, could equal that of the witty, elfin, shy, romantic Lutyens. By charm, perseverance and talent he built up unrivalled connections among the more progressive wing of the Edwardian establishment. He wooed and dazzled them: visitors to his buildings today are still seduced.

As a young man, Lutyens had the good luck to be taken up by Gertrude Jekyll, best known now as a garden designer but an out-and-out Arts and Crafts figure who only turned to gardening as her eyesight failed in middle age. This dumpy, initially intimidating woman, wearing small, wire-framed spectacles, her grey hair pulled back into a bun, was forty-six when the twenty-year-old Lutyens first met her at a Surrey tea party in 1889. She had been an artist and craftswoman, had known Ruskin and Morris, and possessed strong ideas about architecture, some of which she instilled into her protégé when he built a house for her, Munstead Wood. Jekyll took Lutyens on drives around the Surrey lanes, discussing the old local tile-hung, hipped-roofed farmhouses and cottages.

Lutyens himself was a West Surrey boy. The tenth child of an officer in the Indian army, he had grown up in a ramshackle, arty family – his grandfather had been a painter. As a boy he had been delicate; it prevented him from going to public school, like his brothers, and he always regretted the lack of social confidence he suffered as a result. It was obvious from his early teens that he would become an architect. Gifted with an exceptional visual memory, as well as an innate understanding of three-dimensional form, he developed a novel way of recording the old buildings that he saw – sketching them, not on paper, but on a piece of glass held up to the subject, the lines being drawn with a sharpened edge of soap. He did not need sketchbooks, and despised the reliance that Ernest George, the fashionable country-house architect in whose office he served a brief apprenticeship, placed on them. Lutyens already had the elements of Surrey's tumble-down buildings distilled in his mind, and they formed the basis of his early style.

Aunt Bumps, as Lutyens called Gertrude Jekyll, had many friends. She introduced him to them, and it was the foundation of his practice. By the turn of the century, Miss Jekyll – to use her usual designation – was contributing to *Country Life*, a magazine that had been created in 1897 to celebrate the life of the country house. Again, she made an introduction, this time to its proprietor, Edward Hudson. Hudson and Lutyens, both of them tongue-tied, got on famously.

The early issues of *Country Life* celebrated old crafts, picturesque duck ponds, gnarled rural characters, horses, hunting and dogs. But the magazine also reflected some of the changes that were overtaking Surrey and everywhere else without disapproval. Odd though it may seem now, it was rather a progressive magazine, championing a new way of life – the small house near London, the motor car that made week-ending more convenient, the game of golf, the collecting of mellow, genuinely old furniture. Edward VII's plutocratic friends, with their flashy gilt furniture, elaborate driven game shoots and gambling, were rarely mentioned. Every week *Country Life* would publish a long article on a fine old country house, or perhaps a new one: thanks to developments in printing, they could be illustrated with handsome photographs, lit and processed with the subtlety of watercolours. Lutyens, mostly building for rich businessmen, barristers, politicians and the occasional aristocrat, was soon an integral part of *Country Life*'s world. 'Huddy', as Lutyens called Hudson, made it his mission to promote Lutyens's work in his magazine. He also commissioned no fewer than three country houses from him, as well as the *Country Life* office in Covent Garden in London.

Marsh Court was designed for another friend, Herbert Johnson. Like Hudson's Deanery Garden, it has a Jekyll garden – a sunken garden around a pond, and a pergola accompanied by rills and alcoves of thin, closely laid tiles. But Johnson's garden was fairly small in relation to the size of his house, not being his major interest. Johnson made his money from stockbroking. It was not considered to be a completely gentlemanly activity at the turn of the century, but money came easily, and he dedicated the rest of his life to sport, later covering the walls of his ballroom with the trophy heads of animals shot in Africa. The site of Marsh Court was chosen for its proximity to the Test, popularly regarded, not least by Lutyens, as the finest of English trout rivers. Fishing was a pastime that Johnson shared with Lutyens, a country boy at heart. 'I worked all the morning and then after lunch went out to fish,' he wrote in a letter during a solitary dinner at Marsh Court in September 1905. After tea he nearly caught a whopper, but it got away. It was often a 'happy day' for Lutyens when he visited Marsh Court.

Marsh Court was larger than many of the new houses featured in *Country Life*, and further from London. But contemporaries would have seen it as radical. For one thing there was the clunch. Inside the house, the use of pegged oak is almost extravagant. Oak was the Arts and Crafts material par excellence. Architects who wanted to dissociate themselves from the modern industrial world rejected commonplace iron nails in favour of oak pegs, which bristle from the staircase at Marsh Court. One of the bedrooms has a crown post roof. Door hinges were hammered by black-smiths, in the old-fashioned way. Carved flowers and animals appear in odd places; like the hinges, they were not given the high polish that might suggest the use of a machine; the marks of the carver's tools are still visible. Oak even intrudes into the bathrooms, with their enormous towel rails, as thick as elephants' legs; the floors are made of oak trellis, so that surplus water pours through the holes in the floor into lead drip pans underneath.

Many of the ceilings are decorated with garlands of grapes. In the eighteenth century, Jackson and Sons pioneered a composite of paper pulp mixed with glue which could take fine detail from wooden moulds; the Adam brothers used it for their nervously busy geometrical ceilings. Lutyens rejected this material in favour of the old, more blobby form of plasterwork used in the seventeenth century, and recently revived by Ernest Gimson. This is the style of the ceiling of the broad entrance passage, which runs along the front of the house at right angles to the front door.

There is a door from this passage, not opposite the front door because Lutyens, at this stage of his career, opposed symmetry, and besides the room it goes into preserves the glimmer of a notion of a great hall (and is therefore entered at one end.) The great hall had been revived by paternalistic Victorians, who wanted somewhere to feast the tenantry and uphold the other duties of a Christian landowner. By the Edwardian period it had morphed into something altogether more relaxed: the living hall. The term *lounge* was sometimes used: a place, as the term implies, where you didn't have to sit up straight. The living hall became almost a badge of the new architecture, signifying that a new state of social evolution had been achieved.

Lutyens's hall at Marsh Court is not quite of this kind; it is difficult to find a point of difference, architecturally, between this room and the drawing room next door. They are part of an enfilade of three rooms along the south side of the house (the third is the dining room), opening into each other in a way that works very well for entertaining large parties. Seventeenth-century rather than Georgian in style, these rooms are not Arts and Crafts, but rather a precursor of Lutyens's revived English Renaissance style, which – nodding towards Sir Christopher Wren – he punningly called 'Wrenaissance'. The dining room is luxuriously panelled in walnut. Classicism would become the High Game which Lutyens played, outside as well as inside, when building Heathcote in Yorkshire (1906) – 'hard labour, hard thinking', as Lutyens called it – and its successors. At the rather earlier Marsh Court, it may have been a requirement of the client.

The billiard room forms part of a suite of rooms known as a male preserve; with a nearby gun room and room for the removal of rain-soaked sporting clothes downstairs, it would, in a big Victorian house, have communicated with a corridor of 'bachelor bedrooms' for the legions of young, and not so young, men who came to shoot, having not yet found mates. Marsh Court is not on this scale, but the concept survives. The billiard tables sit on a giant carved slab of – what else? – chalk.

Gertrude Jekyll was not the only woman to take Lutyens under her wing; another was Barbara Webb, living at Milford in Surrey, and she it was who introduced Lutyens to his future wife, Lady Emily Lytton, the daughter of an earl, now deceased, who had been Viceroy of India. The Lyttons were then living at Knebworth, a big country house, in straitened circumstances, so the couple had to wait until the young architect was earning enough for them to marry. Meanwhile, the bashful Lutyens expressed his romantic devotion to his love by designing a little casket covered in green leather, full of emblems of their future life together: an anchor, symbolizing hope; a brass pipe stopper (Lutyens always had a pipe in his mouth: the stopper evoked the pipes that would be smoked by the domestic hearth); a heart; a crucifix; a tiny Bible accompanied by a magnifying glass and so on. Among them was a sketch for the house that he hoped they would build. In letters he would doodle pictures of himself as a knight errant, carrying a T-square. The marriage finally took place in the church in the park at Knebworth in 1897; the couple spent their honeymoon in Holland, where already a hint of future differences emerged on the beach at Schreveningen. She liked looking at the sea; Lutyens hated it, and sat next to her, his chair facing the other way, firmly towards the land.

With Lutyens constantly called away to country houses such as Marsh Court, Emily felt neglected. Through some French clients of her husband's called Mallet she became enthralled by the new religion of Theosophy and fell, platonically, into the arms of the handsome young Krishnamurti, the Indian boy whom the Theosophists had identified as the next incarnation of the Maitreya Buddha. This brought Lutyens much pain. But in a letter to Emily he had to admit, 'Architecture takes me away from you in some ways.' That was literally true of his punishing round of site visits, but architecture was also a country of the spirit for which his wife had no passport.

Critics have said that, despite their bathrooms, Lutyens's houses are not very comfortable to live in; that may be because he had never been very comfortable at home himself. And there was more discomfort to come. Within a couple of years the First World War had shattered the well-upholstered, dreamy world of his client base. Afterwards came commissions for war memorials, New Delhi and the Midland Bank headquarters – but few houses. Two stand out. The first is White Lodge on the Cliff at Roedean in Sussex, which Lutyens remodelled for Victoria, Lady Sackville; she became an eccentrically close friend, possibly a lover, whom he called MacSack (she called him MacNed). The other is a mill house, extended to become an integral part of a water garden; the main room is a T-shaped living hall, with windows at the sides of the crossbar to throw natural light onto what was, in effect, a stage. On the stage played the dramatic Hungarian cellist painted by Augustus John in a lava flow of red dress: Guilhermina Suggia. Plumpton Place in Sussex was the last of the houses that Lutyens designed for his old friend Edward Hudson. Huddy at last had found love.

17. A Brewer's Hymn to Empire
Elveden Hall

As you make your way along the A12, through that sandiest, scrubbiest part of Suffolk known as the Breckland, where prehistoric man dug mines for flints, you feel that something big is just round the corner. Big is exactly what Elveden Hall is. It announces itself with a memorial column, capped by an urn, that is visible at the end of a mile-long straight of road.

When the column was new, it was possible to climb the 146 stairs – lit by slit windows in the fluting of the shaft – to a viewing platform on top of the Corinthian capital. From there you could see across the tops of the trees to the water tower, two miles distant, with a small mountain range of roof ridges and a copper dome marking the Hall itself. The dome which stands over the entrance front was a piece of rhetoric that the architect, William Young, was unable to resist. He was engaged on the tub-thumping, neo-Baroque War Office in Whitehall when Elveden was on his drawing board – although the effort to complete that official commission led him to neglect his health, and he died in 1900, leaving the house to be finished by his son Clyde. The dome is empty. So now is the Hall itself.

The gorgeously plump knoles, sofas and daybeds; the medal cabinet designed by Sir William Chambers; the ranks of coalscuttles and water canisters . . . all were auctioned by Christie's at a four-day sale in 1984. Stencilled notices to American airmen could still be seen on the walls, a memory of the wartime requisitioning from which the house had never wholly recovered. For all this, Elveden still spoke boldly of the English house at a high-water mark of imperial self-confidence. Here was its zenith of elaboration and comfort. The romantic Lutyens and the shy Edward Hudson, arriving from one of the former's subtle, oakily austere houses in the Home Counties, would have shivered metaphorically – just as the Christie's team shivered physically as they catalogued the unheated house that freezing January – if they had come here.

Yet even Lutyens and Hudson would surely have recognized that Elveden is also a tour de force. Although the copper dome may be false, there is another dome in the house, the one that surmounts the chilly splendour of the Indian Hall: a monument to the British Empire which seems all the more extraordinary for its Edwardian owner's apparent lack of contact with India. Scarcely less remarkable were the 'servants' offices' – the housekeeper's rooms, the kitchens, the boot rooms – which drove the domestic machine forward; all were demolished after the Second World War.

That owner was Edward Cecil Guinness, 1st Earl of Iveagh, the great-grandson of Arthur Guinness who founded the brewery. Iveagh typified something of the new values governing grand late Victorian and Edwardian society, particularly that which centred on Edward VII himself. Iveagh was very rich and understood the tastes of royal guests at a time when comfort and sophistication were becoming more important than ancestry. Edward VII stayed at Elveden (whose luxurious atmosphere impressed Henry 'Chips' Channon even after the First World War) over every other New

Year, alternating with Chatsworth. But Iveagh was not a dinosaur; unlike his brother Lord Ardilaun, who sold his stake in the brewery and, following the traditional route to social acceptance, bought land, he stayed close to the brewery, and worked. He kept at it. In her diary for 1882 Lady Iveagh noted that her husband had 'so few of the pleasures or enjoyments that other young men have and hating his buisness [*sic*] he is obliged to work at it like a slave'. His marriage to 'Dodo', as she was known, had been a love match; she was a cousin of limited means.

When Iveagh had bought the estate in 1894, there had already been a house on it, most of which dated from the era of Prince Duleep Singh. By turns sad, cruel, devout, romantic and, in later days, revoltingly obese, the Prince had come to England at the same time as the Koh-i-Noor diamond, now part of the Crown Jewels. The British, in the shape of Lord Dalhousie, had entered the Punjab at a period of factional infighting, during which most of Singh's relatives had died. Singh became ruler at the age of five; Dalhousie removed him from the throne in return for a pension from the East India Company. Queen Victoria was enchanted by him when he arrived in London. She felt considerable trepidation at showing him the Koh-i-Noor, which had been reduced to half its original size by cutting in the European manner. (The moment when he did see it again was described by one witness as 'I may truly say . . . to me one of the most excruciatingly uncomfortable quarters-of-an-hour that I ever passed'.) Duleep Singh was encouraged to play with the royal children, and later the Prince of Wales would stay with him at Elveden, beginning the association that would continue into the era of his successor there. Singh had the house remodelled for his marriage in 1864. Even *The Times of India* called the bride, a half-Abyssinian and half-German girl, 'interesting rather than handsome', and she was hopelessly ill equipped for her role, having been chosen from a mission school – according to one of those engaged in the quest – expressly for her ignorance of 'fashionable aristocratic life'. Singh transferred his attentions to waitresses, chorus girls, the chemin-de-fer table, and partridge shooting in Suffolk.

Outside, Duleep Singh's Elveden, designed by the unspectacular John Norton, looked like a large town house in Kensington. Inside it was considerably more exotic. Norton 'had the gratification', as *The Builder* called it in November 1871, 'of being instructed to decorate the interior with pure Indian ornament'; Singh, who had never been paid his full stipend by the East India Company, was becoming increasingly conscious of his patrimony. Sadly his son, Frederick Duleep Singh, who wrote a useful paper on the 'history and antiquities' of Elveden, thought the Indian work insufficiently extraordinary to merit more than a passing comment; the ceilings, he wrote, 'were copied from the palaces of Lahore and Delhi'. This remark conceals what must have been one of the most remarkable interiors in Britain. Nearly everywhere was encrusted with Indian-style ornament made out of plaster, with a cast-iron balustrade to the staircase, which was lacquered in sealing-wax red. Messrs Powell of Whitefriars studded the drawing room with shards of silvered convex glass.

One can only hope it made Duleep Singh happy; the costs of the project sunk him financially, and he ended by re-embracing his old religion, taking up his claim to the Punjab throne, flirting with Russia, living increasingly abroad and signing himself in a letter to the Prince of Wales, 'Sovereign of the Sikh Nation and proud implacable foe of England'. It was a pathetic gesture of defiance, for he had no serious support outside his native country, and his attempts to return there were frustrated with absurd simplicity by the British police. After the death of his abandoned first wife, his second marriage was to a young English girl who called herself an actress. He died in Paris. It was a condition of one of his money-raising expedients with the India Office that Elveden was sold.

William Young's scheme built a mirror image of the Maharajah's house, joined to the original by a central dome (though, typically for this date, the new wing was not quite identical – the Gothic Revival's dubious gift to Edwardian classicism). The result was enormous, at a time when houses were tending to become smaller. One has a feeling that not all the rooms had a real purpose. The former morning room, for instance, became, somewhat obscurely, the 'old study'.

The plans for Elveden had been finished by the time of William Young's death; Clyde Young was then thirty years old. Elveden had been preceded by another house commission from a millionaire member of the Marlborough House set, the 5th Earl Cadogan, for whom William Young remodelled Culford Hall, half a dozen miles away. East Anglia, which offered the pleasures of Newmarket and shooting and had the royal blessing of Sandringham, was very attractive to the Edwardian rich; another arrival, at the stud farm Moulton Paddocks, was the financier Sir Ernest Cassel. Clyde Young must have made a good impression at Elveden. In about 1910 he designed Pyrford Court in Surrey for Lord Iveagh's son, the 2nd Earl.

After William Young's death, Iveagh's agent, Colonel G. W. Addison, wrote to Clyde about the new arrangements for work on Elveden. While his 'father's design, speaking generally', was 'to be adhered to', and the building operations remained 'entirely in your hands', Iveagh reserved the right to consult J. M. Brydon 'without any additional charge other than travelling expenses'. This was another establishment choice, Brydon being the architect of the other great Whitehall building of these years, the enormous new Government Buildings on the corner of Great George and Parliament streets.

Iveagh would have poop-pooped up to the new Elveden in a shiny new motor car. He was an enthusiastic motorist, having the experimental rubber blocks that were to have made up the floor of the *porte-cochère* changed to wood, as rubber would have been damaged by the 'oil which drips so much from the motor cars'. A flight of steps led up to the octagonal entrance hall, panelled in wainscot. The ceiling was in the 'Adam' style, and it seems that the idea of the room may have been taken from Robert Adam's engraving of the mausoleum of the Emperor Diocletian at Spalato, which is circular, but with a similar use of attached columns with arches above. The marble for the columns caused immense problems. While the alabaster for the caps and bases was easy to obtain, Verde Antico from Ireland – Irish Green – was difficult to find in large blocks without vents; the quarry was owned by Americans who sent almost their whole output of long stones across the Atlantic. It was decided it would be best to have green Cipollino at Elveden instead.

After the sombre entrance hall, opening the wainscot double door into the Indian Hall, with five south-facing French windows at the other end of the room, can make one blink. The Indian Hall is almost completely lined with white Carrara marble, in contrast to the plaster of Duleep Singh's rooms – which, with their more colourful, if tawdry, decoration, perhaps showed a greater feeling for the real spirit of India. Iveagh's is an astonishing private monument to the vision of Empire, even given the taste for grand marble-lined spaces among the very rich (a younger generation nicknamed Sir Ernest Cassel's entrance hall in London 'the giant's lavatory'). Elveden stands alone in terms of scale and conception. Emotionally it anticipated Imre Kiralfy's vision of spotless white palaces, domes and towers which became the architecture of the 'White City' Franco-British Exhibition of 1908 (the first published views of the idea appeared in *The Graphic* in February 1905, less than eighteen months after the Indian Hall was completed).

The Indian Hall is in every respect an astonishing structure. Photographs of Indian palaces in family albums suggest that Iveagh may have travelled in India, but since they are all of architecture they could equally – and more probably – have been obtained in England with the Indian Hall in mind. The most remarkable thing is the thoroughness with which he went into the scheme. The cost of over £70,000 was prodigious, and the details were designed under the eye of Sir Caspar Purdon Clarke, then director of the recently renamed Victoria and Albert Museum. When the work was over, Purdon Clarke proposed an inscription that explains part of its purpose, which was 'to reproduce, in England, the best examples of Moghul Architecture'. Like the Victoria and Albert Museum itself, it was conceived – by Purdon Clarke at least – as essentially didactic.

Duleep Singh's decoration had been typical of Rajput palace architecture of the time, impure to a scholarly eye, but consistent. The eclecticism of Iveagh's Indian Hall mirrors that of the decorative scheme throughout the house, and of the furniture. In the columns supporting the galleries, for instance, Islamic types are juxtaposed with ones of Hindu origin and thus a thousand years earlier in style. The effect is like putting Romanesque next to Rococo, and should be seen in the light of the 'comparative method' of nineteenth-century architectural history and museums. That the wealth of detail does not get out of hand is due to the Youngs' controlling, neo-Baroque sense of space, which gives the room a unity more familiar in Western than in Indian buildings.

Purdon Clarke was well suited to the challenge of Elveden, having both been trained as an architect and had wide experience of India and the East. In 1874 he had begun a two-year posting in Tehran as the superintendent of works for the British consular buildings there. Then he acted as architect to the Indian section of the Paris Exhibition of 1878. His first work at South Kensington had been with Indian objects. As an architect he had been active in the 1880s, designing a number of buildings associated with South Kensington – such as Alexandra House, for students of the Royal College of Music, and the National School of Cookery – as well as two works in Indian styles: Lord Brassey's Indian Museum in Park Lane (1887) and the Indian Palace at the Paris Exhibition of 1889.

Purdon Clarke was able to show Young drawings from the Museum collections and to recommend books, notably the Maharajah of Jaipur's 'magnificent work on Indian architectural details' which had recently been produced by Colonel (Sir Samuel Swinton) Jacob. True to the improving mission of the V and A, Purdon Clarke arranged for specimens of columns from Delhi to be sent to Farmer and Brindley of Westminster, the best-known firm of ornamental stone carvers at the turn of the century. When a loan of Indian inlaid marble was sent from South Kensington to the Buxton Museum, he organized local manufacturers to make copies in case that type of work should be used.

The Indian Hall is in the form of a cross. Around three sides runs a gallery, supported on arches at the north and pairs of coupled columns to the east and west. Four arches spring from the first-floor level to carry the great dome. The pendentives required special thought as in India 'the lines do not follow the sides of an Octagon,' Purdon Clarke advised. The pattern of concentric bands was possibly suggested by the Dilwara Temple of Mt Abu, of which there is a photograph in Iveagh's albums. The cusping to the underside of the arches, flowing like great ribbons of marble, may have been inspired by the Dewan-i-Khas in Delhi.

Some use of colour was contemplated at the beginning, with Purdon Clarke remembering how 'delicate inlays' gave 'an appearance of comfort which was quite absent in the Pearl Mosque in which the decoration was entirely of carved white marble set in rich mouldings'. But, as he wrote to Colonel Addison on 15 November 1900, 'At Elveden the difficulty is in knowing where to stop the colour and this can be met by doing without it altogether.' And they went without it in the Duleep Singh rooms, too; those were all painted over.

For all the scholarship, the effect of the Indian Hall is of a Taj Mahal – most iconic of Indian monuments for Western visitors – magically transported to the cold heathlands of Suffolk. It was a building extravagance, and the first thought of a modern visitor in winter may be how it was ever heated. Elveden had underfloor central heating to all except Lord Iveagh's room, and ducts were even laid there in case the increasing desire for comfort should conquer the ingrained fear of stuffy rooms. Such a system might have been effective elsewhere, but it could not contend with the refrigerating effect of the Indian Hall, where there were only two fireplaces, one to either side. While the design of the marble superstructure is engaging, the grates are not especially large. In her memoir *Seventy Years Young*, Lady Fingall, the wife of a hunting Irish peer, remembered the Indian Hall as the coldest room in England (an accolade for which there was stiff competition). On the decorator's ground plan marking the original position of the furniture, it is noticeable that the space in the centre was left almost empty, with all the chairs and sofas grouped close to the fireplaces.

With a floor sprung with railway buffers, the Indian Hall could serve as a ballroom. But its day-to-day use was as what Edwardians tended to call a living hall, and it could be called the ne plus ultra of the form. Guests assembled here before dinner, to the accompaniment of Cassano's band from London playing in the gallery. Except for one or two ornaments, the Indian style did not extend to the furniture, as it had in Duleep Singh's rooms. The emphasis was rather on a luxurious degree of comfort: the armchairs and daybeds here and throughout the house being extremely well padded and sprung and mostly supplied by Maples. Colour was provided by velvet upholstery in pale greens and burgundy reds, and by the use of old Italian or Portuguese embroidery to make cushions and panels for chair backs. These cushions were in many ways the prettiest things in the house. A number of altar frontals were uncovered during the cataloguing for the 1984 sale; they seem originally to have been draped over the backs of settles (like antimacassars) and arranged on the lids of the two grand pianos that stood in the apse. Large eighteenth-century red-lacquer

Dresden vases stood either side of the north doors, and between the arches were screens of old Spanish leather.

With Elveden, we enter the age of the interior-decorating firm, which now provided the controlling eye on the fitting out of rooms which would once have been provided by architects. They thrived on eclecticism, bewildering house owners with limitless possibilities of choice and frustrating architects whose vision tended to be more singly focused. Eclecticism had to some extent mutated since the days of 18 Stafford Terrace. Linley Sambourne had mixed furniture of different dates within the same room, judging the effect by eye. This approach had not died away altogether: look at the mixture of furniture in the Indian Hall. However, it was also fashionable for the rooms of grand houses to be treated as a kind of menu of styles, each providing an historical flavour that suited its use.

The heavier styles – Queen Anne or early Georgian – were thought appropriate for dining rooms, where cigars were smoked and port consumed after dinner. The Elveden dining room, panelled in walnut, was hung with Brussels and Gobelins tapestries, suggesting to Purdon Clarke that the furniture should be Chippendale, since Sheraton

> was more in touch with Louise 16th and the following Empire style
> and therefore more suitable for the Boudoir with its Boucher panels.
> The Dining Room at Elveden is a somewhat difficult room to treat
> and in my opinion should conform with the general style of the house
> and be made as comfortable as the Queen Anne or Early Georgian
> period will permit.

John Keyse Sherwin's painting of the installation banquet of the Order of St Patrick at Dublin Castle in 1783 occupied the whole of the west wall; Lord Iveagh, who was a member of the Order, bought it in 1916. That he loved pictures can be seen from the sixty-three works of art that make up the Iveagh Bequest at Kenwood in London; they include masterpieces by Vermeer, Rembrandt and Gainsborough, although fine tapestries were preferred to such serious art at Elveden.

Work on the dining room did not finish on time and threatened to disrupt the carefully planned social arrangements. 'I really do not know what to do,' Iveagh wrote to Addison on 6 September 1903. 'We have a large shooting party coming to us before the end of this month and my wife will want quite 10 days before that time to furnish and arrange the room . . . If we have to entertain a large party in the present dining room – a thing which I do not for a moment contemplate – the inconvenience will be very great and I should be put to the expense of fitting up a temporary hot plate.' The last party was held in December 1938 when the Hon. Patricia Guinness married Alan Lennox-Boyd. 'The dining room very gorgeous with gold griffins and pale green orchids all down the table & Patsy with her diamonds round her neck,' wrote Freya Stark in a letter. 'Everyone a little hectic except Lady Iveagh [wife of the 2nd Earl] who keeps her perfect and beautiful calm.' Across the corridor from the dining room, Lady Iveagh's room was Louis Seize, to suit the Aubusson tapestries as Purdon Clarke had advised, but Lord Iveagh's room was a not wholly successful mixture of 'Adam' and Jacobean, panelled in oak. A 'cosy corner', as it would have been known, was formed by two full-height Ionic columns standing forward of the fireplace, and there was a spiral staircase to give access to Lord and Lady Iveagh's bedroom suite on the first floor, which ran the whole length of the east wing.

Whose eye marshalled this great catholicity of taste? Not, it would seem, that of the opulent decorating firm Lenygon and Morant, though the judicious combination of colour, old furniture and comfort was very much in their line; there is no evidence that they worked at the house. Trollope's the builders had a decorating wing, and some of the rooms were left in their hands. But for most of the principal rooms the Iveaghs went to the Edinburgh firm of Morrisons. We have seen that Iveagh favoured safe choices in architects; when it came to landscape gardening, for instance, he wrote to the Office of Works for suggestions. Morrisons had in their way a comparable reputation in decorating, the principal with whom Iveagh dealt – Mr Reid – having won the contract for decorating and upholstering Pullman railway carriages. Reid did so well out of this type of work that he was able to build himself a castle on the outskirts of Edinburgh – Lauriston Castle – although his unfortunate wife was mortified to discover that Edinburgh society would still not call because she was 'trade'.

The effect of the furniture and tapestries was, as the magazine *The World* commented on 18 December 1901, 'set off by orchids, palms, flowering plants, and the electric light' – the last thought to add particular lustre. The ubiquitous country-house visitor Augustus Hare grumpily commented upon the 'electric piano which goes on pounding away with a pertinacity which is perfectly distracting'. The gossip writers lapped it all up: Elveden was 'an appallingly luxurious mansion', purred *Mayfair* in 1910. They were not just thinking of the decoration, of course. A lot depended on the now demolished servants' wing, which was planned around two courtyards and, like so much at Elveden, unusually big. The stables, water tower and kitchen gardens formed a vast complex, and the real business of the estate, shooting, was pursued on a scale that would have impressed even Duleep Singh. The biggest recorded bag was in 1912, when five guns killed 3,247 birds. Lady Fingall stood next to the future George V when he shot two partridges coming towards him, turned and took another two behind. She slapped him on the back and they danced around together for joy. A note pinned to the game book for 15 November 1899 in the royal shot's own hand records that his personal bag for that day was 368 pheasants, 127 partridges, 28 hares, 51 rabbits and a pig [*sic*]. Having used 1,200 cartridges, he calculated his success rate as 52.08 per cent. In 1906 a party of seven – including Edward VII and the Prince of Wales – killed 4,310 pheasants in three days.

   Lord Iveagh also rebuilt the village, and after the First World War had W. D. Caröe, architect to the Church Commissioners, add a bell tower in Lady Iveagh's memory and a war memorial cloister connecting it to the church. The giant column that it used to be possible to climb is another war memorial. Designed by Clyde Young, it is, despite the post-First World War date, a completely Edwardian gesture, and an appropriate memorial to Lord Iveagh himself, who, although he lived until 1927, was spiritually so at home in the Edwardian age.

18. The Semi and the Suburbs
7 Blyth Grove, Worksop

There is a flat black case at the top of 7 Blyth Grove, Worksop. I opened it when I was sitting amid the many neatly catalogued boxes of paper in the attic during my research for this book. It contained the chain of office belonging to William Straw, president of the Worksop and District Grocers' Association. It radiates the confidence and self-approbation of a Victorian shopkeeper who had made his way in the world, qualities that seem not to have been transmitted to his sons, who became reclusively obsessed with the past, hoarding the ephemera of a world that might otherwise have been forgotten.

Mr Straw came from Mansfield. Born in 1864, he appears to have studied at J. Malty and Son's Commercial and Mathematical Academy there; the copybook in which he practised his hand-writing survives. So does his post-office savings book: first deposit 5s on 22 December 1865. (By 1887 he had accumulated £79 5s 11d.) Apprenticed to a grocer and tea dealer called Peggs, he prospered sufficiently to own his own shop in a Georgian terrace in Worksop.

A photograph shows him outside it, face lugubrious with moustache, white apron nearly to the ground, a fine display of hams hanging, without any regard for twenty-first-century ideas about food inspection, outside the shop window. Cadbury's Cocoa announces itself in decorative writing on the window glass, and no fewer than three posters proclaim the presence of garden and flower seeds; Mr Straw had become a seed merchant as well as a grocer, perhaps inspired by his own passion for his allotment. He lived over the shop with his wife Florence and two boys, William and Walter, until in 1923 the shopkeeper and his family projected themselves into the middle classes. They moved to a house with a name wrought into its gate – Edgecliffe – as well as a number (7 Blyth Grove), in a road of semi-detached houses with gardens that wound up from another road of quite substantial houses hidden by trees. There were fields at the back and vegetable gardens on the plots that had not yet been developed.

The story of the English house has reached the suburbs. And not before time. As a word, *suburb* has been around for centuries. Chaucer speaks of suburbs, but not with any affection; they were places where honest citizens trod with caution. A degree of regulation and order prevailed in cities, protected and circumscribed by their walls. But the land immediately outside the city tended to be colonized by all those occupations which the city authorities sometimes needed, sometimes tolerated, but could not stomach living among: slaughterhouses, tanneries, prisons, brothels and, later, bear pits and theatres. Southwark, London's first suburb, was not subject to the sort of controls imposed on the City itself. Such rules as did govern it were entangled in the excessive number of bodies that exercised jurisdiction over different parts or activities; these included the Bishop of Winchester, who attempted to regulate the behaviour of prostitutes, one of his dictates insisting that a woman who was paid for sex should spend the whole night with her customer. By the time of Samuel Pepys, however, the environs of

London had come to be appreciated for other charms. Pepys himself spent the year of the Great Plague living 'merrily' at Greenwich; his friends there – shipbuilders, merchants – had handsome houses with orchards, but could be rowed up to the City or the Court whenever necessary. (Shooting the rapids formed by the narrow arches of London Bridge was exciting for those who felt up to it.) Epsom, 15 miles south of the capital, was further away, but – having established itself as a spa – could attract a London crowd to settle there by the time Daniel Defoe visited in 1724:

> Men of Business, who are at London upon Business all the Day, and moving to their lodgings at Night, make the Families, generally speaking, rather provide Suppers than Dinners: for 'tis very frequent for the Trading part of the Company to place their families here, and take their Horses every Morning to London . . . and be at Epsom again at Night.

In what sounds like a perfectly agreeable way, commuting had now begun.

Commuting has always been something of a British disease. On the Continent, the threat of marauding armies kept the citizenry crowded within their city walls. The British could risk living more expansively. Even before the coming of the railway, 'great parcels of stockjobbers' could stay at Brighton, observed William Cobbett: 'They skip backwards and forwards on the coaches and actually carry on stockjobbing in Change Alley though they reside in Brighton.' Of course Brighton was, and just about is, too far away from London to be a suburb. Norwood, though, was a different matter; it was there that Mr Spenlow, the solicitor to whom Dickens's David Copperfield was articled, lived with his daughter, the future Mrs Copperfield; a phaeton with high-stepping horses would take him from his home to Doctors' Commons and back every day. One Friday evening Copperfield was driven down for the weekend and was enchanted by the effect of *rus in urbe*. 'There was a lovely garden to Mr. Spenlow's house,' writes Dickens in the persona of his hero. 'There was a charming lawn, there were clusters of trees, and there were perspective walks that I could just distinguish in the dark, arched over with trellis-work, on which shrubs and flowers grew in the growing season.' The house itself was what the Victorians would have called a villa.

The term *Villa* also has a history, coming, as we have seen, from Italy, and being particularly associated with Palladio. As the eighteenth century wore on, the word drifted socially downwards, until by the last quarter it was generally used of gentlemen's houses that lay close to cities. These residences were not enormously large, they were likely to be surrounded by a few acres of ornamental parkland, but not landed estates, and their object was pleasure. The Thames Valley west of London was a great breeding ground. To begin with, the preferred style, like the word, was Italianate – classical, but perhaps with a twist, such as that introduced by John Nash (the great aficionado of the villa) in evoking that picturesque incident of so many paintings of the Campagna, the fortified farmhouse. But there was no stylistic monopoly. Horace Walpole's Strawberry Hill at Twickenham, a crucible of the Gothic Revival, was also a villa, built bang next to the London road. In the nineteenth century, 'villa' was used to enhance the status of a motley assortment of dwellings, often of dubious stylistic pedigree – a flavour of which can be tasted in the Old English and Anglo-Norman, as well as classical, designs in P. F. Robinson's *Designs for Ornamental Villas* (1827). The details became odder, the styles more eclectic, and by 1850 the villa had settled itself comfortably down in the suburbs: a substantial middle-class dwelling, not without a hint of pretension. It was still there in 1905 when Edgecliffe was built.

As it happens – and Edgecliffe's developer may well have been unaware of the fact – the years around 1905 represent a high-water mark of the suburban ideal. Among a socially progressive intelligentsia, suburbs appeared to offer a new model for living, an antidote to the ills of the city. The Victorian city had come to be seen as a monster, belching smoke from its thousands of coal fires, clattering with the noise of carriage wheels, and devouring the health of its inhabitants. By 1900 the worst of the tottering 'rookeries' like Jacob's Island, Bermondsey, in *Oliver Twist* had been swept away, but there were still slums, and nothing had been done to improve the quality of the air. Campaigners were beginning to realize that tuberculosis and other diseases were associated with lack of fresh air and sunlight. As William Morris put it,

> Forget the spreading of the hideous town;
> Think rather of the pack-horse on the down,
> And dream of London, small, and white, and clean,
> The clear Thames bordered by its gardens green.

Hermann Muthesius, a German architect who wrote about the English house in 1904–5, found that this new paradise had been created near Turnham Green in west London, in the shape of a Queen Anne Revival suburb created after 1875. Bedford Park was nothing less than the 'starting-point of the smaller modern house', which had subsequently disseminated itself across the whole country. The developer, a cloth merchant with artistic connections called Jonathan Carr, commissioned designs from top architects – the mildly racy E. W. Godwin, then the massively successful Richard Norman Shaw, finally (after delays in settling Shaw's bills) Shaw's elegant, understated protégé E. J. May. The theme is red brick, great tall chimney stacks, terracotta garnishes, white-painted balustrades around rooftops and balconies, and big window bays. These are spacious houses with spreading plans: unlike the traditional London house – 154 Tachbrook Street, for example – the kitchen is not in the basement.

But it was not the architectural style which distinguished Bedford Park, so much as its spirit. From the start it was an arty sort of place.

The social regime was, by Victorian standards, relaxed. There was a church, of course, though it hardly looks like the conventional Gothic Revival offering. More of a signature was the Art School. The other leading institution was the tennis club, where men and women of all ages could meet informally and perhaps try their hand at what was still a newly invented game. Tennis was to become an important middle-class activity. 'The possession of a tennis ground has become such an imperative social necessity,' wrote the *Spectator* as early as 26 July 1884, 'that every wretched little garden-plot is pressed into the service, and courts are religiously traced out in half the meagre back-gardens of the suburbs of London, even though the available space is little bigger than a billiard-table.' It was always necessary to arrange tournaments, to meet friends and perhaps even to find future partners in both senses of the word – a prefigurement of the Miss Joan Hunter Dunn generation, when to be 'furnished and burnished by Aldershot sun' was a fashionable sign of good health. (In the 1890s Sir George Sitwell told his most unsporting daughter Edith that 'there is nothing a man likes so much as a girl who is good at the parallel bars.')

There was also something self-consciously villagey about Bedford Park. This faux rustic quality became a recurrent note in the suburban tune. The estate which the estate agent William Webb laid out at Purley near Croydon from 1888 had a village green and a smithy, and for a time geese were kept. With houses standing on broad, winding roads lined with trees and flowers, residents 'not only had the enjoyment of their own premises in desirable seclusion,' wrote Webb, 'but ... it may appear as though they are in one large garden of which their own holding is part.' Further out from London the view might well be extended by the managed landscape of a golf course, golf having captured the imagination of a public unequipped for, or bored by, traditional field sports. The idea that became *Country Life* was born during a game of golf at the Walton Heath club in Surrey (the editor's office is still decorated with grisailles of tweedy, pipe-smoking golfers).

'One large garden . . .' Webb's words encapsulate the tone of two pioneering concepts which influenced planning for a century. The first was the Garden City. Housing and community buildings would stand next to architect-designed factories in a setting that was more or less rural. This was the vision of the City clerk-turned-stenographer Ebenezer Howard. As a young man, Howard had hoped to make a success of farming in the United States; he did not, but along the way he encountered Frederick Law Olmstead's ideas for town planning. Returning to England, Howard published a book, *Tomorrow: A Peaceful Path to Real Reform* (1898), established a limited company, raised capital, organized the purchase of a landed estate in Hertfordshire and held an architectural competition, the last being won by the firm of Parker and Unwin. The result was Letchworth Garden City. Unlike Bedford Park, roads were laid out to follow the contours of the landscape and respect old trees. Self-conscious beauty was mixed lightly with socialism. There was an inn (of course), but the inn sold no beer, alcohol being banned from the precincts of Letchworth until 1958. The tone was caught by W. Percival Westell, an early resident and the first curator of the Letchworth Museum, who saw this 'quiet rural retreat for the town worker' as also providing 'a haven of refuge for the artist, the sculptor, the musician, the literary man or woman, and those who have ceased to ply either wares or brains, and, what is more important, perhaps, proper housing for the industrial population'. George Bernard Shaw came and spoke; artists came and settled; the sandal-maker George Adams, who had at one time been gardener and beekeeper to Edward Carpenter, poet, Fabian and homosexual, was on hand to provide footwear. Other garments were produced by the Spirella company, an American manufacturer of ladies' corsets, which built a factory in 1912.

'One of the great social problems of today is the ways and means of finally sounding the death-knell of Slumdom,' announced Westell, 'and even if Letchworth has not yet efficiently solved the question, the fact remains that a step has been taken in the right direction when one realises the squalor of the crowded garret and the misery of the filthy alley.' There was a golf course at Letchworth, naturally, and 'good cricket, hockey and football clubs'. And in the manner of many writers about decoration, architecture and topography before the First World War, Westell was not ashamed of making wild claims in favour of the health-giving properties of the place: 'The oxygen given off by the pines away in the west is borne on the bosom of the wind and floats over the Garden City.' Soon Howard had founded another Garden City, at Welwyn nearer London.

The second revolutionary concept was the Garden Suburb, which bore unique fruit at Hampstead in London. The kinship is obvious. Hampstead Garden Suburb was begun two years after Letchworth Garden City, and Parker and Unwin were again called upon to design it. Its origins, however, were rather different. The stimulus was the preservation of, rather than the improvement of, living conditions, though the latter soon became part of it. Rich in her own right, her father having made a fortune from selling macassar oil for men's hair, Mrs Henrietta Barnett was married to the founder of Toynbee Hall in the East End of London, where undergraduates from Oxford and Cambridge went to teach the poor. She also was a formidable organizer. Living in Hampstead, she made a cause out of saving the landscape north of the Heath, then on the point of being overwhelmed by uncontrolled sprawl along the route of the Northern Line of the underground. After a fund-raising campaign, part of an estate owned by Eton College was presented to the London County Council as an extension to the Heath. Mrs Barnett then persuaded the College to sell the rest of its 243 acres to the Hampstead Garden Suburb Trust, a charitable body set up to develop the land on the principles of Letchworth. It was to be a model estate in which 'people of all classes of society, of all sorts of opinions, and all standards of income' could live 'in helpful neighbourliness'. As at Bedford Park, the Hampstead Garden Suburb firmament was illuminated by a galaxy of sparkling architects. Lutyens designed a church and a vicarage. When his 1909 church design was rejected by Mrs Barnett as being too big for its surroundings, he exploded in a letter to fellow-architect Herbert Baker, calling his patroness a 'philistine' with 'no idea beyond a window box full of geraniums, calceolarias and lobelias, over which you can see a goose on the green'. (They agreed to a compromise, or – as Lutyens put it in his journal – 'Mrs Barnett was vanquished.') The Church of St Jude stands on the Central Square. This was one respect in which Hampstead Garden Suburb was an improvement on Letchworth; Letchworth tends to be all *sub* and no *urb* – however attractive the streets, they float free of any significant centre. Hampstead Garden Suburb had a core.

The Garden City and the Garden Suburb were brave new departures, a democratization of the Picturesque principles that we encountered at Endsleigh Cottage, and as such radically different from most of the housing built in the late nineteenth century. The latter consisted of streets built strictly according to the requirements established by prevailing by-laws; modest bay-fronted dwellings lining roads that are exactly sixty feet wide provided a solid standard of accommodation for artisans, but the cumulative effect is monotonous. They were different, too, from Edgecliffe. Blyth Grove is not wholly without Picturesque aspirations: note the word *Grove*. It winds; the houses have gardens. But the development was not utopian, high-minded socialist or arty; there was no attempt to make it cohere stylistically; plots were sold to be developed individually. The style of Edgecliffe, with its harsh red brick, spiky gables and mustard-grained woodwork, could not even be described as sub-Bedford Park. If anything, it echoed – however distantly – Pugin. Nevertheless, like the Garden City and Garden Suburb, it represented a bid for escape from the city centre to a vaguely defined outer limit. (The problem being that, as so many suburban residents have found, the outer limit is not static. When Edgecliffe was built, it was indeed on the edge, if not of a cliff then of Worksop. It looked out over fields. But the edge moved. It now looks out over other houses.)

'Worksop is a market town, situated in a wide valley formed by gently rising hills, that run from east to west,' wrote a local historian in 1854. 'From the north it has a very pleasing appearance.' There was a railway station and a towering, dramatically plain Norman church, a survival from Worksop Priory; red-brick streets were set off by an unusual number of poplars and a background of 'finely wooded hills' which ultimately joined up with Sherwood Forest: 'It is altogether a pleasant, clean, and cheerful looking town; and has well-built, wide, and commodious streets, and good houses; although more are wanted of the middle class character.' Some extraordinarily grand families had country houses round about, and owned land in the town – several dukes, a smattering of earls – and there was at one point plenty of hunting. But this aristocratic connection left little mark. There were no ambitious episodes of town planning, no stately statues, little patronage in the shape of public buildings. By the end of the nineteenth century, Worksop had come to be associated principally with one thing in the minds of the great families round about: coal. It became a mining town. The income helped sustain the ducal ways of life, but before long the dukes themselves had stopped going there. Although more distinguished in terms of history, Worksop came to be little different from Eastwood, the Nottinghamshire town in which the novelist D. H. Lawrence grew up. The Lawrence family pursued a similar, although more roundabout, domestic path to the Straws. From the modest 8A Victoria Street in which the novelist was born, they moved to an end-of-terrace house in what is now Garden Road, with a more generous garden. Respectable from the front, it backed onto a squalid alley, which was Mrs Lawrence's *bête noire*. This occasioned another move, this time to Walker Street – 'a house on the brow of the hill, commanding a view of the valley, which spread out like a convex cockle-shell, or a clamp-shell, before it', as Lawrence described in *Sons and Lovers* (1913). The final move took place when Lawrence was nineteen, and brought them to the salubrity of a semi-detached house, 97 Lynncroft. Lawrence hated all suburbs: he called them 'horrid little red mantraps'. Nevertheless he seems to have felt a quiet pride in the family achievement.

Edgecliffe was another semi-detached. In this it was typical of many suburbs. The semi had begun the onslaught that would make it the defining building type of new development in the 1920s and 1930s. There were benefits of economy: by joining two dwellings together, the builder saved on the cost of construction, and also on space. But the householder could still enjoy access to a back garden; there was a side door, to which delivering tradesmen were directed, as well as a front door for family use; unlike the terraced house, the semi redeemed wife and servants from running downstairs to a basement kitchen and up again to the dining room. Edgecliffe's original occupants would have employed some kind of domestic help, probably on a daily basis: above the door to the kitchen is a small board for the electrically operated bells that rang from front door, dining room, drawing room, bathroom and two of the five bedrooms. But already the supply of cheap labour that ran the Victorian house had begun to dry up. Employers were conscious of the need to save labour. Before long there was talk of a 'crisis'. Most inter-war semis were built to operate without any servants at all. (In 1911 some houses in Harrow were advertised as 'specially designed to meet the requirements of a small family not wishing to incur the worry and expense of keeping a servant.')

Even in 1905, the semi was a well-established building type; it had been around since the seventeenth century. A street of semi-detached houses had been built in Highgate in London in 1688: the fact that it was called The Grove suggests a typological kinship, however remote, with Blyth Grove. By the 1790s a whole estate of semis (the Eyre estate) was being built in St John's Wood. They might well have been called semi-detached 'villas', a term often used in the early years, which suggests something about their origins as well as their social pretensions. The purlieus of London provided a congenial habitat. In 1823 the landscape gardener and encyclopedist John Claudius Loudon designed one in Porchester Terrace, living in half of it himself and publishing the result in *The Suburban Gardener and Village Companion*. (Confusingly he called it a 'double detached villa', but we know what he meant.)

As at Blyth Grove, Regency semis were built in symmetrical pairs; unlike Blyth Grove, they were classical in style, capped with a pediment and the awkward lack of any other central emphasis often being made good by a false window or plaque. By 1859, the form had become so familiar that the Hon. Emily Eden could write a fashionable novel about it, called nothing less than *The Semi-Detached House*. Unfortunately Eden gives little clue as to the appearance of the eponymous semi; eclecticism was now in full spate, flooding domestic architecture with all manner of historical references and sweeping the semi-detached residence along in its stream. Bedford Park introduced the idea of the non-identical twin: for a while it was no longer de rigueur for the two halves to mirror one another. The houses were big enough to take the disparity. In more modest streets, the attractions of individuality were outweighed by a general restlessness of effect, and by the time that Blyth Grove was built, the semi had settled back into its natural condition of symmetry. There on the whole it remained, though dressed up in a villagey trim of hipped roof, tile-hanging and half-timber. Osbert Lancaster satirized this style, the rather too familiar face of the inter-war suburb, as 'By-Pass Variegated'.

Edgecliffe is not particularly remarkable as a building of 1905; it acquires its interest from the time when William and Florence Straw moved in, in 1923. William Straw died suddenly, working on his allotment, in 1932. His wife seems to have been devoted to his memory, since she did nothing to remove or rearrange his possessions: his tobacco pouch and pipes remained where they always had been, hanging beside the mantelpiece in the parlour. His coat and hats were left on their pegs in the hall. The date on the calendar was not changed. After her own death in 1939, William and Walter Straw showed themselves to be equally conservative. William had been to university in London, and for some years taught English at the City of London College. He commuted down every week, returning to Worksop in time for the evening meal on Fridays. Although he eventually stopped teaching, he kept on his digs and continued to go down to London as before. There were no servants at Edgecliffe by this time. So on his mother's death, he stopped his London arrangement, and came home to keep house. Walter took on the grocer's shop in the marketplace.

The brothers kept Edgecliffe just as their parents had known it. In the main bedroom, Mr and Mrs Straw's clothes were carefully laid out between sheets of newspaper to preserve them, the paper being changed from time to time – though not after 1969, the date on the newspapers that are now there. The books that William, the university man, bought – often first editions, sent through the post in brown-paper parcels that were sometimes put straight under the bed without being unwrapped – show a passion for local history. J. C. Atkinson's *British Birds' Eggs and Nests* (1861) rubs shoulders with Alison Uttley's *Country Things* (1946) and *A Dictionary of the Sussex Dialect* (1875). It extended to an admiration of Lawrence (*Apocalypse*, *The Virgin and the Gipsy*), though it is hard to think of more dissimilar spirits.

The washing, until William's death in 1990, was still performed as it always had been, water being pumped by hand into a big stoneware sink, made by Hodgkin and Jones of Sheffield. It was heated in a large copper tank with a coal fire underneath it, and clothes were pounded and twisted in a zinc tub using a wooden 'dolly' (looking a bit like an inverted hat stand.) The bathroom was spare and unheated – not a room to linger in. There was a lavatory, perhaps an introduction from the elder Straws' time. Certainly they had updated the downstairs lavatory, reached from the garden. Originally it had been an earth closet, equipped with a special door from which the night soil could be removed. This was replaced with a water closet.

In the attic the Straws kept the tin hats they had worn as air-raid wardens during the Second World War. Like other people who had lived through that time of privation, they did not waste more than they could avoid. They left an upstairs store cupboard, stocked with a motley assortment of provisions – you never know what may come in handy – which now seems an evocative tableau of semi-detached life: baked beans, Bovril, spices, icing sugar, a large tin of Fowler's Pure Cane West India Treacle, a jar of 1938 goose fat, Carnation evaporated milk, jam, tinned potatoes (why did they buy them, when they grew their own?), Libby's pineapple slices, baking powder, Camp coffee with its picture of a Scottish officer being served by a native batman, many tins of sardines . . . But what is striking is not the quantity of stuff in the house but its relatively manageable volume. You could still walk into the rooms even though they contained the unedited accumulation of fifty years. The Straws' was a frugal generation. A bathroom cupboard bulges with old pairs of striped flannel pyjamas.

One of William Straw's pleasures was to haunt the sale of country houses that were being broken up in the mid-twentieth century. For someone distressed by change, the disappearance of the old families from the area must have seemed dismal, even if it gave him the opportunity to view their possessions and, occasionally, to buy something. This may have been why he left much of his own estate to the National Trust (never expecting, one imagines, that his sanctum would be shown to the public, for surely he intended the bequest to be sold). The Dukeries – as the area around Worksop was known – had moved, like the rest of Britain, in the direction of the suburb. Expectations were rising. The First World War had rattled the social fabric and loosened its joints. A growing army of clerks and accountants, tradesmen and shop walkers, wanted better than their parents had known. The motor bus, the underground railways and the commuter train made it possible for them to have it.

There was no mechanism in place to bring order to this sudden rush of democratic demand. The road system could not cope with the numbers of cars that piled onto it. Long queues of traffic snaked across beauty spots such as the South Downs every weekend. When a network of arterial roads was built to pump traffic into and out of the big cities, verges were quickly lined, sclerotically, with semis. These were new houses for a new way of life, overlooking a new lot of roads along which a new form of transport was roaring, growling and coughing its cheerful way. It seemed to be a modern solution. The architect Clough Williams-Ellis was one of the first campaigners to voice dissent, suggesting that these roads were the tentacles of an octopus which was strangling England. The town of Peacehaven on the Sussex coast epitomized the formlessness of a development free-for-all. In 1914 a property developer and one-time gold prospector, Charles Neville, drove up in his Hupmobile motor car and the next year bought the beginnings of an estate that would, by 1924, stretch along the coast for five miles. A natural showman, he launched a competition to have his new settlement named. New Anzac-on-Sea, the winning submission, did not stick, and during the war the site was ploughed up to grow food.

But during the 1920s Peacehaven grew in its amoeboid, loose-limbed way to become bigger than the county town of Lewes. There were no planning restrictions. Householders built what they wanted (often bungalows), where they wanted, often with vacant lots in between. To architects and a left-leaning, Continentally inspired intelligentsia, aware of Le Corbusier's vision of tower blocks surrounded by parkland in France, this ultimate expression of individual choice was anathema. Lovers of the countryside were equally shocked. There had to be some rules. They began to be introduced in the 1930s. Ribbon development was banned in 1935. Minimum standards for houses and streets were laid down. But for many people the ideal remained a new house, with a garage and a garden, built on a road that led only to a round of tarmac on which they could turn the car. The front door opened onto a private utopia of electricity, fitted kitchens and vacuum cleaners, of oak-panelled dining rooms, 'bijou baronial halls' in Hendon and 'old-world' inglenooks at Hinchley Wood.

Alan Jackson, in his book *Semi-Detached London* (1973), recalls the ritual, performed on one Sunday afternoon a year or two after moving in, of displaying the new semi to admiring relatives and friends:

> Supplied with the names of road and house on a letterhead printed at cut price by the newly established local stationer, the tourists would find themselves veering wildly around the maze of rutted builder's roads, stepping between piles of bricks and prefabricated window frames, trying not to trip over the plankways used for running wheelbarrows between the dumps of materials at the roadside and the building plots. In vain would they make enquiries about their destination from the equally disoriented and widely scattered inhabitants of the new estate busily clearing their front gardens. Eventually the bright and clean new semi would be found, stark and clinical in its treeless, shrubless setting, a carpet of browning turf beneath its proud window bays.

There followed the tour of the garden, the proud boast (*pace* Edgecliffe) that 'they can't build at the back of us', the inspection of struggling plants. Strength was recruited by a large tea of 'cold meats, tinned salmon and lettuce, many cakes, sponges and tarts, perhaps some jelly, trifle or blancmange'. Afterwards came the demonstration of the new radio in a room that was too relaxed and up to date to be called a parlour; in an echo of the Edwardian living hall it was designated the 'lounge'. Perhaps another meal was served before the visitors, unable to find their way back to the railway station, discovered that they had missed their planned train.

'Gaily into Ruislip Gardens/Runs the red electric train . . .' John Betjeman mourned the passing of rural Middlesex as a 'lost Elysium', and yet came to recognize the suburbs as an essential ingredient of the English scene. Writing *The Castles on the Ground* (1946) from wartime postings around the Middle East, the architectural critic J. M. Richards evoked the order, neatness, silence, comfort and security of the English suburb with poignant particularity. 'The dog summoned from the shadowed porch, the cheerful tea table, the quiet between the passing car lights; there is the essence of the modern English domestic scene,' he concluded. 'For better or worse the English in this generation are becoming a nation of suburban dwellers, and the typical background of domestic life is now the winding road system of the suburban jungle, no longer the maze of city streets and slums where Dickens laid the scene of his stories nearly a century ago.' Fifty years later the 'invincible green suburbs' were still a touchstone of Englishness that Prime Minister John Major saw fit to evoke in his most famous speech.

Mr Major, however, was out of step with the Prince of Wales, whose ideas on this subject chimed harmoniously with thinkers at the other end of the architectural spectrum, such as the apostle of space-age modernity, Richard Rogers. However attractive their gardens and recreation grounds may be to families with young children, they can be a prison to teenagers and old people who do not drive cars. Houses are built too far apart to allow their occupants to walk to shops, cinemas or doctors' surgeries. The suburbs do not coalesce easily into communities, where the needs of all ages are met and where wage-earners, commuting long distances to work, can arrive home in time to read their children stories before bed. They are wasteful of land and often too expensive for the teachers, police, garage keepers and gardeners who make them work. They are not energy-efficient. But Betjeman was right. They are a part of the English psyche. They are still being built.

19. Building a New Britain
The Amersham Prefab

It is April 1947. The Second World War ended two years ago, but Britain is still waiting for the fruits of peace to swell. There are shortages of everything – meat, eggs, petrol, building supplies. But in Finch Lane, at the point where the Buckinghamshire town of Amersham meets open fields, there is excitement. It is not just the bluebells, the catkins, the appearance of May blossom. Into this hitherto bucolic environment – the lane is named after Britain's smallest bird – are trundling lorries from nearby Rickmansworth. They are unloading the components of some new and radically un-rural houses: three lorryloads to a house, forty-six houses altogether. The houses are raised quickly, each in less than a day. There is nothing Old World about them, with their low-pitched roofs of asbestos-cement tiles, their corrugated walls, their unsentimentally rectangular proportions and their staring glass windows. But housing is in such short supply that some families have taken the law into their own hands and occupied the redundant Nissen huts at The Vache, a country house at Chalfont St Giles in Buckinghamshire. To young marrieds who have spent the last few years with their parents, one of the new kit-like dwellings represents very nearly everything that they ever wanted. Certainly enough for now. In the way of things, that 'now' would stretch out into what must sometimes have seemed a 'nearly for ever'.

Houses of this type, designed to last a maximum of fifteen years, have survived for more than four times that period in some parts of Britain. The Bryannts, the first to move into 6 Finch Lane, at a rent of 13s 10d a week, did not stay more than a year. But the house, now in the Chilterns Open Air Museum, survived on its original site until 1987, and the Brants, who succeeded the Bryannts, stayed throughout the life of the building.

6 Finch Lane is a prefab. Students of the genre might call it a Universal House Mark 3, to distinguish it from other types: the Arcon, the Spoon, the Tarran and others. But for once the trade names never caught on. The term *prefab* had a resonance which appealed to the public. It sounded modern. The families who moved into Finch Lane did not do so, one suspects, with feelings of desperation at being able to find nothing better. They embraced the mass-produced, industrial concept. They had seen white-walled, flat-roofed houses before, in the Hollywood films that they watched at the Odeon cinemas, another breed of white-walled, modernistic structure. The prefab was a little corner of modernity in an exhausted, antiquated country. It had a plumbed-in kitchen, an inside lavatory, central heating of a kind and two bedrooms. It might have been equipped with Utility furniture, the range produced during the Second World War to provide cheap, sensibly designed items at a time when most factories had been turned over to the war effort. Who could have wanted more than that?

The essence of a prefab was off-site manufacture. Its component parts were made in factories. Only the concrete base on which the house sat had to be laid on site. Thus the walls of 6 Finch Lane contain twenty-six units, each a metal frame filled with moulded-asbestos sheeting on one side and plasterboard on the other. These units were bolted together and then bolted onto a pressed-steel base. Once the elements had been delivered to the place of construction, the house could be assembled quickly; during an early trial, building work began at 6.00 in the morning and the Mayor of Croydon was eating lunch inside the completed prefab a few hours later.

Prefabrication is not entirely new to the story of the English house. As we have seen, the wooden frames of some medieval houses arrived as kits. Victorian Britain exported iron homes and churches for erection in the colonies. But modern prefabs incorporated a range of novel materials. The most striking – though not 6 Finch Lane – were built of aluminium panels. After the Second World War, this was one of the few materials not in shortage. Concrete was suited to mass production, since it could be poured in large sections, and did not require craftsmen to spend much time on it. This was a departure. British householders, as we have encountered them, have been people of generally conservative taste, but this is as nothing to the conservatism of the methods by which houses were built. Few pre-First World War materials would have been unknown to the Romans. Now Britain was embarking on a phase of experiment.

The first signs of it had appeared in the 1920s with architects adopting the new look that had been pioneered on the Continent. This was a style which reflected the Machine Age. Lines were square, roofs were flat, walls were white – as though they had been built out of concrete, albeit the concrete effect was often only a plaster skin over brick (a kind of twentieth-century stucco) or, in the case of Charters in Berkshire, a luxurious house from the 1930s, Portland stone. The sash window was abandoned in favour of metal casements. To show the revolutionary new possibilities of steel joists, windows were sometimes deliberately placed at the corners of houses, which would have dangerously weakened the structure of traditional buildings. This was the Modern movement, which architects claimed was not so much a style as the inevitable consequence of developments in building technology: the only way to build in the twentieth century, the only way to live. Convention was thrown to the winds. A new kind of society was being born – rational, machine-based, progressive, intellectually validated by clever writers and propagandists. The harbingers appeared at Silver End near Braintree in Essex, a factory village for Crittall, a company which made those very metal-framed windows, and a number of private houses. Some pioneering blocks of flats were built in Highgate in London. However, the ideal of creating a new society through architecture was far from being achieved by the time the Second World War broke out. Most Modern-movement houses were bespoke commissions for rich clients.

Prefabrication created houses that really did employ the principles of mass production and made them available to ordinary people. That they were modern was only one reason for their appeal. They were also bungalows. The one-storey bungalow was a form that had become popular at the end of the nineteenth century. The name came from India, *bangla* being the Hindi or Mahratti word that means 'belonging to Bengal'. Originally it referred to local huts, with their rippling roofs of thatch and eyebrow-sweep of eaves. The first bungalows to be built in Britain had appeared in Westgate-on-Sea and Birchington, near Margate on the Kent coast, after 1869. They had verandahs and croquet lawns and tunnels to the beach; the tone was decidedly less rumbustious than nearby Ramsgate. There was, however, a bohemian connection; the architect J. P. Seddon invited his friend the poet and artist Dante Gabriel Rossetti to recuperate in a timber bungalow at Birchington, although it has to be said that the sea air did not, on this occasion, do the trick: Rossetti died there at Easter 1882. The architect R. A. Briggs – Bungalow Briggs, as he came to be called – made it a mission to domesticate the bungalow across Britain. That bungalows had enjoyed a special affinity with the seaside did them no harm. The seaside not only meant holidays but fresh air and (except for Rossetti) health.

And then there was the simple fact that the prefab was a house. Living in flats was a dangerously foreign idea to the English. Albany on Piccadilly – a town house redeveloped as Oxbridge-style sets in the eighteenth century – has been a smart address since it was built, but little imitated. Mansion flats had to wait until lifts had been developed to become practicable. They made their first appearance in London near the Albert Hall in the 1860s and seemed to answer many of the problems of middle-class life, particularly the servant question. Between the world wars living in flats epitomized a certain attitude to life: young, modern, smart, irresponsible. (Evelyn Waugh has Brenda Last take one, decorated by the ghastly Mrs Beaver, to pursue her affair with John Beaver in *A Handful of Dust*.) But they never caught on outside a metropolitan élite. Before the Second World War, Mass Observation found that the people they questioned were strongly attached to the ideal of the house. These results were repeated in surveys after the war. 'There can be no doubt . . . that flats are unpopular with the great majority of the English people,' concluded one of them. 'In the present survey, for every one person who said that he would like to live in a flat, ten said that they would like to live in a small house or bungalow.'

Gardens were also part of the ideal concept of home. Nearly everybody who was questioned in a pre-war survey conducted in Birmingham wanted one. This was not simply for the joy of gardening with flowers. During the Second World War, every spare parcel of land was dug up to grow vegetables, and gardens continued to play a practical role in feeding the family for years afterwards. You could sit in a garden, put the children's swing in it, dry the washing there, potter in the shed. One of the dividends of peace was a surplus of Anderson shelters, or domestic air-raid shelters, which were supplied to many new residents of prefabs to use as sheds. They made a convenient coal store if nothing else. However modern the prefab may have looked in some respects, it still generally had a stove to burn coal (though probably not an open fire). Communal gardens, which to some architects seemed to offer a better solution to the need for open space, by allowing a greater sweep of park to walk and play in, were no substitute for the individuality of the back garden.

Gardens were not, it is safe to say, uppermost in the minds of the planners who devised the prefab; they were a benefit that arrived more or less by accident. Other aspects of the estates on which they were placed reflected the thought that had gone into public housing since 1900. Local councils had been given the power to clear slums within their boundaries by the Artisans' Dwellings Act of 1875. The Housing of the Working Classes Act of 1890 had encouraged them to build model estates of their own. The London County Council, founded in 1889, led the way. They built a number of sober but superbly crafted estates, the Old Oak estate in Acton, begun in 1911, being architecturally one of the best. (Though not in terms of the accommodation offered, perhaps. At this date the policy was to provide homes only for those whose needs could not be met elsewhere; the houses therefore were rather small, so as not to compete with the private sector.) Government subsidized Councils to provide housing after the First World War in the drive to provide half a million 'homes fit for heroes'. They took the form of rather austere two-storey cottages, built amid privet hedges and grass verges, placed in groups of four or six, often around cul-de-sacs; larger groups would be disposed in a geometrical pattern. Architecturally their simplified Georgian character – symmetrical brick façades, sash windows, hipped roofs – caused them to be called 'boxes with lids'. The style persisted throughout the 1930s. What a departure the prefab made from it!

But prefabs were arranged on the ground in much the same way that boxes with lids would have been. The rule book to which local authorities worked was often good, derived from the Garden City movement. They were experienced in fitting buildings to land-scapes. Sometimes prefabs were put down in places that would not normally have been developed, such as parks or derelict ground; this provoked criticism. Equally the very suddenness with which prefabs arose was apt to disconcert local residents, familiar with the scene before the new homes had materialized so quickly. To the people who lived on the prefab estates, their settings often seemed very pleasant. And there was a pioneering spirit about them, too: they were mostly occupied by young families. Children could run in and out of each other's houses, without fear of the few motor cars. Mothers – it was generally the wife who stayed at home while her husband went out to a job at a factory – found plenty of support in what became strongly bonded communities.

Again, this advantage had probably not been foreseen; the men from the Ministry had other things on their mind. The Temporary Housing Programme, announced in March 1944, killed two birds with one stone. Hundreds of thousands of families across Britain had been bombed out of their houses during the Blitz. They were often still doubled up with other families, in cramped and difficult conditions. As the end of the war came into sight, the government could address itself to some of the challenges that Britain would face in peacetime. One priority was to provide a quick solution to the immediate housing problem. Many materials would be in short supply, imports diminished by the loss of shipping, road and rail transport would be disrupted, and much of the workforce would still be under arms. Another priority was to ensure that factories which had hitherto been working all out to produce armaments did not suddenly fall idle when no longer required by the military. The workforce needed new forms of employment. In one Home Counties factory, the *Picture Post* found 'orders for bomber wings are nearing completion. Meanwhile, prototypes of wooden bunga-lows are being made, embodying principles adapted from aircraft work.' The first prototype – an all-steel version – was exhibited to local authorities at the Tate Gallery in London in May 1944.

Woodwork at 6 Finch Lane is painted sage green, inside and out; the metal-framed casements and interior walls are cream. These were some of the few colours available from the limited post-war palette, others being shades of milk chocolate and Great Western plum. The front door gives into a hall, not enormous – the whole house is only 31 feet wide, 21 feet deep – but big enough for a workman's bicycle or a coach-built pram. From here, the door to the right opens into the living room, its floorboards darkened by the man of the house, the centre of the floor being a square of linoleum. Some householders decorated their floors with home-made rag rugs, carpets being unavailable. There are built-in cupboards (sage green, naturally) – quite an advantage given the shortage of furniture. The fireplace contains a stove, to burn coal or, more probably, coke; behind the stove is a back boiler, kept warm by the fire, providing warm water. Warm air circulated around an airing cupboard and a not very efficient heating system, emerging tepidly from ducts near the ceiling.

Next door, oh wonder, there is an Electrolux refrigerator. Perhaps this is only necessary; it is hardly possible to keep anything cold during a warm spell. Even so, it is a luxury far beyond the reach of most pre-war housing. Prefabs worked on electricity, not gas, because it was easier to install. The Belling cooker was electric, and so was the wash boiler: a drum that heated water to boiling point, for washing whites – father's dirty overalls, the sheets from the beds (no coloured sheets then), underclothes (ditto). The back door to the kitchen opens onto a corrugated-iron Anderson shelter: the garden shed. If we return to the hall, the lavatory and bathroom are round a corner – anyone emerging from the bathroom would not immediately be seen if the front door was open. Both stand near the kitchen to minimize the use of copper pipes in the plumbing (copper was in short supply). To the left of the hall are two bedrooms.

The prefab – or rather prefabs, given the ten or so different types that went into production – was not without fault. There were problems of condensation and, eventually, corrosion of metal window frames. Production lines did not switch seamlessly from making armaments to supplying house parts. The latter turned out to be more expensive than had been predicted (this was particularly the case with the aluminium bungalow, the one best adapted to factory production). These supposedly temporary buildings were in fact shacks without much insulation or sound-proofing: families who shared the same water pipe found they could communicate in code by switching on and off the cold tap.

Nevertheless they became loved. This may have been because there was little else on offer. Families who had been allocated a prefab were advised to move in quickly and put up curtains, or other people would be clamouring for it. Curtains . . . that perhaps was the key. However basic and flimsy in terms of construction, the prefab was a box which residents could decorate according to their personal ideas. Greg Stevenson's affectionate *Palaces for the People: Prefabs in Post-War Britain* (2003) contains many images of proud prefab owners for whom factory production did not preclude hydrangeas, net curtains, floral chintz and photographs of favourite dogs. Some Phoenix-type prefabs in Birmingham had already been fitted with cottage front doors before their occupants moved in. As a determined effort was made by local authorities to eliminate the last of the survivors at the end of the twentieth century, the prefab came to represent something special and enduring in the British psyche: the make-do of Austerity combined with the irrepressible home-building instinct of ordinary people.

Although 160,000 prefabs were put up, they made no more than a modest contribution to the housing programme. Four million new homes had to be built. Prefabricated techniques of construction were brought into play, but not to provide bungalows with their own gardens. One local authority after another saw the future as the high-rise flat, despite all the evidence of its unpopularity with the people who were expected to live in it. Blocks of flats could be built quickly. They were also bathed in a vision of the new way of living promoted by Le Corbusier in pre-war France and adopted with missionary zeal by the post-war architectural establishment in Britain. People had become used to being bossed around during the war. Now whole communities huddled into church halls while the bureaucrats told them where they would live. The dilapidated, bomb-damaged terraces in which they had struggled on, with neighbourly stoicism and cockney humour, could have been rehabilitated. Instead they were swept away and replaced with concrete walkways, broken lifts and a sense of isolation. This was not entirely the architects' fault; Councils were too mean to employ the concierges who might have prevented vandalism. But architects were convinced that they knew better than the public whose domestic existences they controlled, and believed that the world at large would come round to their way of thinking in the end. That did not happen.

A tower block in London called Ronan Point collapsed in 1968. That year the construction of Trellick Tower, thirty storeys tall, was started near Paddington Station; it became a symbol of every-thing the public loathed about high-rise flats. It was supposed to be a vertical community, with nurseries and game pitches at the bottom of the tower, but the nursery had to close when teenagers dropped objects onto the roof. The architect Ernö Goldfinger (Ian Fleming borrowed his name for his most famous James Bond villain) never repented, however, and died, in 1987, embittered at the rejection of his work. But times had changed. Prince Charles had already told the Royal Institute of British Architects, on the occasion of its 150th anniversary in 1984, that planners and architects had 'consistently ignored the feelings and wishes of the mass of ordinary people in this country'. Families who had been forced out of terraced slums to live hundreds of feet up in the sky had at last found a champion, the reputation of the Modern movement collapsed, and Britain once again rediscovered itself as a land of pitched roofs, brick walls and clipped hedges. Appropriately, 6 Finch Lane, having outlived its intended lifespan, found its way to a museum.

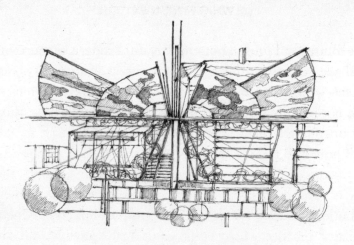

20. Whatever Next?
The Butterfly House

House as metaphor. House as work of art. House as expression of an individual's imagination. We have not encountered anything like the Butterfly House in the story of the English house before. Its approach is through the leafy, manicured lanes of deepest Surrey. The walkway that sweeps us up to the entrance is composed of rounded, lava-like sections. This is the egg. The path is lit by a vine-like tangle of fibre-optic cables through which wisteria has started to weave itself. The ramp rises up, precipitating us into the heart of the chrysalis – the enveloping cocoon of home. From here the view opens out, the house dissolves into glass, we are drawn onwards and almost feel we are taking wing. Going through the conservatory, we *are* taking wing: huge sails, decorated with diaphanous patterns, unfold above us, shading the windows from the sun, exuberantly unfurling over the landscape. This is a very colourful house, a very sophisticated house in some technical respects: a house which expresses a philosophical commitment to protecting the natural world. Welcome to the twenty-first century.

The Butterfly House is one family's thrilling adventure in light and shade, colour, pattern and caprice. Laurie Chetwood, the architect, who designed it for himself, his wife and children, admits that it is something of an indulgence: 'We did not have to worry about offending a client.' For Chetwood, architecture is a combination of heart and head. The head is the rational part, concerned with such matters as cost control and return on investment; there is plenty of head in the award-winning projects for supermarkets and distribution centres which are the stuff of his firm Chetwood Associates' practice. Heart is the emotional content of the project, the mood it induces, the sheer sensuous pleasure it conveys. Sometimes the heart must be allowed to rule the head. Sir John Vanbrugh, Gilbert White, the Duchess of Bedford, Linley Sambourne – they would all, in their own ways, have seen the point. 'Form follows function' was one of the mantras of the Modern movement and that, says Chetwood, was right for its time: 'Many people were poor and needed the basics of life. We have got beyond that now. Emotion is itself a function.' Many people – certainly those sufficiently well off to commission architect-designed houses – lead busy, stressful lives, and their down time is often at the mercy of mobile phones and the email screen. They have more and more material possessions, little time for themselves, their families, their spirits. Beauty deserves to be a priority.

In a sense, the Butterfly House exemplifies the modern condition rather more than Chetwood might have liked. There was a house on the site before – a Canadian kit house which, having appeared at an Ideal Home Exhibition in the late 1930s, was reassembled here. It had a pitched roof covered in cedar shingles, the sort of box-like rooms in which one can imagine pioneers huddling through a Canadian winter, and windows that were too small to do justice to the view. After sixty years on a Surrey hillside, the shingles were peeling from the roof, and its lack of insulation in no way conformed to modern ideas about energy conservation. It was not visible from the road, but for all that the local planners insisted it was kept. Chetwood accepted the inevitable, and at the heart of the Butterfly House the original kit house survives as a symbol of the homeowner's frustration. If it had not been there, the butterfly might have taken an even more ravishing form – perhaps flying straight out from the hillside. But to me, the sight of the butterfly emerging from, and enveloping, the banal, four-square structure that preceded it has a meaning that is in some ways even more relevant to the times. Don't let officialdom get you down.

The interior of the kit house has been cleared. Partitions have been torn down to create a single space, divided only by oval columns or, to use Chetwood's word, aerofoils, which act variously as storage bays and home-entertainment centre. The stairs float upwards as a series of organically shaped plates, dotted with holes for the light to get through. Just one detail to suggest the style of the decoration: the kitchen table is made up of five glass sheets, kidney-shaped, each slightly different from the one below. There are no mechanical fixings to hold them together. Inside, they are inter-penetrated with rods at different angles, each angle having been carefully calculated on a computer so that the whole structure locks securely together. On the end of each rod is a specially designed rubber sheath, so that the sharp point does not mark or break the glass it touches. There is a joy in this table – the joy of an extraordinary thing being imagined and carried through with precision. You won't find one at Ikea; not now, not ever.

So how did we get to the Butterfly House? Little about the English house was colourful in the 1950s, 1960s and 1970s. Suburbia was still on the march; I grew up in houses built during these decades, geographically not so far from the Butterfly House though a world away in form and spirit. In the cities, when whole swathes of Georgian and Victorian terraces were condemned, swept away and replaced by tower blocks, journalists who attended some of the meetings at which Council officials doled out new addresses to bewildered communities – old people and young families being sent to live twenty storeys above the street – still recall the experience with horror. Some Blitzed communities were uprooted and sent to the New Towns – Basildon, Bracknell, Crawley, Harlow, Hatfield, Hemel Hempstead, Stevenage and Welwyn Garden City were the eight around London – built from 1946 as a late flowering of the Garden City movement. These and others like them were promoted with biblical fervour by their admirers. 'No jerry builders will be permitted in Peterlee,' trumpeted E. W. Clarke, the engineer and surveyor for this mining town in County Durham;

> . . . only the best is good enough. Let us, therefore, close our eyes on the nineteenth-century degradation and squalor, and let us look with unseeing eyes on the sordid excrescence of the first decade of this century, let us blind ourselves to the septic and ugly building wens and ribbons perpetrated and planted on us between the wars, but let us open our eyes and look brightly forward and onward to the new town, the new living . . . Peterlee.

Occupying 22,000 acres of what had been good hunting country in Buckinghamshire, Milton Keynes was the last settlement in this tradition. City of a Thousand Roundabouts, set amid what for years were glades of white plastic tubes protecting young trees, some of its early 'neo-vernacular' housing was admirably designed, but the concept of Milton Keynes came to seem flawed: spread out over so wide an area, it relied too heavily on the motor car.

These were decades of despair for the country house, often struggling to recover from being requisitioned schools, hospital or military bases during the Second World War. The nadir was reached in the 1970s. Inflation, super tax, Prime Minister Edward Heath's three-day week, the sheer difficulty of making anything work when you had to wait months for a new telephone line, get the candles ready for the next power cut, and freeze rather than switch on the oil-fired central-heating boiler, knocked the stuffing out of country-house owners. They reinforced the received wisdom that the country house was a hopelessly outmoded building type, fit only to accommodate a boarding school or hospital. In 1974 the Victoria and Albert Museum staged an exhibition on the destruction of the country house to catalogue the toll of demolitions; some houses, it was revealed, had been blown up to make a spectacular finale to a party. Advertisements in *Country Life* – showcasing what was regarded as the most desirable property in the country – featured architecturally unambitious houses in low-maintenance gardens, near to London, preferably accessible to a golf course, while large country houses appeared with the dread tag 'suitable for institutional use'.

The change came in the 1980s, that noisy era of Lawson booms and Big Bangs. Entrepreneurs came out blinking into the sunshine of deregulation. It was said that corporate shooting was the new golf; it became socially acceptable to be rich. The old guard may have looked down their noses at a chap who had to buy his own furniture, but Michael Heseltine revelled in his country house – throwing out avenues, planting an arboretum, commissioning Quinlan Terry to build an orangery. It was a statement of conservative principles. The advertising pages of *Country Life* burst into colour. Pride of place was given to ravishing little country houses, architecturally exquisite, set amid gardens which were themselves located within parks surrounded by small estates – their stables full of hunters, their brooks begging to be fished, their hedges fat with pheasants. The loads-a-money generation had found its home. The British country-house style, trumpeted abroad in the *Treasure Houses of Britain* exhibition staged at the National Gallery in Washington in 1986, not only colonized the drawing rooms of Manhattan; at home, ruched blinds could be seen hanging in the windows of terraced houses in Fulham and newly privatized

Council houses in the Midlands. The country look became a national ideal. Laura Ashley had conquered the world.

That era in turn passed during the 1990s. The wind that blew New Labour to power in 1997 carried some stylistic straws along with it. The new government espoused the values of 'Cool Britannia', visually typified by the spare style of Peter Mandelson's bachelor pad in Notting Hill in London (the arrangements for financing the house later caused his first resignation, further evidence of the role that property had come to occupy in the English psyche). The furniture store Ikea democratized the aesthetic. The metropolitan values now in vogue found expression in the New York-style lofts that were created in warehouses along the Thames; a company that epitomized this trend was actually called the Manhattan Loft Company. One of its coups was to create an apartment block next to Bankside Power Station, which was to become the ultimate loft when converted into the Tate Modern. Chintz sofas and festoon blinds flew out of the window; Minimalism came rushing into the vacuum. The price of what auctioneers call brown furniture collapsed overnight. Country-house hotels, which had burgeoned during the 1980s, underwent an identity crisis, going modern, sweeping out the layers of artfully contrived clutter and replacing it with plain paint surfaces and simplicity. ('It's nothing but a fornicatorium,' sighed one former country-house owner, returning to his family seat after it had been stripped out and converted to the country extension of a fashionable London club.)

Thoroughgoing Minimalism did not last long; it was too uncomfortable for that. Like any virus it mutated. Taste did not revert to the classic style of the 1980s; instead it discovered a new eclecticism, perhaps incorporating one or two old pieces of furniture, but showing them almost as sculpture as part of a spare, modern aesthetic. There were contemporary paintings, not Gainsboroughs, on the walls. Georgian dining tables which would once have fetched £10,000 in Christie's South Kensington were now given estimates of

£500. Who wanted dining tables? In many houses dining rooms are used only at Christmas; for the rest of the year they become, at least, a kind of auxiliary study: don't think of eating there unless you first clear away the briefcase, piles of papers and laptop). Increasingly, in the age of the barbecue, entertaining takes place outside. Estate agents say that gardens have come back into vogue.

The most important room in the twenty-first-century house is the kitchen: food is the modern sacrament, and the kitchen is its temple. Previous generations of owners, if sufficiently well to do, never went into the kitchen, an unwelcoming space occupied by a cook. Now the family cooks in it, eats in it, watches television in it; the children play in it. This has reached such a point that owners who entertain on a large scale will probably need two kitchens; the caterers cannot use the main one, because there are too many people in it already. The scullery that would have been de rigueur in a house from the 1920s or 1930s has disappeared.

In the country the modern kitchen may in big houses be part of a complete family wing at one end of the house, occupying the position that would traditionally have been taken by the service wing (as at Elveden). This is the place to put the gym (increasingly a desideratum), along with the games room and swimming pool. A new requirement of some houses is the second study, for the wife in a two-income marriage. The trend for second studies has been driven forward by the ubiquity of computers (difficult to work in a room in which someone else is playing a computer game). Children will of course have their computers in their bedrooms, which are a law unto themselves; like other bedrooms, they are likely to have their own bathrooms or shower rooms – showers generally being preferred by teenagers. Each of the bedrooms of an architect-designed house will have an adjacent bathroom; expectations in this matter have percolated down to speculative houses, which often have more than one, whatever their size. Increasingly the bathroom has become a leisure room –

a place where people spend rather more time than is strictly necessary for brushing teeth.

A house with a family wing and second kitchen is not going to be small. In fact it is noticeable that since 2000, big country houses have got even bigger, just as London houses at the top end have got ever more dizzyingly expensive. The Barclay brothers' Breqhou Castle in the Channel Islands and Lord Rothermere's Ferne Park in Dorset, both the work of the arch neo-classicist Quinlan Terry, are on a scale rarely seen since the Second World War. A new house has been started at Ashby-cum-Fenby, not far from the seaside town of Cleethorpes, in the rather unfashionable county of Lincolnshire; according to the architect, Keith Bradley, '. . . the floor area of approximately 40,000 square feet will be about the same as Castle Howard or Hardwick Hall.' The eco-friendly theme of the building is comparable to the headquarters that Bradley designed for the National Trust.

Since the 1990s, farmhouses in beautiful locations have been as popular as conventional country houses, resplendent with architecture. Most rich people do not want to show off that way any more; they value security. With a farmhouse comes a quantity of outbuildings; the last thing they will be used for is farming. Instead, they make ideal spaces for gyms, cinemas and party rooms. On the other hand, part of the charm of a country home is the animals that can be kept there. 'How to say no to the first pony' is a question that many country-based fathers ask themselves, usually without finding a convincing answer. A few chickens, an organic vegetable patch, a pig or two – proper, Hugh Fearnley-Whittingstallish food, grown at home so that you know what went into it, is one of the great luxuries of today. Naturally the peasant culture stops at the back door; you would not want it to conflict with the touch-screen technology which now enables country-house owners to lock all the doors from the bedroom and set the central heating from their mobile phones.

So the story of the English house has in some ways come back to where it started. In building a detached chamber block at Boothby Pagnell, the de Bothebys were pursuing comfort and privacy. You may say that comfort is a priority for any house builder: who would intentionally build an uncomfortable house? Perhaps it would be better to say intimacy; Elveden was an exceptionally comfortable house in the Edwardian period, but with all those servants hardly intimate; intimacy – the desire to enjoy one's home by oneself, with only one's family for company – is an essential ingredient of the modern ideal. Architects say that clients who commission them to build large country houses rarely want staff, other than a nanny, to live in (though others may live over the garage). Nor, on the whole, do they want large numbers of guest bedrooms; guests who come to dinner are not generally encouraged to spend the night. We all lead busy lives. Even families rich enough to employ staff, which takes the sting out of cooking, washing up and making beds, regard weekend parties as a complication they do not need. 'Guests now get the worst bedrooms,' comments the architect Robert Adam, 'unlike in the old days when owners wanted to show off their best rooms and views to their guests.' (Though it isn't always like that. According to Angus Morrogh-Ryan of De Matos Storey Ryan, some owners decorate their guest rooms like boutique hotels: '. . . it is the room you would like to have but couldn't bear living in every day of the week.') A second floor for children is very popular. As Adam observes, 'People always say that children will like the sloping roofs; there will be a back stairs for the children to have direct access to the kitchen.'

Celebrities and the super-rich have been increasingly drawn to the countryside in recent years: fed up with being doorstepped by paparazzi, they hide themselves away at the end of long drives. We have also come back to the theme of individuality, the sheer exuberance of the carpentry of the Clergy House at Alfriston and the brickwork at East Barsham Manor. The outstanding feature of the English house in the second half of the twentieth century was the mortgage. In 1945, forty per cent of all households in Britain owned their own home; now that figure has risen to nearly seventy per cent. We have become, in Margaret Thatcher's phrase, a 'property-owning democracy'; houses represent a very large investment for many families. Not surprisingly, we also seem to have become obsessed by them, to judge from the amount of space devoted to property in newspapers and makeover programmes on television. The Englishman's house is his retirement plan. Because of the investment it represents, it is cherished as never before. Cherishing adds personality, though rarely so much as we have seen in the Butterfly House (owners are worried about selling on houses that are too outré to satisfy popular taste).

There is a new dimension, though, which we have not seen much before: sustainability. The world is turning green, and the English house along with it. Of course, many of the houses in this book have been sustainable; there was no Waitrose in the seventeenth century, and even Thomas Bayly, living on the High Street of a town such as Marlborough, would have eaten his own vegetables and eggs. The stucco-fronted houses of Regency Ramsgate generally had their own wells; they did not require water to be piped to them from reservoirs as they do today. What *is* new is the attitude that it is morally wrong to waste the earth's resources.

Housing is said to account for some thirty per cent of Britain's carbon-dioxide emissions. Modern house builders who are sensitive to public anxiety about climate change want their buildings to make as little impact on their environment as possible. They do not have much choice about it: it has become a priority of the planning system. This affects the technology of the house: how it is heated, how it is lit, how it is cooled. It is possible to build houses that are not merely carbon neutral but carbon positive: that is to say, their net effect is positively to reduce greenhouse-gas emissions (thanks, for example, to using hemp-based

insulation which locks up carbon that is absorbed while growing). Some of the apparatus for green generation is easier to install
in the country than in the town. Geothermal heating, whereby
pipes are buried underground to keep water at a constant
temperature which then only needs topping up, requires space.
So does a decently sized windmill. On the other hand, solar
panels and the micro combined heat and power generators that
are said to be in development – effectively mini power stations
that can go under the stairs – are as suitable for the town as
anywhere else; terraced houses have the advantage over detached
ones of losing less heat. In the case of some architect-designed
houses, prioritizing the green agenda dictates the form that the
house takes: through the use of grass banks and roofs laid with
turf, it is possible for the building to merge completely with its
surroundings, to the extent that visitors hardly spot it until they
have arrived at the front door. This shows a sensitivity to landscape – again, partly enforced by the planners – to which Gilbert
White might have responded. In the summer of 2007 an
eco-community comprising tents, felt-covered yurts and canvas
benders which had sprung up on a 42-acre farm in Devon was
awarded planning permission, much to the chagrin of local
residents whose attempts to build more conventional housing
had been disallowed over the years. The ideas behind such low-
impact, carbon-free living – 'permaculture', to use a jargon word
from the 1970s – are swimming through the hippy fringe towards
the mainstream.

The Butterfly House exemplifies nearly all the themes I have just
traced. It is, however flamboyant, a family house. It is a house to be
visited by guests, but they are unlikely to find much space to stay
the night. The Butterfly concept emerged out of an ecological
survey commissioned before the house was designed, which
revealed that the site – with its mixture of trees, meadow and
garden – was likely to be a butterfly paradise. Since then the hillside

has been planted with buddleia and other butterfly-attracting shrubs. Rainwater is recycled along tendril-like drains twisting in and out of the fibre-optic cable beside the entrance ramp and disappearing into industrial-sized orange-juice containers (a cheap and practical solution) which are buried underground. Air is blown through the water to cool it. The house is a hymn to the wondrous beauty of nature. It is also almost theatrically at pains to minimize the footprint it leaves.

Tread softly, for you tread on a broken world. Dream deeply – as the Butterfly House does – and perhaps we can imagine it restored. Dream of beauty. Volume house builders rarely do: in a seller's market, they compete with each other for sites that can get planning permission, then offer miseries of architecture. Exceptional houses such as the Butterfly House demonstrate what can be done when imagination is given free rein. It cannot be beyond hope that one day a more creative approach will be applied to the norm. Whether the result would look like a thousand Butterfly Houses, who knows? The master of volume house building, in the Victorian period, was Thomas Cubitt. His houses still make comfortable and happy family homes. Going forward sometimes means going back.

Further Reading

All books mentioned here were published in London unless otherwise specified.

An Ordinary London Terraced House

Everything you could possibly want to know about Thomas Cubitt can be found in Hermione Hobhouse's magisterial *Thomas Cubitt, Master Builder* (1971). Robert Bakewell's manual *Observations on Building and Brick-making* was published in 1834. Edward Dobson's *Treatise on the Manufacture of Bricks and Tiles* (1850) was reprinted in facsimile by the George Street Press, Stafford, in 1973 (ed. Dr Francis Celoria). The quotation from Trollope comes from *The Small House at Allington* (1864). Don't look for evidence of Pimlico *d'autrefois* in *Passport to Pimlico*: the location shots were filmed in Lambeth and Vauxhall in south London.

I. Boothby Pagnell Manor House

Readers who want to know more about medieval building techniques should visit the Château de Guédelon in northern Burgundy, a new castle that is being built as faithfully to the old ways as possible. Philippe Minard and François Folcher have produced a book about it: *Guédelon: Fanatics for a Fortress* (Geneva, 2003). Of course, it's better to visit.

The best guide to English building materials remains Alec Clifton-Taylor's *The Pattern of English Building*, first published in 1962. See also *English Stone Building*, which Clifton-Taylor wrote with A. S. Ireson, scion of an old family of stonemasons, in 1983. I am grateful to David Smith for showing me the Building Stones collection at the Natural History Museum in London, assembled in the 1830s to help decide which stone to use for the Houses of Parliament. John Allen Howe's *Geology of Building Stones*, first published in 1910 and reprinted in 2001, has not been bettered as an introduction to the subject.

An authoritative study of medieval domestic architecture is provided by Margaret Wood's *The English Medieval House*, first published in 1965. However, Wood was writing before archaeology revealed the presence of a separate hall at Boothby Pagnell. The latest thinking on the subject can be found in Edward Impey's 'The Manor House, Boothby Pagnell, Lincolnshire', in *Country Life*, 29 July 1999. W. J. Blair's 'Hall and Chamber: English Domestic Planning 1000–1250', in Gwyn Meirion-Jones and Michael Jones, eds, *Manorial Domestic Buildings in England and Northern France*, published by the Society of Antiquaries in 1993, gives further context.

2. The Clergy House, Alfriston

I became interested in the Clergy House as the first building acquired by the National Trust. The absence of carbon or tree-ring dating, not to mention any contemporary documentation, makes it a tantalizing house, even though it is not a specially early survival. Some of England's oldest timber-framed structures have been identified by John Walker, in 'Late 12th and Early 13th Century Aisled Buildings: A Comparison (Part 1)', *Vernacular Architecture*, XXX (1999), pp. 21–52, as having been built before 1230. They comprise seven halls (Fyfield Hall, mentioned in chapter 1, being the earliest), a barn and a bell tower. The halls are not all grand, manorial structures, but include a cottage (Westwick Cottage, near St Albans in Hertfordshire, only 28 feet long and dating from 1184–1219) and two farmhouses (Newbury Farmhouse, at Tonge in Kent, 1182–1227, and Sycamore Farm, at Long Crendon in Buckinghamshire, 1205).

I am grateful to Dr Annabelle Hughes for having discussed the Clergy House with me. My thanks also to Benedict Gummer for sharing his knowledge of the Black Death. More about medieval Sussex can be found in John Lowerson's *A Short History of Sussex* (Folkestone, 1980). Alan Savidge's *The Parsonage in England* (1964) provides a history of clergy dwellings, whether or not the Clergy House was built to be one. Christopher Dyer's *Everyday Life in the Middle Ages* (1995) is the starting point for anyone interested in the social background to the period, just as R. W. Brunskill's many books on traditional and vernacular architecture are the first port of call for students of the country's more humble domestic buildings. His *Timber Building in Britain* (1985) and R. J. Brown's *Timber-Framed Buildings of England* (1986) unfold the mystery of carpentry. Brown believes that the Clergy House could have been built for a priest or priests because of possible separate access to the service wing. Further context is supplied by M. W. Barley's *The English Farmhouse and Cottage* (1961). Thomas Wright's *The Homes of Other Days* (1871) may now be old-fashioned, but contains many enjoyable aperçus.

There is a charming picture of the Clergy House in W. Galsworthy Davie's *Old Cottages and Farmhouses in Kent and Sussex* (1900), a book that illustrates the wonderful variety of house types in this corner of England alone. The National Trust did not cast a pall over the house in the early years. According to Felicity Ashbee's *Janet Ashbee: Love, Marriage, and the Arts and Crafts Movement* (2002), Janet Ashbee honeymooned there with her husband, the designer C. R. Ashbee, in 1898: 'The weather was perfect, especially for swimming, and she cast off her stays before her first bathe with CRA in a symbolic gesture. She never wore stays again.'

3. East Barsham Manor

Jeremy Musson described East Barsham in *Country Life*, 26 February 2004. His *The English Manor House* (1999) is a visual treat for anyone who loves old houses. Nathaniel Lloyd is the father of brick studies, his *A History of English Brickwork* having been published in 1925. (It was Lloyd who employed Lutyens to restore Great Dixter in East Sussex between 1910 and 1914, work which included the moving of a Wealden house from the village of Benenden.) More recently, Jane A. Wright wrote *Brick Building in England from the Middle Ages to 1550* (1972), while R. W. Brunskill's *Brick Building in Britain* appeared in 2006. The provisions of Sir Henry Feymor's will are quoted in Nicholas Cooper and Marianne Majerus, *English Manor Houses* (1990).

Readers whose imagination has been stirred by my account of The Grange in chapter 10 may be interested to know that A. W. N. Pugin illustrated East Barsham in his book *Examples of Gothic Architecture* (1838). It was then known as Wolterton Manor House, and already badly dilapidated.

4. Buckland Abbey

I wrote about Buckland in *Country Life*, 28 July 1988. The best account of the Grenvilles remains A. L. Rowse, *Sir Richard Grenville of the Revenge* (1937). For an archaeological analysis of the site, see C. Gaskell Brown, 'Buckland Abbey', *Devon Archaeological Society Proceedings*, 53 (1995), pp. 25–82. The conversion of the abbey of Titchfield into a house is described by W. H. St John Hope in 'The Making of Place House at Titchfield, near Southampton, in 1538', *Archaeological Journal*, LXIIII (1906), pp. 231–44. I also found the following helpful: J. Kew, 'The Disposal of Crown Lands and the Devon Land Market, 1536–58', *Agricultural History Review*, XVIII/2 (1970); R. B. Outhwaite, 'Who Bought Crown Lands? The Pattern of Purchases, 1589–1603', *Bulletin of the Institute of Historical Research*, XLIV (1971); Joyce Youings, 'Drake, Grenville and Buckland Abbey', *Trans. Devon. Assoc.*, 112 (1980), pp. 91–9.

5. Lodge Park

My article on Lodge Park that appeared in *Country Life*, 13 March 1968, was updated by Mary Miers (*Country Life*, 18 May 2000). Lieutenant Hammond's description of Lodge Park, pinpointing the date, is contained in L. G. Wickham Legg, ed., *A relation of Short Survey of 26 Counties, Observed in a seven week Journey begun on 11 August, 1634 by a Captain, a Lieutenant and an Ancient* (1904). The crucial section of this account was published in a letter from Jeffrey Haworth in *Country Life*, 31 August 2000, p. 70.

The history of the Dutton family can be found in *Memorials of the Duttons of Dutton in Cheshire, with Notes Respecting the Sherborne Branch of the Family* (1901). Mark Girouard's article on Tudor and Stuart hunting boxes, 'Arcadian Retreats for the Chase', was published in *Country Life*, 26 September 1963. Paula Henderson's article 'Life at the Top' (*Country Life*, 3 January 1985) is a fascinating account of the Elizabethan and Stuart taste for roof-top living (see also her book *The Tudor House and Garden* [2005]). I notice that the tradition continued: it was the lawyer Mr Tulk-inghorn's habit to walk on the leads outside his tower room in

Dickens's *Bleak House* (1852–3). An account of field sports in Stuart England can be found in Gervase Markham, *Country contentments: or, The husbandmans recreations containing the wholesome experiences, in which any man ought to recreate himselfe, after the toyle of more serious businesse* (1615).

Christopher Gilbert discovered that James Moore made furniture for 'ye Lodge' ('James Moore the Younger and William Kent at Sherborne House', *Burlington Magazine* [March 1969], pp. 148–9). For the architectural background to Lodge Park, read Giles Worsley's *Classical Architecture in Britain* (1994), and *Inigo Jones and the European Classicist Tradition* (2007).

6. The Merchant's House, Marlborough

I am grateful to Sir John Sykes for introducing me to the Merchant's House. For this chapter I have drawn on Jerry Sampson of Caroe and Partners' *Marlborough: The Merchant's House Report* (1994) and J. C. Green's BA dissertation 'Seventeenth Century Fire Disasters: A Study of the Great Fire of Marlborough, 1653' (Birmingham University, 1998). For Francis Freeman, see K. Maslen, *The Life of Francis Freeman of Marlborough* (c. 1600–1671). *Take Heed in Time, or a Briefe Relation of Many Harmes which Have of Late been Done by Fire in Marlborough* . . . (1653) was reprinted in 1991 for the Merchant's House. Clarendon's low opinion of Marlborough is quoted in A. R. Stedman, *Marlborough and the Upper Kennet Country* (Marlborough, 1960), p. 134.

The architecture of Marlborough High Street is analysed in *Victoria County History: Wiltshire*, vol. 12. Pentices were common in the Middle Ages, according to Kathryn A. Morrison, *English Shops and Shopping* (2003). The date of Pepys's comments on Marlborough is 15 June 1688. Marlborough's great fire can be compared to the conflagration that consumed Warwick; see M. Farr, *The Great Fire of Warwick, 1694* (1992).

7. Vanbrugh Castle, Greenwich

Kerry Downes, the biographer of Vanbrugh, described the Maze Hill compound in his article 'The Little Colony on Greenwich Hill', *Country Life*, 27 May 1976, pp. 1406–8. A further account can be found in W. E. L. Fletcher, 'The Maze Hill Estate of Sir John Vanbrugh', *Transactions of the Greenwich and Lewisham Antiquarian Society*, VIII (1978), pp. 136–42. See also Neil Rhind's *Blackheath Village and Environs, 1790–1970*, II (1983), and Laurence Whistler, *The Imagination of Vanbrugh and His Fellow Artists* (1954), pp. 200–206.

A good history of the sash window is provided by *See Windows*, the second in a series of conservation advisory booklets produced by the Building of Bath Museum and Bath City Council (1994). The London Building Act of 1709 was superseded by the London Building Act of 1774 which required that windows should be fully rebated. This became a national requirement in 1820.

8. 19 New King Street, Bath

Tim Mowl and Brian Earnshaw's *John Wood* (1988) is a masterly account of an architect who was more complex than his buildings seem to suggest. Ralph Allen can be explored through Benjamin Boyce's *The Benevolent Man: A Life of Ralph Allen* (Cambridge, MA, 1967). The classic book about Bath architecture is Walter Ison's *The Georgian Buildings of Bath* (1948). Others include David Gadd, *Georgian Summer* (1971); Charles Robertson, *Bath: An Architectural Guide* (1975), p. 141; and Graham Davis and Penny Bonsall, *A History of Bath* (Lancaster, 2006). Bath also has a museum specially dedicated to its architectural history, the Building of Bath Museum.

Constance A. Lubbock published *The Herschel Chronicle* (Cambridge) in 1933. Mrs John Herschel brought out *Memoir and Correspondence of Caroline Herschel* in 1876. Fanny Nelson's comment about Bath prices is quoted by Brian Little in *Bath Portrait* (Bristol, 1961).

9. The Wakes, Selborne

David Standing, the head gardener of Gilbert White's House and the Oates Museum, knows more about the garden than anyone. I am grateful for the opportunity to discuss it with him.

Richard Mabey published his biography *Gilbert White* in 1986. He also edited the journals and published them in three volumes (1986–9). David Watkin's history of the Picturesque movement, *The English Vision*, appeared in 1982. I have also drawn on the following sources: Dr Celia Fisher, 'The Restoration of Gilbert White's Garden at Selborne', *Hortus* (2001); Paul Foster and David Standing, 'Landscape and Labour: Gilbert White's Garden, 1751–93', Selborne Paper No. 2 (2006); and Gwyn I. Meirion-Jones, 'The Wakes, Selborne: An Architectural Study', *Proceedings of the Hampshire Field Club Archaeological Society*, XXXIX (1983), pp. 145–69.

Gilpin's views on forest scenery are quoted in Brian Short, *England's Landscape: The South-East* (2006). Shenstone's *ferme ornée* was published in 1765 by Rovery Dodsley in *A Description of The Leasowes*.

The twentieth-century decorator David Hicks would have approved of White's wooden eyecatchers, since Hicks used a two-dimensional obelisk in his Oxfordshire garden; being attached to a wheelbarrow, it had the advantage over a solid version in that it could be moved from one location to another.

Isabel Colegate's *The Pelican in the Wilderness* (2002) is a history of hermits in landscape parks.

10. 10 North Street, Cromford

I wrote about Cromford in 'The Legacy of Richard Arkwright', *Country Life*, 8 September 1983, pp. 590–92. I am grateful to the Landmark Trust for showing me Caroline Stanford's notes on 10 North Street; they own the house. See also *Arkwright and the Mills at Cromford*, published by the Arkwright Society (rev. edn 1977). The diaries of John Byng, Viscount Torrington, were published in four volumes in 1934, with an abridged edition by Fanny Andrews published in 1954. There are several accounts of Arkwright's life, R. S. Flitton's *The Arkwrights* being the most recent (1989).

Uncertainty over water in Cromford explains why Masson Mill was built on the Derwent. The findings of the clergyman in Saffron Hill were published in William Bardwell's *Healthy Homes and How to Make Them* (1854). The gift of 'fine Milch Cows' etc. was reported by the *Derby Mercury* in July 1783 (quoted by Stanford).

11. Endsleigh Cottage

The classic account of the Picturesque movement is Christopher Hussey, *The Picturesque* (1927). This is also the theme of David Watkin's *The English Vision* (1982), which is written from a scholarly perspective.

John Cornforth wrote about Endsleigh in *Country Life*, 9 and 16 October 1997, when it was a fishing club; I returned to the house after it had become a hotel (*Country Life*, 9 February 2006). The house had earlier been described by Christopher Hussey, *Country Life*, 3 and 10 August 1961. I wrote about the 6th Duke of Bedford's garden buildings at Woburn in 'Park and Garden Building and Woburn – I and II', *Country Life*, 31 March and 7 April 1983. Wyatville's biography has been written by Derek Linstrum: *Sir Jeffry Wyatville, Architect to the King* (Oxford, 1972). *Letters to Lord G. William Russell from various Writers 1817–1845* (3 vols,

1915–19) reveals how the next generation thought about the 6th Duke's extravagance. In 1832, the Marquess of Tavistock, the future 7th Duke, wrote to Lord George William Russell, his brother, that 'if my father goes on squandering and borrowing at the present rate, there will be nothing left soon for any of his family in a short time.' W. J. Hooker's contrasting opinion can be found in *Copy of a Letter Addressed to Dawson Turner, Esq., F.R.A., and L.S., &c. &c. on the Occasion of the Death of the Duke of Bedford, Glasgow* (1840). More about Woburn can be found in Georgiana Blakiston, *Woburn and the Russells* (1980).

12. The Grange, Ramsgate

I am grateful to Stephen Davies for introducing me to the joys and mysteries of Ramsgate. His *Thanetalia*, privately published for family and friends, have been liberally quarried for this chapter. The quotation about cannibalistic lodging keepers comes from *Punch's Guide to the Watering Places* (July 1842). Jane Austen remembered Ramsgate in *Pride and Prejudice*; it was where Wickham attempted to elope with Miss Darcy. Austen's comment about Mrs Bridges can be found in a letter of September 1813, quoted in David Waldron Smithers, *Jane Austen in Kent* (Westerham, 1981). The jeremiad against stucco and the evil hour in which it was invented comes from Charles Eastlake's *Hints on Household Taste* (1868). Information about the paddle steamers comes from G. H. Davidson, *The Thames and Thanet Guide*, 4th edn (n.d.). Dickens expressed his low opinion of Ramsgate in a letter to John Forster in September 1839. The description of bathing comes from the anonymous *All About Ramsgate and Broadstairs* (1864).

At Ramsgate, Wilkie Collins would usually stay with his housekeeper and presumed mistress on the West Cliff, but sometimes he would be joined by his 'morganatic wife' Martha Rudd, and on those occasions he moved to the East Cliff. The presence of the young Van Gogh, who stayed in Spencer Square in 1876 while working as a drawing master, was a comparative breath of respectability. That year he wrote to his brother, Theo, claiming to be 'a child of the pine woods and of the beach at Ramsgate'.

Since I began this book, Rosemary Hill's definitive work on Pugin has appeared: *God's Architect: Pugin and the Building of Romantic Britain* (2007). In 1999, Hill wrote *Pugin and Ramsgate* for the Ramsgate Society. The comment by Pugin's doctor is quoted in Caroline Stanford, ed., '*Dearest Augustus and I*': *The Journal of Jane Pugin* (Reading, 2004). The information about John Hardman Powell is from Alexandra Wedgwood, ed., 'Pugin in His Home: A Memoir by J. H. Powell', *Architectural History*, XXXI (1988). The Grange is now owned by the Landmark Trust.

13. Mechi Farm

The trials of John Butcher have been revealed by John Broad in 'Housing the Rural Poor in Southern England, 1650–1850', *Agricultural History Review*, XLVIII/2 (2000), pp. 151–70. Other works I found helpful for this chapter are James Malton, *An Essay on British Cottage Architecture* (1798); John Birch, *Country Architecture: A Work Designed for the Use of the Nobility and Country Gentlemen*, 1874; and John Gloag, *Mr Loudon's England* (1970). Model farm buildings are discussed in Susanna Wade Martins, *The English Model Farm* (2002). For more about chickens, see Bonington Moubray, *A Practical Treatise on Breeding, Rearing and Fattening All Kinds of Domestic Poultry, Pheasants, Pigeons and Rabbits* (1815). Cochin mania is described in a novel by C. M. Yonge, *The Daisy Chain* (1856). The Landmark Trust owns the Poultry Yard and Fowl House at Leighton Hall, over the Welsh border, which were built for a Liverpool banker, John Naylor, in 1861. The notes for the house written by Charlotte Haslam are a rich vein for the historical poultry fancier. The Victoria County History have put an accessible guide to Warter on the internet; find this at: http://www.englandpast.net/education/warter_index.html.

The principal source for the buildings at Mechi Farm, Blenner-hasset, is William Lawson's *Ten Years of Gentleman Farming at Blennerhasset with Co-operative Objects* (1874). The review quoted at the end of the chapter comes from *Harper's New Monthly Magazine* (November 1875), pp. 895–9.

14. 18 Stafford Terrace, Kensington

Linley Sambourne House, 18 Stafford Terrace, London W8, is owned by the Royal Borough of Kensington and Chelsea. The Sambourne Family Archive can be consulted at Kensington Central Library in London. The diaries of Marion Sambourne formed the basis of Shirley Nicholson's *A Victorian Household* (Stroud, 1994).

The French visitor quoted in the first paragraph of this chapter can be found in Charles Eastlake's *Hints on Household Taste* (1868). Steen Rasmussen wrote *London: The Unique City* (1937). For Sambourne's photography, see Robin Simon, ed., *Public Artist, Private Passions* (2001). The drudgery that faced country girls working as servants in London can be gathered from Liz Stanley, ed., *The Diaries of Hannah Cullwick* (1984). Marion owned a manual on household management, *Family Fare or the Young Housewife's Daily Assistant*, written by an author using the pseudonym Cre-fydd – the copy was from the 7th edn (1874 – the year she married). The Pooters shared their taste for music-hall turns with another resident of Holloway, Cora Crippen, whose hopes of a more vibrant life than one spent running a lodging house and married to a dentist's medical advisor led her to join the Music Hall Ladies Guild. She was murdered by Dr Crippen.

15. Brantwood

I wrote about Brantwood in *Country Life*, 26 July and 2 August 1984. In those days, it was possible to stay in the house and enjoy the Lakeland view from Ruskin's bathtub. The Ruskin papers, which used to be housed at Bembridge School on the Isle of Wight, are now in the University of Lancaster.

A window onto Ruskin's life at Brantwood, rehanging pictures, putting fossils in a new order and worrying about madness, is provided by Helen Gill Viljoen, ed., *The Brantwood Diary of John Ruskin* (1971). Information about the contents of Brantwood (for example, the Turner ring) can be gleaned from the Sotheby sale catalogues (1931). For Brantwood's place in the aesthetic of the Lake District, see *The Discovery of the Lake District: A Northern Arcadia and Its Uses*, the catalogue of the 1984 exhibition at the Victoria and Albert Museum in London. There are too many biographies of Ruskin to list, but in some ways the most useful remains W. G. Collingwood (1889). Other publications that I have drawn on for this chapter are: James S. Dearden, ed., *The Professor: Arthur Severn's Memoir of Ruskin* (1967); Sheila Birkenhead, *Illustrious Friends: The Story of Joseph Severn and His Son Arthur* (1965); James S. Dearden, *Facets of Ruskin* (1970); James S. Dearden, 'Printing and Brantwood I and II', *Book Collector* (Winter 1978), pp. 515–32; (Summer 1979), pp. 236–51; Barrie and Wendy Armstrong, *The Arts and Crafts Movement in the North West of England*, Wetherby (2005).

16. Marsh Court

Christopher Hussey's *The Life of Sir Edwin Lutyens* (1953) is perhaps the greatest architectural biography ever written. It should be read in conjunction with the three great volumes of plates entitled *The Architecture of Sir Edwin Lutyens* by A. S. G. Butler

(1950). The RIBA's collection of Lutyens's drawings and letters can be consulted in the Victoria and Albert Museum.

Several other books have appeared since the 1950s which elaborate on parts of the story that could not be told so soon after the architect's death, or which reinterpret Lutyens for a new generation. Architectural studies include Peter Inskip, *Edwin Lutyens* (1979); Roderick Gradidge, *Edwin Lutyens* (1981); and Gavin Stamp, *Edwin Lutyens* (2001). The 1981 Lutyens exhibition at the Hayward Gallery in London is remembered in a catalogue. Lutyens the man emerges vividly in Mary Lutyens, *Edwin Lutyens* (1980). Clayre Percy and Jane Ridley, eds, *The Letters of Edwin Lutyens to His Wife Lady Emily*, was published in 1985, and Jane Ridley, *The Architect and His Wife*, appeared in 2001. The horticultural context is provided by Jane Brown, *Gardens of a Golden Afternoon* (1982), and the same author's *Lutyens and the Edwardians* (1996) sets Lutyens in his time.

The Arts and Crafts movement can be explored in Peter Davey, *Arts and Crafts Architecture* (1980), and Margaret Richardson, *Architects of the Arts and Crafts Movement* (1983). I wrote about Le Bois des Moutiers, the house in which Lady Emily first encountered theosophy, in *Country Life*, 21 and 28 May 1981.

17. Elveden Hall

Duleep Singh's life is recounted in Michael Alexander and Sushila Anand's *Queen Victoria's Maharajah* (1980). The embarrassing moment with the Koh-i-Noor is described in Edith Login's *Lady Login's Recollections* (1916). The architectural background to Lord Iveagh's Elveden is described by me in *The Last Country Houses* (1982). Shooting played a big role in the Edwardian country house: for this, see Jonathan Garnier Ruffer's enjoyable *The Big Shots* (1977). When the contents of Elveden were sold by Christie's in 1984, they produced a seven-volume sale catalogue, including an historical account by me. I am grateful to the present Earl of Iveagh for showing me the house, empty but admirably maintained and surrounded by beautiful parkland.

18. 7 Blyth Grove, Worksop

I would like to thank Andrew Barber of the National Trust for showing me 7 Blyth Grove and sharing his experience of it. I found Daniel Defoe's description of Epsom in Nicholas Taylor, *The Village in the City* (1973). For the architecture of the twentieth-century suburb, see Paul Oliver, Ian Davis and Ian Bentley, *Dunroamin* (1981). Histories of the semi can be found in Alan A. Jackson, *Semi-Detached London* (1973), and James D. Murphy, *The Semi-Detached House* (Dublin, 1977).

The 1854 historian who described pre-industrial Worksop was Edwin Eddison, in *History of Worksop with Historical, Descriptive and Discursive Sketches of Sherwood Forest and the Neighbourhood*.

The variety of William Straw's interests can be seen from the headings under which the National Trust has catalogued his collection of newspaper cuttings and other material: St John the Evangelist Church; Windmills; Coronation Glove tradition; Clumber and the Newcastle family; Public rights of way; Local history – Worksop; Recipes and domestic tips; Archaeology; English Language; Everest; Fine Arts; Heraldry; W. R. Inge, Dean of St Paul's Cathedral; Horace King, Speaker of the House of Commons; London and London University; Nottingham; Sutton-in-Ashfield; Chesterfield Canal; English Literature; Famous men; Gardening; Humour; Jam Making; D. H. Lawrence; Monarchy; Portlands and Welbeck; Religion; Wine and beer making.

In *London: The Unique City* (1937), Steen Eiler Rasmussen lauded the low density of British cities: 'The English example is amazing, for their great industrial cities, in which each family has its own house, have been created without any difficulty, – and

London, the largest city in the world, is the very type of the scattered city.' It is a view that would find less favour today. Clough Williams-Ellis campaigned against ribbon development in *England and the Octopus* (1929).

19. The Amersham Prefab

For the history of prefabs, see Brenda Vale, *Prefabs: A History of the UK Temporary Housing Programme* (1995); Greg Stevenson, *Palaces for the People, Prefabs in Post-War Britain* (2003); R. B. White, *Prefabrication: A History of Its Development in Great Britain* (1965). I am grateful to the Chilterns Open Air Museum for access to their archive.

Utility furniture represents the first and only time that government attempted to take control of domestic taste, with the help of progressive designers such as Gordon Russell and Enid Marx. Interestingly, the Bryannts seem to have rebelled: they appear to have had an old-fashioned iron bedstead in their bedroom, according to an oral record in the Chilterns Open Air Museum. Bungalow Briggs spread his influence through *Bungalows and Country Residences* (1891), which went through five editions. For the history of the bungalow, see Anthony King, *The Bungalow: An Indian Contribution to the West* (1982).

Mass Observation's findings are contained in *An Enquiry into People's Homes* (1943). The push to house returning servicemen after the First World War is described in Mark Swenarton, *Homes Fit for Heroes* (1981).

20. The Butterfly House

A virtual tour of the Butterfly House can be taken courtesy of the website provided by its creator, Laurie Chetwood. Find this at: www.butterfly-house.co.uk.

The excited quotation about Peterlee comes from F. W. Clarke's *Farewell Squalor* (1946). Figures on household ownership come from Roger Burrows, *The Joseph Rowntree Foundation: Poverty and Home Ownership in Contemporary Britain* (2005). I am told that the phrase 'property-owning democracy' was first used by Anthony Eden.

Index

Acknowledgements

I would like to thank the owners and administrators of the houses I have been lucky enough to visit while researching this book – indeed throughout my career – without whose generosity it could not have been written. I have tried to acknowledge the help of the scholars with whom I discussed various subjects in the notes; I apologise to any I may have left out, but I am sincerely grateful to them all the same. My colleagues at *Country Life*, particularly in the architectural department, have been an unfailing source of support. I would also like to thank my agent, Zoe Pagnamenta, and my editor, Richard Atkinson, as well as Andrea Belloli and Mai Osawa.

Since my wife and family live in one of the families in the book I am doubly grateful to them for having allowed me to invade our own privacy, as well as having tolerated the absences (in the study, if not other parts of England) which are an inescapable part of writing architectural books.

NOTE ON THE AUTHOR

Clive Aslet joined *Country Life* in 1977, and is now Editor at Large. He writes extensively for national newspapers, and often broadcasts on radio and television. His first book, *The Last Country Houses*, was published in 1982. His most recent book was the highly acclaimed *Landmarks of Britain*. An authority on British life, Clive is well known as a campaigner on countryside and other issues. Married with three children, he divides his time between London and Ramsgate.

NOTE ON THE TYPE

The text of this book is set in Linotype Stempel Garamond, a version of Garamond adapted and first used by the Stempel foundry in 1924. It is one of several versions of Garamond based on the designs of Claude Garamond. It is thought that Garamond based his font on Bembo, cut in 1495 by Francesco Griffo in collaboration with the Italian printer Aldus Manutius. Garamond types were first used in books printed in Paris around 1532. Many of the present-day versions of this type are based on the *Typi Academiae* of Jean Jannon cut in Sedan in 1615.

Claude Garamond was born in Paris in 1480. He learned how to cut type from his father and by the age of fifteen he was able to fashion steel punches the size of a pica with great precision. At the age of sixty he was commissioned by King Francis I to design a Greek alphabet; for this he was given the honourable title of royal type founder. He died in 1561.